W9-DFO-480

Indian New England Before the Mayflower

Menotomy: A drink from a spring. Sculpture by Cyrus Dallin.
Town Hall Park, Arlington, Massachusetts.

Indian New England Before the Mayflower

Howard S. Russell

University Press of New England

Hanover, New Hampshire
and London, England, 1980

The University Press of New England

Brandeis University

Clark University

Dartmouth College

University of New Hampshire

University of Rhode Island

Tufts University

University of Vermont

Preface

Marcus Aurelius gratefully acknowledged the examples of tutors, relatives, and friends from whom he acquired the personal qualities he valued. "From Rusticus," he writes, he had learned "to read with precision and not to be satisfied with general statements." In offering a description of New England's Indians as they lived when Europeans first met them, I affirm this purpose. I have tried to present the natives as neither savages nor heroes, but fellow human beings, living at a particular time in a particular environment. In this endeavor to provide a truthful picture I have had the help of many friends, living and departed. Some few are mentioned here.

Let me first pay tribute to New England's earliest explorers, Verrazano, Champlain, John Smith, and a score of literate sailors, and next acknowledge my debt to Pilgrims and Puritans; settlers, travelers, military men, and missionaries; and the accounts all have left us. A surprising number of them, in the midst of crowded lives, took time and trouble to describe in writing the new land and the characteristics and way of life of its peoples.

A second background source is the modern archaeologist and scientist. New England is fortunate to be the home of several active archaeological societies, each sponsoring physical excavations and publications that continually add to our perception of prehistoric man, his habits and environment. To these societies, their officers, and the contributors to their publications, and along with them to local and professional anthropologists, geographers, linguists, botanists, and other specialists whose studies may be specifically recognized in the bibliography, I am greatly indebted.

Beyond such general attributions I mention with special gratitude a few of the groups and individuals who have provided help:

Membership in two organizations for over a third of a century has been a continued stimulus. The Massachusetts Archaeological Society, through the courtesy of its curator, Maurice Robbins, its editor, Dena M. Dincauze, and its officers and trustees, has generously allowed me my choice among the illustrations that have appeared in its *Bulletin*. The artist responsible for many is the *Bulletin's* long-time editor (now retired), William J. Fowler. He has not only acquiesced in their use but kindly read and criticized portions of the text. The second organization is the nationwide Agricultural History Society, whose Executive Secretary, Wayne D. Rasmussen, an authority on Indian agriculture, has offered repeated advice and encouragement. One of the Society's members, Jonathan Gell, was generous with critical counsel on anthropological aspects of the script.

Special appreciation is due Albin Webber, who from my crude pencil sketches developed the accurate maps. Robert Schuette, my hometown publisher, loaned the excellent diorama photographs which he originally took to illustrate an earlier article of mine appearing locally some years since. For other illustrations, individual credits appear on the appropriate pages.

From the anthropological field, encouragement for publication came from Margaret A. Towle of Harvard and Peru, who insisted that an earlier version of the manuscript should be published, and from Richard Evans Schultes, until recently head of Harvard's Botanical Museum, who also kindly suggested Walton C. Galinat of the University of Massachusetts Experiment Station as collaborator. Dr. Galinat has provided important advice and assistance, though a heavy load of research and teaching made actual collaboration impractical. In botanical matters the aid of his associate Josephine Stewart Starbuck has been of great value.

It would be difficult to measure the contribution of Professor William A. Haviland of the University of Vermont, who generously opened to me his "The Original Vermonters" manuscript (in press) and his pertinent notes; he criticized my manuscript and in particular widened my appreciation of the Abenaki culture of northern and Down East Indian life.

For the cooperation of the Boston Athenaeum and its ever helpful staff, and the Harvard and Massachusetts State libraries, I am deeply indebted. My local library staff have found answers to numerous textual questions, and have obtained rare volumes for me. Reference librarians and state college anthropologists or archaeologists in every New England state have cheerfully helped.

Beyond all these, my gratitude goes to Mrs. Russell for providing the comprehensive index and for proofreading; and to her and our daughter Constance S. Russell for unlimited interest, patience, and helpfulness; to my efficient typist, Carol Kassabian; and to my student neighbor and messenger J. Christopher Flowers. For any merit this volume may have as to style and typography the credit goes chiefly to my publishing mentor, David Horne, and his ever helpful staff.

Wayland, Massachusetts   H.S.R.
October 1979

Contents

List of Illustrations

Foreword

The maps show the sites of New England's reported native Indian villages (over 325) and the principal pathways which served their inhabitants. No site or path is intentionally included for which the author has not, from long study of documents, local histories, and personal correspondence, found evidence that it was in use at or about the time the French and English first explored and settled the area.

Omitted, for example, are villages in the upper Housatonic Valley believed to have been earlier inhabited and again Indian-occupied in the eighteenth century. Also omitted are several of John Eliot's Christian Indian settlements, as well as the villages that must once have surrounded Lake Champlain and such inviting harbors as Newport's and Boston's but at the time of English settlement had apparently, for one reason or another, been given up.

As to native paths, only the principal throughways reported as being in common use are shown. In Maine these are chiefly in the southwest: in eastern Maine deep rivers and chains of lakes with occasional portages made travel by water the practical method; and paths were chiefly local.

Incomplete though the maps undoubtedly are, I hope that they will dispel the too common notion of native New England as peopled by a handful of savages wandering in a trackless wilderness.

The word "Indian" as used in this book refers to the native inhabitants of New England at the time Europeans first met them. It is a misnomer inherited from the earliest explorers and map makers of the New World, which they had hoped would be India. To call the natives "Amerinds," as some writers have done, merely compounds confusion, for Amerigo Vespucci was not the discoverer of either new continent.

Use of the geographic term "New England," the inhabitants of which are here described, is obviously a matter of convenience. The tribesmen who once made it their home had no conception of a corresponding geographic or political entity. Each tribe had its own reasonably well defined territory and its separate tribal government.

The spelling of the names of individual tribes, persons, and geographic features are (or have earlier been) subject to wide variations, the result of attempts to render native speech sounds in twentieth-century printers' symbols. Hence, spelling in this volume may be found to differ from that of other published studies. None of this variation or misnaming, however, need becloud our understanding and appreciation of the natives whom the Europeans met, or of their homeland.

Part One

BACKGROUND

1.

The Region and Its Resources

An inviting coast, a productive soil, and a considerably developed and populated countryside. That is the impression one receives, almost without exception, from observations left by the earliest visitors from the Old World to the shores of the area in the New World now called New England, during the century that preceded English settlement. These observers of the sixteenth and opening seventeenth centuries were mostly adventurers, seamen, and fishermen, and it should be remembered that it was always spring or summer when they made their appraisals of the new country. But all who have left records found the land itself attractive and the waters that lapped its beaches congenial.

The native inhabitants whom they met, strange in customs, food, implements, and costumes, they termed savages; yet most, they acknowledged, were not nomads but apparently well settled. Physically they were pleasing to look upon, and their intelligence deserved respect. Their housing was simple, as was that of Europe's lower classes at the time; their agriculture was developed enough to require precise description. They were offshoots of the great Algonquian family of tribes which stretched from the Carolinas to Canada north of the Great Lakes and on into the western plains. Though of one blood and, along the Atlantic and in New England, speaking dialects from a common language, no common bond provided unity or precluded war.

New England's landscape, with its eroded mountains, boulders, drumlins, sand, gravel, and hundreds of lakes, is of glacial origin. For thousands of years a miles-deep burden of ice gripped most of northern North America, including New England. Between 12,000 and 30,000 years ago, possibly in two separate migrations, adventurous Asians had been able to reach unpeopled Alaska from Siberia over ice or by a land bridge now covered by the water of Bering Strait.[1] In the new environment these early comers found sufficient food and shelter to exist. In time the less frigid climate to the south encouraged them to renew their migration. Eventually not only had they peopled western North America and Central America, but in South America their descendants had spread to the chill of Tierra del Fuego.[2]

Radiocarbon dating of archaeological remains shows that between nine and ten millennia ago man began his domicile in New England.

What had drawn him appears to have been the presence of large animals, caribou especially, which fed on the arctic tundra that had succeeded the glaciers as the ice retreated north, and which man in turn fed on.[3]

Eventually most species of this big game vanished, and with a warming climate new plants appeared on land and new species in the sea. Man became at first a gatherer of seeds, fruits, and roots. As plants and trees took over the landscape, he learned to make the seeds digestible by grinding them between stones. At the shore he dug clams, when at length these appeared. Marine life diversified, and he learned ways to spear seals, even to hunt whales that found sustenance in the chilled seawaters. On land he invented traps, pitfalls, and weapons to obtain reindeer and later deer, bear, and smaller game, as these too worked north. In rivers and streams he speared fish or guided them into weirs, then dipped them out. The beaver appeared, to dam streams and provide a habitat congenial for rushes, berries, and wild rice.[4]

Food for humans could now become more varied, and their diet more substantial. Trees had taken the place of tundra, and, no longer dependent on caves, man could provide himself with better shelter. With trees came an increase in nuts and fruits, in handles for tools, in better weapons.

Though man depended chiefly upon gathering wild fruits, seeds, and nuts and upon hunting game, hunger—even starvation—might in unfavorable terrain remain a continual threat. Indeed, as population increased but before cultivation opened a more dependable means of food supply, it is unlikely that in the whole of North America more than a few million people could have found sustenance.[5]

It was not in the Northeast, however, but on the great land bridge that joins the two American continents and in the west of South America that agriculture had its origin, at least 8,000 to 9,000 years ago. Human assistance in the growing of maize, America's most important and valuable cereal, and the selection of superior varieties goes back at least 7,000 years. The improvement and propagation of wild beans began in Central America about the same time.[6] These were but two of the food plants with which the inquisitive inhabitants experimented.

The list of cultivated vegetables native to the Western Hemisphere includes maize; beans; squash; potatoes, both white and sweet; peanuts; manioc, the source of tapioca; the cacao, whence came chocolate and cocoa; sunflowers, a source of food today in northern Europe; tomatoes; peppers, sweet and hot; pimento; eggplant; several melons; and other vegetable foods. Seventeen, at least, of the seventy-two vegetables commonly listed in seed catalogues originated in the American continents. Among fruits used as food in the western world but un-

1. Arnold Spring rock shelter, Greene, Rhode Island. Evidence suggests use by humans over thousands of years. *Massachusetts Archaeological Society Bulletin*, 30 (1969), 1.

known to Europeans in medieval times are pineapples, persimmons, papayas, guavas, avocados, some crabapples, and various berries. Among nuts, the pecan, butternut, and hickory are American. Commercial products considered to be of American origin include tobacco and chewing gum. Add to these the dyes cochineal and indigo as well as hevea and guayule rubber and cotton, found in both hemispheres. Hundreds of American flowers and ornamental shrubs and a multitude of medicinal plants previously unknown also enriched the world's horticulture and pharmacopoeia. From the tropics came cocaine, quinine, arnica, and vanilla. New England itself produced witch hazel, slippery elm, and sassafras. The Indian found medicinal uses for many native plants the virtues of which have been forgotten. Others have been superseded by modern drugs. Among American flowers are zinnias, marigolds, dahlias, cosmos, tuberoses, and many orchids.[7]

To recite such lists is to make clear how abundantly the voyages of Columbus and his successors enriched the modern world in diet, horticulture, commercial products, and medicine. The gold and spices the explorers so desperately sought become insignificant compared to the wealth they found growing. Today "Four-sevenths of the agricultural production of the United States, measured in farm values, consists of economic plants domesticated by the Indian and taken over by the white man."[8]

Among the thousands of plants used in some way by American Indians, about two hundred species were under their cultivation in the Western Hemisphere, including about one in four of our garden esculents and nearly fifty of the crops sufficiently important to be listed in international agricultural statistics.

Most American cultivated plants were developed by the tribes of Central and South America, especially of Mexico and the highlands of the Andes. There maize, the staff of life for a large proportion of western inhabitants, as well as beans and squash, had been under cultivation for thousands of years. It is believed that various strains of maize evolved more or less simultaneously from the seeds of tall native grasses in a number of places in Mexico and Central America. To select and refine the characteristics of three hundred or more types of this plant must have taken several thousand years.[9] It was the native Indian who accomplished this feat.

Archaeologists have established the great antiquity of such cultivated crops. In the arid lands of Peru and Chile and in caves in Mexico and the dry American Southwest, ancient maize kernels, ground meal, and corn cobs—as many as thirty varieties of maize in Peru alone—have been discovered, as well as rinds and seeds of pumpkins and squash, kidney and lima beans, peanuts, sweet and white potatoes, roots and tubers of manioc, and cotton lint. From food remains in Southwestern caves, it is estimated that maize, found also at other sites, was grown in this area as early as 4,500 years ago. Agriculture, more specifically horticulture—the encouragement, selection, and growing with hand tools of fruits, vegetables, and plants for food—must have been well established in North America two thousand years before the rise of Greece and Rome.[10]

Through these thousands of years the peoples of Mexico, Central and South America, and the American Southwest had been selecting from wild flora and domesticating the wealth of food plants. They had also evolved complex systems of government, erected great buildings and centers of worship, devised well engineered systems of irrigation, and become proficient in the decorative arts.

Nearer New England, in the Ohio Valley, peoples now called Adena and Hopewell at length appeared. Before and during the Christian era they constructed massive, carefully conceived earthworks which still bear testimony to the moundbuilders' energy and religious zeal. In what is now New York State, a group of Iroquois Indian tribes evolved a confederacy, the Five Nations, the success of which demonstrated an advanced state of political development. This alliance is said to have been a model for the federal plan of the United States.

To New England, by contrast with Mexico and Central America, cultivation of the soil—the permanence of habitation, and the advance in the arts and government which it makes possible—had come late, so recently that the arrival of cultivated plants was still a subject of strong local tradition. Dwellings were simply constructed, government was solely tribal, and agriculture was limited to a half-dozen crops. Most of the tribes whom the French and the English met had been in New England for at least a thousand years. A few, perhaps, were recent comers. Among all these tribes, differences in geography, climate, and tradition led to differences in food, housing, and mode of life. Their life and characteristics will be the subject of the remainder of this volume.

2.

The First Europeans

Who visited New England first:— Scandinavian Leif Ericsson or other Norsemen; John or Sebastian Cabot from Bristol (Venetian navigators in the service of the English); Portuguese Gaspar and Miguel Corte Real; Estevan Gomez of Spain; enterprising seamen out of Brittany or Britain's west coast city of Bristol; or others—is difficult to prove from any document available. At any rate, in 1524, only three decades after Columbus discovered the New World and two years beyond Magellan's voyage through the strait that bears his name, an Italian adventurer in the service of Francis I of France, Giovanni de Verrazano, not only cruised the New England coast but set down for his king the earliest adequate description of the land. Penetrating five or six leagues (twelve to fifteen miles) into the interior, he found the country "as pleasant as it is possible to conceive," with "open plains as much as twenty or thirty leagues in length, entirely free from trees"; and so fertile, he judged, "that whatever is sown there will yield an excellent crop." Coasting east from this inviting area, however, he reports the shore of northeastern Maine to be forbidding, with rocks, evergreen forests, and no sign of cultivation.[1] A decade later, with the second voyage of Jacques Cartier, came the discovery in 1534 of the St. Lawrence River and the beginning of the long ascendency of the French in Canada.

Several English shipmasters are known to have voyaged to New England during the rest of the sixteenth century, but none has left a useful description of the country or its inhabitants. Opening the next century, however, Bartholomew Gosnold, arriving in 1602 in the *Concord*, out of Dartmouth, reached Maine's Casco Bay. At Cape Neddick friendly natives mapped the coast for him with chalk. Sailing southwest, he crossed Massachusetts Bay, rounded Cape Cod, and set up headquarters at Cuttyhunk in the Elizabeth Islands while he gathered a return cargo of sassafras for medicine.

His contribution to our knowledge is slight, but the visit to the coast in the following summer of Captain Martin Pring is more informative. Pring spent six weeks in Plymouth Harbor loading sassafras, at that time in Europe a high-priced medical panacea. He ate "Pease and Beanes" with the natives, and delightedly watched them dance to the music of a zittern played by a sailor. Pring tells of native gardens planted with vegetables and tobacco, one of which he estimated at an acre. He saw "faire big strawberries" and other pleasing fruits. Before he left, there was enmity between the visitors and the natives, one result of which was the first recorded of Plymouth's innumerable forest fires. Another mariner, George Waymouth, marched inland in Maine over meadows that he called fit for pasture, dotted with occasional oak copses. He, too, noticed strawberries, and several other fruits, together with wild roses, groundnuts, and tobacco; he kidnapped a group of natives on Monhegan Island.[2]

The English were not alone in surveying the possibilities of the coast. French colonists were by now seated in Canada and intent on adding to their dominion. In 1604 Sieur Samuel de Champlain pushed

2. Champlain's map of the Saco, Maine, Indian village. "*A*. The river. *B*. Place where they have their fortress. *C*. Cabins in the open fields, near which they cultivate the land and plant Indian corn. *D*. Extensive tract of land which is sandy, but covered with grass. *E*. Another place where they have their dwellings all together after they have planted their corn. *F*. Marshes with good pasturage. *G*. Spring of fresh water. *H*. A large point of land all cleared up except some fruit trees and wild vines. *I*. Little island at the entrance of the river. *L*. Another islet. *M*. Two islands under shelter of which vessels can anchor with good bottom. *N*. A point of land cleared up where Marchin came to us. *O*. Four islands. *P*. Little brook dry at low tide. *Q*. Shoals along the coast. *R*. Roadstead where vessels can anchor while waiting for the tide." Champlain, *Voyages*, ed. W. L. Grant (1878), courtesy Boston Athenaeum.

south along the coast far enough to give names to the beautiful isles of Mt. Desert and Haute. He ascended the Penobscot to the head of tide, the site of today's Bangor, and the company met a few natives. Setting out again the next year on a leisurely inspection tour, he coasted as far as Nantucket Sound. On his return to France, he presented his sovereign with his "Voyages" and "journal tres-fidele des observations" of the territory, which he named New France but part of which was to become New England. He discussed in detail its coasts, rivers, and soils—the people and their "superstition." He enriched the volume with 22 illustrations and the earliest known (approximately) accurate map of the coast. "All along the shore," he wrote, "there is a great deal of land cleared up and planted with Indian corn. The country is very pleasant and agreeable, and there is no lack of fine trees." On Cape Cod the inhabitants were not so much great hunters as good fishermen and tillers of the soil. The gardens about the villages contained not only corn but beans, squashes, Jerusalem artichokes, and tobacco. At Gloucester during harvest time the following year, the natives tendered vegetables to the visitors. Even more welcome to the French eye and palate were the grapes they were offered. Gloucester, as Champlain depicts it, was mostly open fields and cabins, except for thick woods in two places, one of them Eastern Point, where forest protected the harbor.[3]

Champlain made a detailed map of Plymouth Harbor and its surroundings. He pictures the shore of the bay as largely cleared except for scattered trees. Habitations of the natives with attendant gardens surround the harbor. On only the two points of land at its entrance does he show groves of trees; the rest of the Plymouth Bay terrain is open. The map makes evident an important reason why the Pilgrims, when they arrived a few years later, were to choose this location for their settlement. As one of their chronicles records it, they sited their village "upon a high ground where there is a great deal of land cleared, and hath been planted with corn three or four years ago." At the time of their arrival it was without husbandmen; yet on nearby Cape Cod, in what is now the Chatham area, Champlain shows the harbor surrounded by cultivated land and cabins, except for woods to the east and the extreme northwest; and from his chart of Nauset further north on the Cape's outer shore it is clear that a similar pattern existed there.[4]

The coast was by now the annual destination of numerous European and English fishermen, the rendezvous of the latter Monhegan Island in the Gulf of Maine. In 1614 Captain John Smith arrived from Virginia. He examined the whole coastal area, including Massachusetts Bay and Boston Harbor (missed by Champlain), which he called "the Paradise of all these parts." The shores were well populated, he said, and "many Iles are planted with mulberries and salvage gardens." He counted forty villages between Cape Cod and Penobscot Bay. "The sea Coast as you pass shews you all along large Corne fields." He remarks on two especially pleasant isles of groves, gardens, and cornfields. Who, he concluded, could fail to approve this as a most excellent place for health and fertility?[5]

It was not to remain healthy for its native inhabitants. The English and other Europeans brought diseases against which the natives lacked resistance. Only a few years later a Pilgrim party from Plymouth viewed the same Boston Bay. They counted fifty isles there, some cleared from end to end, others wooded. Most had been inhabited, but the same infection that had depopulated the Plymouth hillsides—formerly considered to have been smallpox, recently thought perhaps bubonic plague—as well as the coast east as far as York River and even the Kennebec, had left these isles empty of cultivators. Not quite all had died, for on the mainland the visitors marched three miles inland and found corn newly gathered. When a few years later, in the mid 1620's, Rev. William Blaxton sat down as first settler on Shawmut and began his garden on the west slope of what was to be Boston's Beacon Hill peninsula, this, like the islands, must have been cleared land; for Anne Pollard, the lively twelve-year-old who was first ashore of the Puritans in 1630, says the place was covered with blueberry and other bushes. As Roger Clap, another original settler, recalled long after, "Governour Winthrop liked that plain Neck . . . called Blackstone's." William Wood in 1633 also describes both Boston and neighboring Chelsea as bare of wood.[6]

Naumkeag peninsula, now Salem, on the North Shore of Massachusetts Bay and site of the earliest Puritan settlement, likewise afforded considerable planting land. Pastor Higginson in 1629 writes from there of "divers plains where there is much ground cleared by the Indians, and especially about the plantation."[7]

Master Thomas Graves—like Captain John Smith experienced in civil engineering—found the countryside "very beautiful in open lands mixed with goodly woods, and again open plains, in some places five hundred acres." This last phrase may have referred to the great salt marshes of Essex County north of Salem, where he lived, though he speaks separately of marsh and lowlands; he also notices many cornfields on the hills.[8]

On the South Shore of Boston Bay, Mt. Wollaston, now part of Quincy, had been cleared of trees. There the Indian chief Chicatawbut had his seat. Close by, Wood reported an extensive treeless plain called Massachusetts Fields, where the greatest sagamore in the country, he said, had lived before the plague. Myles Standish had been introduced still earlier to what appears to be the same spot, the central gathering place of the local tribe. What are now Weymouth and Scituate, on the Bay's South Shore, also had large, open fields. This land, which in 1630 became the seat of the Massachusetts Bay Colony, was therefore not unbroken wilderness. Despite great areas of forest, "the land affords void ground" and "in many places, much cleared ground for tillage."[9]

As to the situation at Plymouth Colony, which included Cape Cod, Captain John Smith on his earlier visit to Provincetown in 1614 had expressed a poor opinion of its woods (they are still mostly poor today); but in parts, the Cape was well cultivated. Coming a little later, after the great Indian epidemic, Captain Thomas Dermer (1619) found along the coast "antient plantations, not long since populous, now utterly void" from the plague. A few inhabitants survived, however, for an exploring party from the company on the Mayflower, upon their first landing on Cape Cod's north shore in late 1620, almost immediately found evidence of human occupation and agriculture, a storehouse of corn. *Mourt's Relation* mentions fifty acres of plain ground there in a single tract, and local historians tell of large open fields suitable for tillage. When the Mayflower's voyagers settled at Plymouth, they found the situation just as Champlain had described it, except for the effects of the epidemic: "It pleased Almighty God to plant them upon the seate of an old towne . . . abandoned of the Indians."[10]

As for the south side of Cape Cod, John Brereton, recounting Captain Bartholomew Gosnold's voyage in 1602, had pictured the landscape near the entrance to Buzzard's Bay as "ravishing," with meadows very large and full of green grass. The islands off Cape Cod all had great cleared spaces. (On Martha's Vineyard, then heavily populated by Indians, traditional native cornhills were still to be seen in the 1930's, along with the mortars in which the grain was ground.)[11]

A Pilgrim party heading west from Plymouth in 1621 on an embassy to Chief Massasoit explored the land beside the Nemasket River through Middleboro (Nemasket) to Taunton. They came upon the sites of several former Indian villages with cleared fields. Turning south along the Taunton River estuary, they found that "thousands of men have lived here who died in the great plague that befell these parts." As they headed for Massasoit's residence on Mt. Hope Bay, they came to few places that had not been formerly inhabited. From other sources it appears that three of his villages were then still peopled.[12]

In future Rhode Island near what was to become Providence, Roger Williams, a decade and a half later, found well cultivated lands and fields lush with strawberries. Two former Indian fields he cultivated with his own hands. Governor John Winthrop observed that the country on the west of the Bay of Narragansett [what Rhode Islanders call

Kent and South counties] is all champaign [level open land] for many miles, and full of Indians."[13]

Here and on the large fertile islands in the Bay itself the Narragansetts had their seats; the infection had not reached them. Williams said that in traveling 20 miles you might come to 20 towns, large and small. De Forest estimates the Indian population here as probably the densest in New England. They were farmers all. On Block Island off the Rhode Island shore, in a military expedition not long after, the English destroyed Indian cornfields to the amount of 200 acres; and Winthrop's history says that the rest was oak sprout.[14]

Conditions were similar along the Connecticut shore. On a punitive expedition against the Pequots, Captain John Endecott, reaching Pequot Harbor, now the mouth of the Thames estuary and the harbor of New London and Groton, Connecticut, ascended a hill and overlooked a number of Indian cornfields, dotted here and there with wigwams, occupying both banks.[15] As the English began to populate the shore of Long Island Sound, they found villages and cultivation at Lyme, Madison, Guilford, New Haven, Milford, and Bridgeport. Milford alone had four Indian villages. When settlers moved west to the mouth of the Housatonic and beyond at Stratford, Shelton, Fairfield, Stamford, and Greenwich, they met with still others. It is no wonder, that Verrazano, as he sailed along the Sound, commented on the multitude of fires that met his eyes.[16]

Original records of town and county local historians describe what early colonists found along the rivers of interior New England. In the valley of the Connecticut, famous in recent centuries for its tobacco, potato, onion, and asparagus farms, the first white settlers came upon wide intervale meadows clear of trees and green with grass. Winthrop tells of a large village on the river's east side at South Windsor and another at East Hartford. Both sides of the Connecticut River were being or had been cultivated, at what are now Middletown, Wethersfield, Hartford, Enfield, Windsor, and Suffield in Connecticut; at Agawam, Northampton, Hadley, Hatfield, Whateley, Deerfield, and Northfield in Massachusetts; at Vernon, and the Oxbow at Newbury, Vermont; across the river at Winchester and Haverhill in New Hampshire; even in the Upper Coos Country (Guildhall and Maidstone, Vermont, and Northumberland and Lancaster, New Hampshire); and perhaps even further north. In western Vermont at Pownal, Arlington, Manchester, about Lake Champlain, and along tributary streams, Otter Creek especially, Indians had tilled fields before white settlement. In the lake itself, Champlain in 1609 noted four fine islands, twelve to fifteen leagues long, which had formerly been inhabited but were abandoned as a result of tribal wars. A Vermont historian mentions a 25-acre clearing in Shelburne at the mouth of the La Platte River.[17]

Pyguag (the Indian name for Wethersfield, Connecticut, and adjoining areas) is reported to have signified "cleared land." Further north, in Massachusetts, the fields the English bought for their Hadley settlement were designated in Algonquian "ground that has been planted." In most of the new river towns, the English were happy to lay out their villages on already open sites which, perhaps generation after generation, the natives had kept treeless, or nearly so.[18]

Due in part to a destructive smallpox epidemic from 1633 to 1635, New England's great central valley was lightly inhabited when the English arrived. Mohawk ravages from the west appear another likely cause; and tradition supports this view. Yet some Indian tribes—good farmers, too—making a pact with the Mohawks, had stayed to cultivate fields there (but, as will appear, the Mohawks later destroyed them). In a single transaction the Pocumtucks of Deerfield sold William Pynchon, founder of Springfield, 500 bushels of surplus corn, the crop of at least twenty acres of tillage, as food for the needy English settlers of Connecticut. All signs point to prehistoric occupation, probably long continued, for even the northernmost part of the productive Connecticut Valley, by peoples who kept its intervales open.[19] Local historians comment that further west in the Berkshire valleys of the Housatonic and Hoosac rivers, Indians—some in historic times—also lived and planted.[20] In western Connecticut, at Simsbury, Farmington, Sharon, Plainfield, Canaan, and similiar interior town sites, the English acquired tract after tract of land already cultivated. From the Indian fields of interior Wabbaquasset, now Woodstock, in northeast Connecticut, generous Nipmucks carried corn on their backs for the seventy miles to Boston as a gift to tide over one of the desperate first years of the English.[21]

Records show open lands and cleared village sites which the English were glad to acquire, with a certain amount of compensation to their previous occupants, all along the Merrimac River and in what are now the Newburys, Amesbury, Haverhill, Lowell, and Chelmsford in Massachusetts; and in New Hampshire at Nashua, Manchester, Concord, Boscawen, and beside the tributary Souhegan (said to mean "cleared but wornout land"), as far north as the shores of Lake Winnepesaukee, and at Lake Ossipee.[22] In Maine, up the Kennebec near Augusta, "we found a gallant Champion land and exceedinge fertile," writes an anonymous explorer in 1607. The Saco area included substantial tillage. A single field of "hoe-land" inland at Canton Point was estimated at 600 acres, one of several open tracts in Maine's Androscoggin Valley. (Samoset, who welcomed the Pilgrims at Plymouth, was sachem of the Pemaquid area east of Bath.) An English mariner, Christopher Levett, has left a picture of southern Maine in 1624. At Aguamenticus (York River) he encountered "good ground, and much already cleared, fit for the planting of corn [grain] and other fruits, having heretofore been planted by the Salvages who are all dead." At Saco the voyagers noted a great quantity of clear ground. Cornfields are recorded as far northeast as the Penobscot, and cleared land beside Lake Champlain in Vermont. Aroostook's settlers are said to have encountered some in northern Maine when that was occupied two centuries later.[23]

It is clear that by the time the first white explorers and immigrants appeared in the sixteenth and seventeenth centuries, and undoubtedly long before, areas open and cleared for settlement, cultivation, or other native purposes were common along New England's seacoast from the Kennebec on the east to the present New York line on the west, and on all the large and some small off-shore islands as well. Inland, open lands were strung at favorable spots along numerous alluvial river valleys in southern New England, spotted beside the principal ponds and lakes and many smaller ones; and on fertile rounded hilltops and southern slopes nearby where conditions were favorable for cultivation and life.

Part Two
THE PEOPLE

3.

The Tribes and Their Distribution

When Europeans first met New England Indians, the natives' political organization was tribal. A chief sachem governed each tribe, and subordinate sachems or sagamores headed its various divisions or villages (called "shires" by William Wood). In southern New England, the chieftainship was usually hereditary, descending through the mother, perhaps to a sister's offspring. Among the Abenaki the choice was more related to the chief's ability to command respect. Among the Narragansetts his authority was almost absolute. A chief might even punish a malefactor with his own hands. Daniel Neal called the system strictly monarchical. Roger Williams says that they planted or moved at the pleasure of the highest or superior sachem. In some tribes, however, among the mobile Abenakis of northern New England, where there was greater dependence on the environment, for instance, the chief's authority was likely to be largely advisory. Though a member of an old chief's family would probably be chosen to succeed him, the new chief's influence would depend to a greater extent on his own character, abilities, and prestige; among Maine's Penobscots and other Abenakis this was normally the case. Indeed, a noted warrior rather than the chief might be selected to lead the tribe in battle. Governor Thomas Hutchinson of Massachusetts Bay in the eighteenth century affirmed that "all persons of the blood royal bear sway in government."[1]

However high the chief's standing, he had a lively regard for public opinion: he seldom exercised his authority in important matters without a careful canvass of his council—"chosen for their wisdom and ability"—and his subordinate sachems, or without attempting to arrive either at unanimity or at least tacit consent. Governor Thomas Sullivan, writing later of Maine's Penobscots, observed that their chiefs and leaders habitually called councils and were governed by their decisions; and a like custom is reported from New Hampshire. If a sachem was too harsh, a tribesman might leave and join another tribe. Subordinates to the sachem were commonly divided into three categories: those of superior blood or attainments; the *sannops*, or commoners; and other persons, perhaps originally captives and not admitted to the tribe or in some respect lacking legal rights. In fact, there was no law in the European sense; tribal custom had the force of law, with public opinion to enforce it.[2]

3. Council Oak, Dighton, Massachusetts. According to tradition, Metacom (King Philip) and his council met in the shade of this widespread tree. Photograph by Howard S. Russell, about 1930.

The elderly were held in honor. Where weighty themes were considered, the members of the council of elders and the subchiefs as well were called in consultation; often all the higher-quality tribesmen participated. Proper consideration might take hours or even days before decision came. The conclave might include women, for they were the food producers and persons of experience and good judgment. In early historic times several instances are recorded in which women of high birth headed New England Indian groups as sachems. Sometimes as widows they succeeded their husbands; others were chosen when an able male of the princely line was lacking. "If there be no sachem the queen rules," Wood explains. At least seven such are recorded in early colonial history: three in Connecticut, two in Rhode Island, two in Massachusetts. They also signed deeds when land was transferred to the English.[3] Promising boys, Daniel Neal states, were purposely trained for membership in what he terms the council of nobles or "Paniese." At tribal sessions eloquence might be the decisive attribute. An able speaker drew admiration equal to that accorded the capable of body or even the brave warrior. At such general sessions unanimity was the objective, and time was taken to achieve it.[4]

Indian society contained certain groups claiming a common origin or blood tie. Ordinarily a common mark or family designation signified membership: among Mohegans, for example, a person might be a Wolf,

Turtle, or Turkey, with the appropriate identifying mark, while the Maine Abenakis used Sturgeon, Bear, Hummingbird, and other designations. Intermarriage within the family group was not acceptable; members of several families might dwell in the same village.[5] The Indians of the whole Atlantic seaboard above South Carolina were of Algonquian blood and shared the same Eastern Algonquian tongue, though with substantial differences of dialect from tribe to tribe: between, for example, the Indians of Chesapeake Bay and the Hudson Valley, and those of eastern Maine and Massachusetts Bay. Including the tribes of Canada and the Plains, McNickle counts, in all, thirteen distinct Algonquian languages.[6]

Boundaries of tribal lands were well known, defined by drainage basins, streams, hills, or other physical limits, traditional and mutually respected. Says Williams: "The natives are very exact and punctual in the bounds of their lands, belonging to this or that prince or people, even to a river, brook, etc." A casual encroachment on a deer park was sufficient ground for hostility, explains a colonial lady (this in New York), "not for the value of the deer or bear which might be killed, but that they thought their national honor violated . . ."[7] In southern New England each tribal domain included village sites, fields for cultivation, at least one good fishing place, more distant hunting grounds, and often a fort or two for defense.

The quality and quantity of lands and resources varied from tribe to tribe, according to each tribe's strength and location. The fishing places at the great falls and at certain oyster beds at the shore appear to have been open to all tribes (see below, page 124).

Though evidence on this subject is scanty, the territory claimed by the tribe seems to have been held in common, not to be alienated except through the chief or recognized tribal leaders after consultation with the tribe. Deeds to white colonists frequently bear numerous signatures, not seldom of both men and women. Each family had for its own use and cultivation as much land for tillage as it would care for. Certain lands might be cultivated in common, for the benefit of a high chief or to provide a store for tribal hospitality. Among the Penobscots the field the family cultivated was theirs as long as they used it, though some tribes assigned lands for the season only.[8]

Weapons, tools, ornaments, and clothing were personal property. So was the family's food, subject to the hospitality customs of the tribe, and the dogs, of which there were likely to be several; for, says Nicolas, their wealth is in proportion to their dogs. The concept of property in land may have begun to appear; Williams notes: "I have known them make bargain and sale amongst themselves for a small piece or quantity of ground," but whether he refers to tribes or to individuals is not clear.

Abenaki families in Maine traditionally passed on maple orchards from one family generation to the next.[9]

Common to all families of the tribe were the carefully protected groves of nut trees, berry fields, deer pasture, and wooded and marshy sources of firewood, and of materials for canoes, housing, baskets, and tools. The sachem was the holder for the tribe of all lakes and streams in its territory. His well stocked wigwam was the center of tribal hospitality. Ancestral ways of life from the long distant past were gradually modified as new conditions arose from new needs.

Beginning at what is today the New York state line, settlements of the Wappingers, related to the New York Mahicans, dotted Long Island Sound shore. A spillover of Mahicans from the Hudson Valley later settled in the Housatonic Valley in the Berkshires, and Mahicans were also domiciled in the Hoosac River area further north.

Easterly along the Connecticut shore resided the Western Niantics; then the powerful Pequot tribe, and their subject Mohegans, who later were to join the English in the virtual extermination of their masters. At the Rhode Island line dwelt a small tribe, the Eastern Niantics.[10]

The populous Narragansetts occupied the shores and islands of the bay which now bears their name, except for the Mt. Hope section to the east. Thence to parallel Buzzard's Bay and across most of Cape Cod were found the Wampanoags, Pokanokets, or Eastern Indians. On the peninsula's easternmost reaches and on Martha's Vineyard and Nantucket lived the related Nausets.[11]

To the north of the Wampanoag territory, about southern Massachusetts Bay and Boston Harbor, a numerous tribe, the Massachusetts, people of the Great Blue Hill, had their seats. Toward Cape Ann the domain of the Pawtuckets began, extending both north to include the lower valley of the Merrimac and its tributaries and east to the sea. To their north lived the Pennacooks.[12]

Still further eastward, scattered here and there in the valleys of Maine's large rivers, dwelt the Abenaki. Their chief divisions centered on Maine's three great river valleys. Beyond these and still in today's Maine the Passamaquoddians lived and hunted. The Tarrantines in the present Nova Scotia raided the coastal Maine and New Hampshire peoples and kept them in fear.[13]

Inland, into what is now Vermont, New Hampshire, even interior Maine, the powerful Mohawks from New York to the westward had extended their influence. When recorded history began, they were collecting tribute also from the Pocumtucks in the Connecticut Valley at Deerfield and Squakheags just above them at Northfield, and south

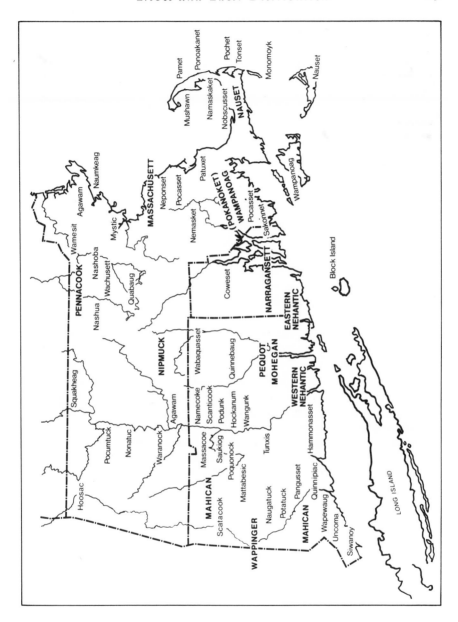

4. Approximate locations of certain Southern New England Indian tribes.

along the Connecticut River, and from the scattered and tribally unorganized Nipmuck villages in interior Massachusetts.

As we have seen, archaeological remains furnish evidence of village sites and agriculture in the fertile valleys of western Vermont, about Lake Champlain, as well as in the upper Connecticut Valley. Yet whether as a result of Mohawk depredations or other causes, only a small number of Western Algonquians were found there by early European explorers.[14]

How great was the native population of the New England area at the 1605 date, say, when Champlain explored it, and before the scourge of imported diseases that came first between 1615 and 1620 and again after the advent of the Puritan influx of the 1630's? F. W. Hodge considers that for the part agricultural, part hunting-and-gathering type of native life, southern New England's population had about reached the maximum possible for its resources. If so, what was that maximum? Willoughby, after "a somewhat extended investigation," concluded that a figure of 24,000 would include New England's whole population previous to the great epidemic that preceded the Mayflower's arrival. Francis Parkman had earlier estimated the fighting strength of all New England in 1600 at 8,000, indicating a population fairly comparable to though somewhat larger than Willoughby's figure. Demographer James Mooney's estimate is 28,000. By contrast, Charles Starbird assigned a figure between 36,000 and 38,000 to Maine alone; and a total of 24,000 is proposed for small Rhode Island by a 1920 historian of that state, though a recent state history allows the predominant Narragansetts but 5,000.[15]

Certain local data offer piecemeal evidence. A Pilgrim party on the way to visit Chief Massasoit of the Wampanoags in 1621 passed through the Middleboro-Taunton-Warren area to Mt. Hope Bay. They saw the remains of so many once occupied villages and such extensive formerly cultivated fields that they concluded thousands of people must have lived there before the plague. Champlain, a decade and a half earlier, had found two hundred natives (presumably adults) at Gloucester, and at the Nauset village on Cape Cod five to six hundred. Yet Nauset was but one of thirty villages, large and small, in the Cape area. As late as 1685 five hundred and eight was the count of adult praying Indians, youngsters not included, at the easterly end of Cape Cod. This would indicate a total of twelve to fifteen hundred if, as is likely, there were nonpraying inhabitants in addition.[16]

Offshore, Nantucket and Martha's Vineyard harbored substantial numbers, as did Block Island. On Block Island in 1636 Captain John Endecott on a punitive expedition claimed to have destroyed two hundred acres of Indian corn as well as the inhabitants' wigwams. Using

5. Approximate locations of certain Northern New England Indian tribes.

explorer Martin Pring's observation of an acre of tillage per family, and even allowing for considerable exaggeration, this would suggest a total of five or six hundred people on that island, and Jennings estimates twelve to fifteen hundred. Thomas Mayhew's missionary letter in 1674 states that Martha's Vineyard then counted 300 Indian families, indicating a population on that fertile island of at least 1,000; but Jennings' figure triples this. The reliable missionary Daniel Gookin writes of three hundred praying "males and females" on Nantucket in 1674, not apparently including children. (The group of small Elizabeth islands had each a few families also). Since the plague seems to have missed the islands named, it appears reasonable to assign these three a total of at least 3,000 people, which would be one eighth of Willoughby's estimate for the whole of New England.[17]

The Rhode Island west-shore neighborhood with its eight Narragansett villages is called by De Forest the densest native area on the whole Atlantic coast, its population set as late as 1674 at 5,000: Roger Williams tells of "thousands" gathering there for games and sports, and a dozen villages, large and small, within twenty miles. Governor Hutchinson of Massachusetts says it was generally agreed that at the opening of King Philip's War the Narragansetts had 2,000 fighting men, which would indicate a total then, of at least 6,000.

Connecticut was certainly well peopled. In the Cos Cob massacre of 1624 the Dutch and English killed a great number, probably six to seven hundred, and at Golden Hill in Bridgeport six hundred Poguonnocks were concentrated by the English in a reservation. A mid-Connecticut historian, on the other hand, asserts that in the Windsor section of the Great Valley alone the natives of ten villages had been able to muster "2000 bowmen," indicating a population just for that fertile area of, say, 6,000. Yet De Forest allows only 6,000 to 7,000 inhabitants for the whole state![18]

Coming north to Massachusetts Bay, Edward Johnson in his "Wonder-Working Providence" accords the Massachusetts tribe 30,000 able men before the sickness—an undoubted exaggeration. A modern writer numbers the single Saugus sub-tribe, (perhaps Pennacook rather than Massachusett) just east of Boston, at 3,000 people. In addition to the shore dwellers, the Mystic River Valley, the Concord River Valley, and the Merrimac Valley each afforded home and farm land for hundreds of Indian families. As a further criterion of settlement, and from study of scores of local histories, I have found Indians resident as modern times began, in over one hundred of Massachusetts' present towns.[19]

For New Hampshire one of its historians, Edwin D. Sanborn, a century ago suggested a figure of four to five thousand natives before English occupation. James D. Squires puts it at less than 4,000.[20]

The missionary Gookin in the mid-1660's offers the result of his inquiries among native informants for the whole New England area west of the Maine-New Hampshire line. The numbers of fighting men he lists add up to 18,000, which—even allowing for exaggeration by his native informants (though Indians were noted for exactness)—would indicate the presence of 54,000 people at least. He does not mention the inhabitants of such populous western Connecticut shore villages as Cos Cob and Bridgeport, to name only two, or the Pocumtucks of the upper Connecticut Valley, called by the Dutch a "great" or numerous tribe numbered by a local historian at 5,000, or the Squakheags to their north. These and some of the inland Nipmucks were apparently beyond his purview.[21]

Considering all the data, and disregarding published estimates that appear improbable, we judge that a total of at least 60,000 natives in what are today the three southern New England states and New Hampshire is not unreasonable. Vermont, formerly populated about Lake Champlain and in the Connecticut Valley, was in the 1600's mostly unpeopled except around Vernon, Brattleboro, Newbury, and Missisquoi.

There remain the valleys of Maine's rivers and their inhabitants. The evidence is meager. Mrs. Eckstorm believed that at the time the

6. Traditional cross-island Indian path, deeply worn. Martha's Vineyard, Massachusetts. Photograph by Howard S. Russell, about 1940.

English arrived in Massachusetts, eastern Maine was largely uninhabited; Mooney, the most quoted estimater of population numbers for North America, accords the whole of Maine but 3,000. Turning to local data, J. W. Thornton quotes sailors' reports on four seventeenth-century Penobscot villages. One had 55 "houses" and 80 men; another 55 and 90 men; a third 30 and 90 men; a fourth, Pemaquid, 100 men, women, and children. Allowing, for the first three, two additional persons for each male would indicate a total population for the four villages as 880. At Sagadahoc there were four more villages. Using the same average per village would bring the total inhabitants for the area he reports to about 1,750 persons. Rufus Sewall claims that the Wauwenocs about Sheepscot Bay had subject chiefs to the west commanding 1,000 to 1,500 bowmen each. Starbird guesses that the Androscoggin Valley may have been home for 5,000 to 6,000. For my own part, from a variety of sources I have been able to locate twenty-three early Indian villages in Maine, with possible mention of others. Using the average per village from Thornton's data, we arrive at a total for the whole of Maine of around 5,000 native inhabitants, chiefly west of the Penobscot River. This does not seem unreasonable, though considering the losses from the 1616-17 plague, it may be far from exact.[22]

The population for the entire area of what is today called New England at the time the English came may therefore have reached a total of 75,000. The precise figures we shall never know.

As to the geographic distribution of native settlement, it is enlightening to recall that the populous southern New England tribes relied largely on tillage for food, and that all except the northeasternmost of New England's Indians were at least in part agricultural people. We should therefore examine the environmental factors that entered into their selection of habitats—in particular water, soil, forest, and frost.

The main centers of tribal population were close to the shore or in the valleys of large rivers. To account for this circumstance, one theory is that the ancestors of the Indians whom the Europeans first met had arrived by sea in their remarkable canoes. A more likely cause seems to be that year in and year out, fish was a considerably more reliable source of food than game, and New England waters held a wealth of fish; also moving waters bring driftwood for fuel. At least as important, however, might be that the Indians' chief cultivated crops—corn, beans, and squash—are all extremely sensitive to a spring frost and at maturity to an autumn frost. The stabilizing influence of the sea or any substantial body of water may lengthen the growing season by two weeks or more at spring planting and again in the fall. With the possibility in much of

New England of a late August frost, this might readily mean the difference between 100 days and 130 days or more for growing crops. A long frost-free season is likewise important for wild berries, grapes, cherries, and nuts, which the Indians also relied on. Hence a comparison of Indian New England habitats with a map of its thermal divisions makes it appear likely that the natives were as aware of the influence of climate on crops as are modern cultivators. Edward Delabarre believed this to be one reason for the concentration of planting fields and population in the region about Mt. Hope Bay, where he records a large area of Indian cornfields. Thus, to the ease of transportation and travel that a waterside location afforded was added a climatic advantage. A map of southern New England's chief cities and towns, so far as they are located beside the sea and the principal rivers and lakes, will closely approximate that of the larger Indian villages of the sixteenth and seventeenth centuries.[23]

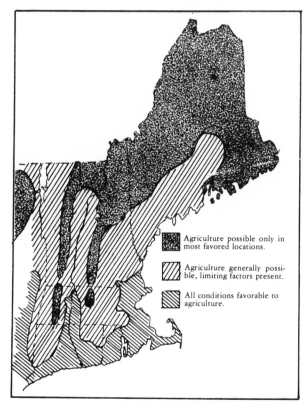

Agriculture possible only in most favored locations.

Agriculture generally possible, limiting factors present.

All conditions favorable to agriculture.

7. Areas climatically suitable for Indian farming. *BMAS*, 8 (1947), 31.

4.

Personal Characteristics

This native inhabitant—cultivator, hunter, fisherman, crafts-man—of whom, in the Massachusetts Bay region at any rate, so few remained when the Pilgrims and Puritans appeared, was "amiable to behold," according to William Wood: "black haired, out nosed, broad shouldered, brawny armed, long and slender handed, out breasted, small waisted, lank bellied, well thighed, flat kneed," with "handsome grown legs, and small feet." Well proportioned and goodly people, John Smith thought; Champlain also called them handsome. "They exceed us in size," Verrazano observed. English, French, and Swiss describe the males as taller than their own countrymen, and very straight. A modern local historian reports that among Squakheag skeletons unearthed in the Connecticut Valley (of a period undetermined) appear "small giants," estimated (perhaps excessively) to have been more than six and a half feet tall; and other exhumed skeletons often indicate good height. By contrast, Captain George Waymouth reports a tribe on St. George's Island whose members were neither tall nor large. But no early account classes the Indians as physically smaller than Europeans.[1] A Connect-icut archaeologist, from observing remains of a considerable series of shore burials, reports an average height of five feet, ten inches.

As to complexion, to one of Captain Gosnold's company the natives appeared dark olive. Others saw them as bronze or tawny, one tribe even black (perhaps painted). None described those they met as aged. To Gosnold they appeared gentle of disposition and exceedingly courteous, but other early visitors suspected deceit or encountered fear and antagonism.

The males were easy to judge physically, for "Naked they go, except a skin about their waist, and sometimes a mantle about their shoulders." Their teeth, gleaming white, were sound and regular, and apparently intact. Few or none were cross-eyed, blind, lame, or hunchbacked; most were well formed and without blemish.[2] No male was bearded beyond a few hairs, but the skins of some bore seared-in embellishments. Wood tells how upon the cheeks of the superior males there were "certain portraitures of Beares, Deeres, Mooses, Wolves . . . Eagles, Hawkes" incised permanently in unchangeable ink, together with round impressions on their arms and breasts, for what purpose he is not altogether certain. The animal designs, Willoughby suggests, were clan insignia.³ Waymouth noted seven Maine males with stripes of blue painted across chin, upper lip, and nose.

As for the feminine aspect, Verrazano, earliest of all, called the Indian female "comely to behold: very graceful and well formed: of a sweet and pleasant countenance" and well mannered. Champlain thought the Cape Cod girls neat in manners and dress; Isaack De Rasieres, a very early visitor to New England from New Amsterdam, considered them attractive, of middle height, and well proportioned, their features finely cut, hair long, eyes black. Several other Europeans, including the Hollander Adriaen Van der Donck, termed them physically well favored, seldom very handsome, and rarely very ugly.⁴

Testimony from early English writers is usually complimentary. Josselyn judged the young ones "very comely, with good features, many prettie Brownettoes and spider-fingered lasses . . . among them." He termed them "slender, limbs cleanly, straight, generally plump as a partridge, and, saving now and then one, of a modest deportment." Like others, he noted their black eyes and even, very white teeth, "which," he adds, "the natives account the most necessary and best parts of man." Gabriel Archer, on the shore of Vineyard Sound, describes a native's wife and daughter as clean and straight-bodied, with sweet, pleasant faces. All observers agree as to their erect carriage and ability to bear great burdens without stooping.⁵

In general the women are reported to be of moderate height; yet as late as 1828, after some observers considered New England Indians to have degenerated, a local historian remarks on a highborn Indian woman on the Connecticut shore nearly six feet tall, muscular, erect, of stately step with piercing black eyes, of polite and commanding appearance.⁶

The youngsters' physiques drew special plaudits. "Their children are never Rickety nor shall you ever see a Bandy-leg'd or Crooked Indian." (Youngsters went bare in summer.) "No fools among Indians, but some born deaf and so dumb." In New Netherland Nicolaes Van Wassenaer called the native children well shaped, few deformed or with natural physical faults. Adriaen Van der Donck had never heard of a native child born blind. This general good health, vigor, and spirit of the young Indian was in marked contrast to the misery of many children reported in the Europe of the sixteenth and seventeenth centuries.⁷ Early New England writers are critical of the freedom allowed Indian children by their elders and of the lack of discipline; but to Indian parents and to the grandparents, aunts, and uncles who often helped rear them, the results of their methods must have appeared satisfactory.

They love them all, Lescarbot testified. Few local explorers say much about the elderly, but the Pennsylvania missionary John Heckewelder writes that there the old were as well treated as favorite children.[8]

The Italian Verrazano, who had sailed the whole Atlantic coast, appears to present a balanced appraisal as he observes New England's natives: "This is the goodliest people and of the fairest condition that we have found in this our voyage; they exceed us in bigness, they are the color of brass, some of them incline more to whiteness, others are of a yellow color, with long and black hair which they are careful to turn and deck up: they are of a sweet and pleasant countenance."[9]

Contemporary judgments as to bodily development and symmetry, even though corroborated from numerous sources, might appear doubtful were it not for the handsome proportions and fine faces of certain remaining descendants of the race, still occasionally to be met on Martha's Vineyard, or at one of the modern Indian neighborhoods of Cape Cod, Connecticut, or Maine.

As to mental capacity, Roger Williams testifies: "For the temper of the braine in quick apprehension and accurate judgments to say no more, the most high and Sovereign Creator hath not made them inferior to Europeans." Wood also found their understanding quick, judgment good, and memory strong.[10] "I have not seen anyone who does not frankly admit that the Savages are more intelligent than our ordinary peasants," wrote Father Paul Le Jeune in Canada; he even suggested that laborers be sent from France to work for the Indians. The Algonquians there, related to the New England tribes, he thought especially acute. Father Pierre Biard noted one difference from the whites: "All their conceptions are limited to sensible and material things . . . nothing abstract, internal, spiritual" (but on this point other observers disagree). In serious matters the Indian was likely to be grave and thoughtful, in sport and competition ebullient. No one doubts his deep knowledge of woodcraft and nature's ways.[11]

In respect to moral attributes testimony is sharply divided. Here we moderns tread on insecure ground if we rely on the writings of Puritan and colonial chroniclers, steeped in the Old Testament and confident of their destiny as God's chosen people. The New England portion of the New World was to them an area He had prepared for His elect. Many early chroniclers, plainly prejudiced, had nothing good to say of the natives. Thievish, deceitful, lazy, improvident, licentious, bloody, murderous, devilish—these are but a few of the derogatory adjectives used by soldiers, frontiersmen, and Puritan divines. Cotton Mather, from his town of Boston, called them wretches and blood-thirsty savages, "the most devoted vassals of the deval."[12] Their ability to remember for years benefits conferred and injuries suffered at others' hands is well attested. Tales of treachery and deceit are numerous; yet there is no lack of reliable testimony in regard to acts of loyalty, and generosity to friends; and their punctuality and scrupulous regard for agreements is proverbial. The Indian sense of personal dignity and his concept of fair dealing were frequently outraged by unscrupulous newcomers. Assuming themselves superior, and with a radically different concept of land tenure, the whites often dislodged him from ancestral fields and hunting grounds, bound him by laws in the making of which he had no part, demanded his allegiance to a faraway king of whom he had never before heard.

Like the colonists who judged him, each native was an individual, with a deep sense of personal and tribal worth. To Europeans who treated them with consideration and respect most natives responded in kind. Awful cruelties are unquestionably to be laid at the door of some Indians. Their deeds of violence fill the chronicles of the 1600's and 1700's: English men and women slain in ambush, scalped, carried off in the dead of winter; children dashed against trees—scores of such tales are recorded in the old writings. Yet it is revealing to recall the words of Rev. Robert Cushman of Plymouth, and then to note the terrible sequel. "The Indians," he testified, "are said to be the most cruel and treacherous people in all these parts, even like lions, but to us they have been like lambs, so kind, so submissive and trusty, as a man may truly say, many Christians are not so kind and sincere . . . they never offered us the least injury in word or deed."[13]

Such are the facts of human nature that later, inflamed by what they considered acts of injustice and greed on the part of the English, descendants of these same kindly Indians were burning houses and slaughtering men, women, and children in the outreaches of Plymouth Colony and through most of the territory of Massachusetts Bay; and in a single act of retaliation, descendants of Mr. Cushman's hearers sold into Spanish slavery King Philip's wife and son of nine years, and executed or sold 180 other Indians he had praised, with numerous similar transactions to follow. Such deeds of the Plymouth (and Massachusetts) authorities appear three centuries later even less pardonable if, as has been charged in at least one case, it was in contravention of the terms under which the Indians had been led to surrender to Plymouth's military representatives.[14]

Nor did these cruel acts stand alone. Much earlier, in a surprise attack in 1643, colonial soldiers had destroyed a whole town of Pequots, one of the most numerous and haughty Indian tribes, though it sheltered women and children along with the warriors; and Hollanders and English had done a similar deed in western Connecticut in 1644. In the Great Swamp Fight in 1675 another Indian fort peopled by hundreds of both sexes and all ages suffered a dreadful fate in a holocaust of fire. Some Puritan divines considered the opportunity for such actions a blessing from the Almighty; and for their part, the Dutch held a public thanksgiving in New Amsterdam.[15] It seems fair to conclude in this quite different day that both the Indian tribes and their European successors exhibited at times some of the best and some of the ugliest qualities of the human race.

5.

Health and Illness

Though Indians are often depicted as persons of superior physical characteristics, they did not escape all ailments of the human race. Some explorers, indeed, thought that because of the natives' rougher life, they were more subject to disease than Europeans. They were inured to cold; yet arthritis, rheumatism, neuralgia, chills and fever, pleurisy ("which all their remedies can't conquer"), and eye troubles from smoky cabins were not uncommon. Wounds sometimes brought on festering sores.

Except for the hazards of warfare and the chase, however, the Indian span of life was likely to be longer than that of most of Europe's people at the time of discovery. Until the advent of explorers and fishermen from across the water, New England's natives were free of the infectious and contagious diseases that scourged the Old World: smallpox, malaria, typhus, tuberculosis, the bubonic plague, diphtheria, measles, probably syphilis, and many others were all unknown. Lahontan observed that the American Indian was "unacquainted with the infinity of diseases that plague the Europeans."

Such effects of malnutrition as rickets and humpbacks, common in Europe, were missing. Some natives, however, were deaf. Teeth, all descriptions agree—and archaeological evidence bears this out—were strong and regular. Those of the elderly, while likely to be worn down from much eating of stone-ground cornmeal, were seldom missing. Toothache, Roger Williams remarks, the natives "abominated."

Indian medicine, moreover, is entitled to respect. One student of the subject, Leaman F. Hallett, ventures the opinion that their healers had a far more comprehensive knowledge of curatives than that possessed by the early English settlers. Using plant extracts and other of nature's remedies, they were especially successful with fractures and wounds; more than one tale has come down from colonial times of successful healing after English attempts had failed. Wood gives the natives credit for rare skill in the use of plants as curatives.[1]

To counteract their ills, the native pharmacopoeia contained a wealth of specifics. Youngken asserts that they were acquainted with cough and cold remedies, emetics, cathartics, diaphoretics, vermifuges, astringents, alteratives, stimulants, narcotics, and antiseptics—all from plant sources. So complete was aboriginal knowledge of their native flora, says Vogel, that some tribe or other used all but a half dozen indigenous drugs now known.

How these herbs and roots produced the desired effect they may not have understood. They simply worked. Youngken lists four hundred and fifty plant remedies and over fifty Indian drugs recognized in present-day pharmacopoeias. Hallett counts sixty-three sources of healing from New England alone. (See below, Appendix.) With fractures and dislocations, their bonesetters, using bark with resin cements, were especially skillful. When captive John Gyles froze his feet, the Indians told him to smear them with a fir balsam salve; in a few days they were well again. The natives had poultices, and they were familiar with massage and adept at reducing swellings.[2]

Particular reliance was placed on the sweat bath, the most common prescription to cleanse the skin and overcome the illnesses of winter. At Stafford Springs, Connecticut, sulphured waters had supposedly curative properties; Maine Indians had a curative mud spring. They anointed their bodies with fish oil, eagle fat, coon grease, and similar emollients against sun, weather, and insects; the hair was dressed carefully with walnut oil.

Among common native plants and trees which Youngken, Hallett, and others list as local sources of remedies for illness, injuries, sores, aches, and pains are balsam fir, birch bark, blackberry, bloodroot, blue flag, butternut, cranberry, wild cherry, elm, hardhack, Indian hemp, wild hop, lady's slipper, white oak, pipsissewa or wintergreen, pokeberry, white pine, sassafras, smooth sumac, tobacco, gum turpentine, and witch hazel.[3]

With the rough conditions met in long, often bone-chilling days of hunting, there needed to be cold remedies. Two sources were ground juniper and jack-in-the-pulpit; another, dogwood bark. A gargle made from the root of the wild blackberry was thought to be a help for sore throat. If a cold affected the lung, the skin could be scarified and a pitch pine preparation applied. Another chest application, good for other soreness as well, came from the inner bark of the wild black cherry, and a third from the bruised root of Solomon's seal. A cherry bark decoction served as a spring tonic. A powder made from Solomon's seal was held to be an antiseptic; milkweed was another source. Spider's web and prince's pine were used as styptics to stop bleeding. Also for bleeding, John Winthrop, Jr., mentions the wool of the rattlesnake weed. Snake bite was not unusual, and for this the root of that plant was the specific, while to draw out venom from a wound made by a poisoned arrow a decoction from unripe cranberries is reported to have been useful. For other sorts of wounds, a boiled moss might be used. Cranberry poultices were considered helpful for various types of sores, as were boiled water-lily roots. Birch bark and pine bark are mentioned for burns (whether natural, shredded, or boiled is not clear) and a balsam salve for bruises.

As a salve, however, what could be superior to balm of Gilead? Wood ashes, too, allayed inflammation, as did poultices of unripe cranberries and smartweed. As a pleasant means of relieving a headache, the victim heated red cedar leaves on fireplace stones and breathed in the scent. Cedar leaves and twigs, both boiled, were thought helpful for fever.

New England Indians had remedies also for digestive troubles. Goose or skunk oil, or a purgative of butternut bark, would clear the bowels; columbine root or cattail flowers ended diarrhea; a cedar leaf concoction relieved dropsy and urinary difficulties. From the elderberry came both emetic and cathartic. John Winthrop, Jr., even tells of a remedy for piles: bear's grease mixed with the powdered shell of the razor fish (solaris). A Penobscot prescription was tea from boiled white oak bark; it was a help also for diarrhea. For suppressed menstruation pennyroyal or blueberry tea were said to be helpful, as was a decoction from the partridge berry plant taken at childbirth.

For fevers the Delawares (Algonquian) relied on dogwood bark. One reason for the custom of using oil or grease as a skin emollient may have been to counteract exposure to poison ivy. Arthritis and rheumatism as a result of an often rough Indian life took their toll. Wintergreen (containing aspirin) was the source of one remedy; another was the blossoms of the pyrola weed. If you were a Penobscot, you would make a tea from sarsaparilla and sweet flag roots. If your trouble was nausea, an external application of bruised ragweed might help. Witch hazel soothed inflammation; sarsaparilla helped kidney function.

The Indian pharmacists were not all "medicine men," as might be supposed from that current phrase (these seem to have acted more as psychiatrists, exorcists, and hypnotists). More likely, they were knowledgeable elderly women, as modern Mohegan Gladys Tantaquidgeon asserts. Nicolar, discussing Maine Indians, said they had no male doctors till the whites came. Medical lore was passed down in the family from grandmother to mother to daughter and kept private. Not all the remedies mentioned here would be known or available to any single tribe or family, but the sources of some curatives reported by colonial observers were never made known to the English. (See also below, pages 39-41 and 43, for pow-wows.)

The women who were adept at medicine would collect the essential herbs, roots, and barks at odd times—never in the dog days but always just ahead; they would dry them carefully in the sun. With bark, only the inner part was used; it was pounded with stones and ground in a wood or stone mortar, and perhaps boiled or otherwise prepared.[4] They even made syringes, so Youngken states, with a hollow bladder for a bulb.

To early English observers one matter of continual wonder was "the extraordinary ease of childbirth" of Indian women. Usually they required little if any assistance. If on a journey the mother-to-be felt labor approaching, she was likely to leave the company and enter the woods. A few hours later, with a babe in her hands, she would rejoin the group. Gookin notes how unusual it was for the woman to run into difficulty. Indian women, he remarks, are "ordinarily quickly and easily delivered, and many times so strong that a few hours after they will go about their ordinary vocations." Byrd, in the South, mentions a North Carolina Indian belief that a diet of bear's flesh resulted in easy childbirth.[5]

The Indian babe was usually very small by European standards, and born white, with black hair, Lechford said. The new-born would be laid in a soft bed of cattail or milkweed fluff, duck feathers, or sphagnum moss. (Among New Jersey Algonquians it might be soft cedar bark.) This would prevent chafing, and the vegetable substances would perform the absorbent function of the English child's diapers.[6]

Meanwhile, in anticipation of the child's advent, it was the father's duty to prepare a smooth flat cradleboard, two to three feet long and about a foot wide, to which the infant could be strapped. The child's covering would be filled with fluff to prevent chafing. The whole could be carried on the mother's back as she moved about, or hung on a nearby branch while she pounded meal or hoed.[7]

The child was not babied. Upon his mother's recovery, after two or three days, the little papoose "travels about with his bare-footed mother in the Icie Clammbankes." In fact, Ralph May quotes a Captain Levittas as saying that to harden them against the cold, Indians had been known to bury their children in the snow.[8] Yet mortality for both mothers and infants was low. If the mother's milk failed (she ordinarily nursed her child for two years) and no wet nurse was available, she would crush hickorynuts into a thin paste, and this baby food would sustain the child.

Ward attributed to the cradleboard, made "in the form of a bootjack," the absence of rickets and crooked limbs among Indian children. Modern pediatricians might not agree, but numerous observers remarked on the absence of deformities in Indian children. "You shall never see a bandy-legged or crooked Indian" has been earlier quoted. Whether this was in all cases due to a healthy life on the part of parents and children, or whether a malformed babe clearly incapable of enduring the physical strain of normal Indian existence was not allowed to live, can be a matter only of conjecture. Teething is said not to have been a serious matter; the child got a bone to chew. Moreover, the whole series of contagious diseases to which European children were subject was missing.[9]

Among Indian men, except as war might cut it off, the life span was substantial: sixty, eighty, even a hundred years or more are recorded. In a considerable series of Connecticut shore burials, most had lived to be forty or fifty. On occasion, when war or catastrophe made necessary a swift and dangerous removal, the elderly and infirm might choose to remain behind so as not to endanger the whole group; the approach of death was normally without fear.[10]

In addition to the health resources to be found in nature, the sweat bath was used as a standard cleanser, vivifier, and cure-all. On the shore of a clear pond or stream near their village the Indians built a circular hut. Sometimes it was partly of stones, with rushes above and high enough to stand in; sometimes a round excavation for the lower part would suffice. For a floor a bed of stones was laid, and on this a fire was built. After the stones were well heated, the burning brands were pushed out and the stones and any remaining coals were dowsed with water, which raised a great steam. Then the whole family—men, women, and children— would crowd in, close the opening, and sit or lie in the mist and heat. For perhaps an hour they would chat or sing while sweat poured out from every part of their bodies. At length everybody dashed out into the close-by water and swiftly cleansed the skin, then applied ointment to every part. Great claims are still heard for the healthful effect of sweat baths, the Finnish sauna being only one example.[11]

Anointing the skin was a help also against mosquito bites. Some colonial writers mention unpleasant body odors arising from the practice; yet H. E. Pulling, who in the nineteenth century grew up among Great Lakes Algonquians, comments on their cleanliness and their enjoyment of scents from balsam, pine, and sweet flag leaves, which they hung about their necks. "When the Abenakis conveyed their land," he wrote, "they reserved the treaty-right to gather sweet-grass forever, anywhere."[12]

There remains for consideration the role of the powwow, as the colonists heard the Narragansetts call their priest-healers. (The term "medicine," indicating power, and "medicine man," denoting physician or priest, is absent from writings about Indians before the nineteenth century.)[13]

Governor Edward Winslow of Plymouth, with some slight medical knowledge himself, considered the powwow to be concerned principally with calling the devil, rather than acting as a physician; and some of

the most prominent seventeenth-century ministers were bitterly contemptuous. For a fair appraisal, one must discount the diatribes of
Puritan divines. As Daniel Boorstin and John Duffy have pointed out,
the ministers—university graduates, the best educated and best read
persons in the colonies, and considered also to be enriched by divine
grace—were often called on for medical as well as spiritual advice.
Disbelief on their part in the efficacy of the methods of the untutored
and heathen Indian powwow would not be unnatural.[14]

Other observers, even some ministers, offer a more balanced view.
"There are among them certain men and women whom they call
powwows," observes Gookin, who knew them well. "These are partly
wizards and witches holding familiarity with Satan, that evil one; and
partly are physicians and make use at least in show of herbs and roots for
curing the sick and diseased." Highly educated Adriaen Van der Donck
of New Netherland reported that the Indians there knew how to cure
"very dangerous and perilous wounds and sores by the use of roots,
leaves, and other little things." A visitor to Plymouth Colony from New
Netherland tells how the young male neophyte was trained to become a
powwow. He was taken to the woods to seek out and learn the
properties of poisonous and bitter herbs and to use them as emetics in
cases of serious illness. John Josselyn in the Bay Colony observed:
"Their physicians are the Powwows or Indian priests." Colonial accounts not infrequently record cures where English efforts had failed;
European medicine then was anything but scientific.[15]

The chanting and drumming and rhythmic dancing that often
accompanied the powwow's ministrations were in part effective, some
later observers noted, by diverting the mind of the sufferer from his ills.
The combined and concentrated attentions of the priest and the whole
company might understandably have a powerful psychological effect.
This would be especially true considering the native belief in numerous
supernatural causes of illness, such as disrespect or offense to nature,
and slights to plants, animals, and natural forces.[16]

Along with the powwow's magic and sleight of hand might go skill
in removing the causes of illness by sucking out poison, pus, or splin-
ters; dressing and poulticing wounds; and administering healing po-
tions. It needs to be pointed out, however, that methods developed
through centuries and effective for the native ills would have been
useless against new, imported diseases like smallpox, unknown in prediscovery New England. Yet whether because of the powwow and his
methods or in spite of them, the customary state of good health among
New England Indians drew admiration from one observer after
another.[17]

Possibly connected with the practices of the powwow or shaman

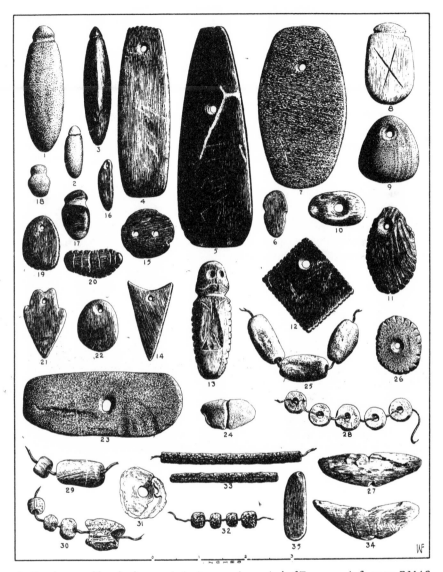

8. Pendants and beads, from archaic times to the period of European influence. *BMAS*, 27 (1966), 50.

are the occasional examples of art in the form of figures incised on smooth rock faces. Some students of the subject conceive that these may have been intended to represent the animal helpers of which each shaman was likely to claim at least one or two. He had power over these allies and could call for assistance.

What is known as picture writing was not common in New England, however. A number of instances are reported on local rock faces: a few in Rhode Island and one in Brattleboro, Vermont, said at the time of Willoughby's book to be covered with dammed river water. He shows photographs taken nearly a century ago of two clear examples of the art at Bellows Falls, Vermont.

Willoughby also shows an interpretation, from the point of view of an Indian archaeologist, of the famous Dighton Rock inscription in southeastern Massachusetts. Various possible origins for this, several of them historical, have been advanced, but their purpose remains in doubt.

Clark Wissler believes that the Algonquians originated the art of picture writing on birch bark. So far as historical sources offer evidence, however, beyond markings on trees or rocks to indicate, for example, claims to hunting territories, the New England Indians appear to have made little practical use of writing.

6.
Religion and Philosophy

Evidence concerning the religion of the original New Englanders is far from plentiful. For the seventeenth-century Puritans who met the natives, trying to provide food, shelter, and government in a strange new land and climate left little room for attention to the beliefs and customs of what remained of the native population. In any case, to the Puritan mind—fixed in its ideas of morality, sin, grace, and redemption and convinced of the superiority of its own beliefs—any Indian religious ideas or exercises were paganism and born of the evil one. Some of the writers who were most sympathetic with the natives called the practices of the Indian powwows diabolical even while praising their success with bones set, wounds made whole, the ill recovered. Indeed, after acknowledging the native doctors' skill, Gookin remarks that "they are reported, and I believe justly, to hold familiarity with the devil and therefore are by the English laws prohibited from the exercise of their diabolical practices."[1]

Persons in some respects as intellectually open as the Mathers, who against fierce opposition pioneered smallpox inoculation in the colonies, had only contempt and hatred for the practitioners of native healing and their religion: "Barbarians and Infidels in whom the Prince of the Power of the air did work as a Spirit," they called them. Yet if virtue, sharing of benefits, and morality are outward signs of religion, the new-come English who had to deal with the natives directly should have found much to praise.[2] Their hospitality drew plaudits. The Indians not only extended a welcome to the stranger and the food and protection of their wigwams by day or night, but, to quote a Rhode Island historian, "with a delicacy that finds no parallel in civilized life sleeping out of.doors to allay the fears or protect the comfort of their temporary guests." Orphans were always provided for, burglary unknown. Rape of an English woman by an Indian was never recorded. The testimony of Cushman, the Plymouth missionary to the Wampanoags, has already been noted; and Catholic Lahontan says of the related Indians of Canada, "They neither quarrel nor fight nor slander one another." Thomas Mayhew agrees.[3]

To the New England Indian all nature, however its various parts might at times appear in conflict, was a single whole, formed, all of it, by the creator and thus to a certain degree sacred. Trees to the Indian were almost like persons, Wissler tells us. Every man, bird, beast, flower, fruit, or even rock had its role and special value as a part of that whole. Hence it deserved respect and, if used by man, appreciation. If the muskrat's winter store of lily roots was raided, the beneficiary of the little animal's foresight must never take all but must leave sufficient to carry the muskrat family to the next season. The muskrats had gathered the roots: they were entitled to a living. If the bark of a white birch was taken for a canoe, the tree received thanks, perhaps a gift of tobacco and an apology. Should the season's crops prove bountiful, the sun, the earth, and the rainmaker deserved gratitude and praise. The principle was live and let live, for the Indian felt himself in the presence of living entities who were as conscious of his existence as he of theirs. As Francis Jennings has acutely observed, the quite different admonition to man in the first chapter of the Book of Genesis to "subdue the earth and have dominion over every living thing that moves on the earth" may have had its influence on the Puritan mind and on our own even though in Genesis the Creator found good everything that He had made.[4] The Indian would have been shocked by certain "sportsmen" who employ an airplane to seek out the winter runs of the deer in the north woods and, from above, using rifles with telescopic sights, are said to slaughter and leave the animals—killing for the sake of killing.

In Indian eyes it was a sin to injure unnecessarily even the least fellow creature. The wild bird or animal, like himself, had a right to life, food, and satisfaction. Some tribes, indeed, held that the animals had been made first and only later developed human form. "With all beings and all things we shall be as brothers," though not credited to a New England Indian, might well have been.

So the bones of the beaver with whose flesh the family had satisfied their hunger and whose fur would help warm their bodies must not be thrown carelessly to the dogs but returned to the animals' native stream. Had not the beaver created the marsh and made a contribution of his flesh and fur? Any waste of the meat of bear, deer, even chipmunk would have been an offense to the slain animal. All was to be consumed lest the creature's soul return to haunt the thoughtless offender. Respect for animals and traditions of kinship with them from ancient times extended to the naming of the Indian blood relatives: the Foxes, Turtles, Bears, and so forth. John Eliot, one of the Puritans who made it their mission to convert the Massachusetts Bay Indians to the Christian faith, took into account this respect for nature in the minds of his charges. While painstakingly translating for their instruction the sacred Bible from which he taught, he acknowledged also the authority of the book of nature "in which every creature was a word or sentence."[5]

To the Indian the whole creation was replete with powers: the sun, the moon, the four winds, thunder, rain; in his own person, the heart, the lungs. For coastal dwellers, Waushakim, the sea, was the great provider. To the Western Abenaki the thunders were seven brothers. Often mysterious in their actions, the forces of nature could not be directly controlled by man, but respect and ceremony might influence and appease them.

Roger Williams counted the "gods" of his Narragansett Bay neighbors: thirty-seven in all. These powers were to be pleased or appeased, not worshiped like the idols made by the hands of men against which in the Bible the prophets warned the Israelites. The New England Indians were not image worshipers; nor did they fear a single devil as the incarnation of all evil, though Lechford concluded that they feared worst the evil god Hobbamono because he did the most harm.[6]

Rather, with elaborate and noisy ceremonies—dances and chants—and with decoration of the person or concealment of identity by masks or paint, the native sought supernatural favor in preparation for planting, the hunt, or battle, or to avoid a god's wrath for misdemeanors. Services of thanksgiving for bountiful harvests and other benefits were never overlooked. Summer supplications for rain had gone before, sometimes lasting days and weeks until showers came. Because these rites were public and often colorful and noisy, they received wondering descriptions from colonial writers who were otherwise contemptuous of the participants and their practices.

The Indian love of dancing is proverbial. Lescarbot tells how they dance to please their gods; to cheer up somebody; to celebrate a victory; to prevent sickness; when they feast anybody; or as thanks when someone else has provided the feast. Always, singing goes along with dancing. The dance can also have a practical purpose: it may be "in honor of the Devil which showeth them their game."

Somewhere in the course of the worshipers' exercises the smoke of the sacred plant, tobacco, was likely to be included. To the Abenaki it symbolized the breath of life. "They think their gods are marvelously delighted therewith," wrote Hariot of the southern tribes. Le Jeune tells of the use of tobacco in Canada: "A great fire was lighted, and the sorcerer threw therein five cakes of tobacco . . . while addressing his prayer to the sun, to the Demons, and to the Pest (a contagion) conjuring them to leave their country and to repair as soon as possible to the country of the Iroquois," their enemies.[7]

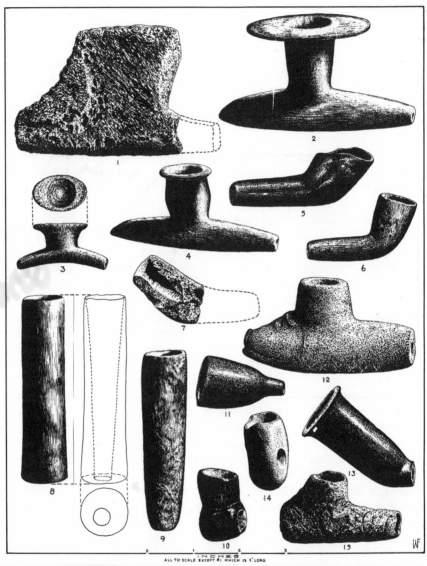

9. Stone pipes, some as old as 500 B.C. *BMAS*, 27 (1966), 46.

Burial customs, too, afford insight into native beliefs. The soul of the departed was believed to journey to the southwest, there to share the delights of the wigwam and fields of the great god Kanta (or Tanto or Kautautowit), where abundance reigns and ancestors offer welcome and feasting. Today's archaeological excavator is likely to find the skeleton of the deceased, if not in a sitting position, at least flexed and

10. Contents of burial pits from Titicut, southeastern Massachusetts. Front teeth are worn from foods masticated. A preference for canoe travel is suggested by the prominent attachment of the arm bones, with only moderate leg-bone attachment. *BMAS*, 20 (1959), 22.

interred with its head to the southwest, perhaps to make easy the departure of the spirit of the dead to its long home. In one such burial the body had been wrapped in bark.

Beside the corpse friendly hands have buried the deceased's most cherished possessions, together with practical items likely to be needed in the country of souls. For a man these might include the brave's weapons on his right, on his left a tobacco pipe; and his axe, stone knife, the stone points of arrows and spear from his hunting equipment, and beads and belts of wampum. The woman's soul would value her necklace of shell beads, her eardrops or brilliants, her basketry and decorated clothing, her bowls and grinding tools. The child's soul would appreciate a tiny pot, a deer antler, and its little toys. All these, along with the highly esteemed red paint, perhaps from central Maine and buried with the body, have been recovered from local graves. The occasional bits of basketry, decorated clothing, armlets, and fishhooks that have escaped dissolution are examples of personal treasures of the less permanent sort. After burial the period of mourning by the bereaved family might last days, months, or even years, according to the depth of affection in which family and friends had held the departed. Funerals (and marriages also) were the occasion, especially in the case of distinguished persons, for the recital of genealogies and encomiums on the accomplishments of the persons concerned.[8]

11. This tiny child's pot went to the grave with her. *BMAS*, 35 (1974), 15.

Part Three

THE HOUSEHOLD

7.

A Place to Live

Within the tribe and forming one of its pillars, the nuclear family was the basic unit of Algonquian life. In southern New England ordinarily a family lived in its own separate dwelling, though two or more families on occasion might combine to occupy a larger structure, each with its own fire and quarters. Among the Abenaki of the north, several related families would be housed in a long house. Each looked after its youngsters and provided its own food (or the bulk of it), together with clothing, tools, and equipment, directly or by exchange. In case of either windfall or dearth, however, sharing was expected and practiced. Marriage was the basis of society, though divorce, while infrequent, was not difficult.

Three diverse sources of information—archaeological remains, observations by early European visitors, and the hundreds of local New England town histories—shed light on the factors that influenced New England natives in their choice of domiciles.

Few New England Indians were by preference nomadic or forest dwellers; most were villagers, and had been for centuries. Like Canadian tribes they preferred a physically attractive spot for a settlement, even a temporary camp.[1] Almost without exception the sites chosen for villages combined a number of advantages: an elevation with a pleasing outlook, yet defensible; protection from the north wind by a hill or copse of evergreens; a clear, flowing spring; and a source of firewood nearby. The site would be close to the sea; to one or more lakes, where fishing was good; to a large river (preferably the confluence of two streams); or, better still, all three. The waters would offer ease of travel and transportation as well as food. Except where climate made agriculture impractical, somewhere in the neighborhood would be found a pine plain or other "light" land that could be readily cleared and cultivated with hand tools.[2] The inhabitants would probably not stay for the whole year at the new village site. They would very likely spend a few weeks at the seashore or at a great waterfall, seeking fish to cure—and also to enjoy pleasant company, games, and contests.[3]

In the villages that Champlain shows on his maps of Plymouth and Cape Cod, the cabins stood separate "without any order of building," each on its own house lot with its own cornfield. Apparently the Wampanoags and the Nausets were not fearful of enemies. By contrast the dwellings he records in Maine's Saco Valley (near the present New Hampshire line) were enclosed by a common stockade to protect against nonagricultural raiders from further east. Some of Maine's agricultural Indians had been forced back into the interior. New Hampshire's Pennacooks are said to have had three forts, and in southwest New Hampshire (in the seventeenth century) the Squakheagues had a fort on a bluff at the river bend on the Connecticut in Hinsdale. Further south, almost to Boston Bay, the local villagers lived in fear of similar depredations, though the Massachusetts tribe did not. Beyond the territory of the Massachusetts and Wampanoags (whose headquarters under Massasoit were today's Warren and Barrington, Rhode Island, later at Bristol), Ninigret had a fort at Charlestown (in historic time), and the Narragansetts in 1675 occupied a closely built winter village in the midst of a great swamp, defended by a

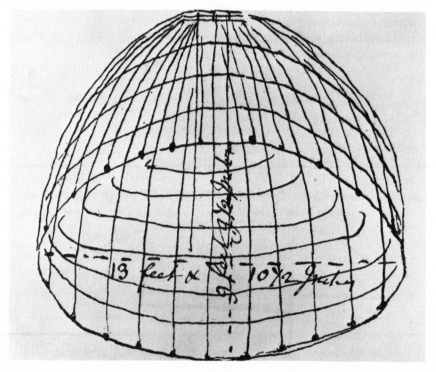

12. Frame of the wigwam of George Wawkeets, of the Nehantic tribe, Connecticut. Drawing (1761) by Ezra Stiles, president of Yale College. Wawkeets and Ben Uncas, a member of the Mohegan tribe, told President Stiles that seven persons could live comfortably in this wigwam. *Extracts from the Itineraries . . . of Ezra Stiles*, ed. F. B. Dexter (New Haven, 1916), p. 131.

palisade. Connecticut River Indians had a fortified town at South Windsor, and there must have been more.[4]

Reasons other than fear of enemies might impel villagers to seek a new site—a plague of fleas or a scarcity of firewood, for example. (Various plants called fleabane were common, but I have found no reference to their use.) When a group of English set up their domicile in the Connecticut River Valley, the local Indians concluded that they had made the move because they had used up the available wood at their previous site.[5] The Indian women sometimes brought firewood from great distances.

In all but northern and perhaps extreme eastern New England, then, the Indian was a villager. The Indian home, the wigwam where the family passed the winter, was no makeshift, but a tight, warm, comfortable dwelling. In southern New England it had vertical sides and was likely to be square or oblong, with a half-moon roof somewhat like that of a modern Quonset hut. In Maine the shape might be round and the roof domelike. A square or round cabin with a circumference of twenty to thirty feet would ordinarily house a single family—two related families at most. The Quonset-shaped house, however, preferred among the Abenaki of the north and also found in southern New England, could be as much as sixty to eighty feet long and twenty feet wide and be home for six or eight families—usually related— each with its own fireplace. Only in eastern Maine would the round wigwam's poles meet at the top in a cone, like the tepee of the Indians of the West. A Maine multiple dwelling might have long, slanted sides meeting at the peak: a double lean-to with the shape of an upside-down V.[6]

To build either single cabin or long house, the men (sometimes the women) cut lithe saplings and set their larger ends in the ground two or three feet apart to outline the cabin's shape. They then bent the tops inward from opposite sides to form a dome or arch, and bound them together with withes. To guard against the strain of New England's occasional raging storms, the risers were laced together with cords or strips of walnut bark—"wondrous tuffe," as one writer described it. For the long house, horizontal poles running lengthwise stiffened sides and roof.[7]

After the frame had been erected, the women covered roof and sides with six to nine-foot strips of bark—elm, chestnut, birch, or oak, lapped like great shingles—sewing them together with a thread of evergreen tree roots, artfully. Instead of bark for roofing, they might fasten on mats "wrought cunningly" from reeds, flags, sedge, or, for lack of better material, cornstalks—and all neatly sewed together, Morton notes, "with needles made of the splinter bones of a crane's legge with

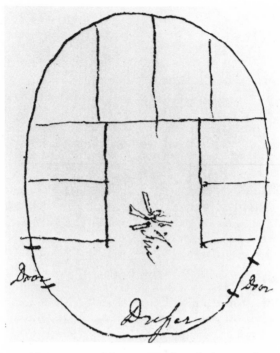

13. The interior of George Wawkeets' wigwam, showing platforms for sitting and sleeping about the fire. Ezra
Stiles drawing; 1761, *Itineraries*, p. 131 (reverse side).

thread of their Indian hempe." For winter the home needed two
thicknesses of mats on both roof and sides, the interior one finely
woven, perhaps decorated also. These rendered the whole house
watertight. The squaw kept it neatly swept with a cedar broom.

At the center of the single cabin's roof, the builders left a
smokehole a foot and a half wide; in a long house there would be
others at intervals. A small fire within would ordinarily keep the room
comfortable—warmer than an English house, Wood says. If smoke
became bothersome, or if a change in wind spoiled the draft, a pull on
a string would raise or lower a mat or skin overhead to windward of the
smokehole. In damp, windy weather, to avoid a smoky interior the
family might heat stones at a fire outside and carry them in to serve as
radiators.[8]

A low doorway on the southwest side with a drop mat or skin let
the members of the family in and out; another, opposite, perhaps
several in a large cabin, could be opened to permit air to draw through
from different directions when a draft was needed. To enter, the mat

or skin was lifted, then dropped into place again so that the draft from the fire might not be spoiled.

In the middle of the dirt floor a circle of firestones formed the hearth; beside it stood "four little crotchets set in the ground, supporting cross sticks, on which were hung what they have to roast" by hooks of twisted withes. Once the fire was going well, a long log might have its end fed to the blaze night and day until consumed.[9]

For decoration the Narragansett women lined their inside walls with "Munnotaubana" (hangings dyed and embroidered). In an arc about the fireplace and reaching to the wall the men set up slatted or split-log horizontal platforms or benches, raised a foot and a half or more from the floor on crotched stakes.[10] On these the women laid deerskins, sealskins "soft as velvet," or woven mats of grass, sometimes decorated in black, blue, red, and yellow. Here the family rested or slept with feet to the fire, and in cold weather kept warm under skins of bear, otter, beaver, or coon. With a fire in the center, the cabin would ordinarily be snug, and ("what no one would believe") for persons inured to cold, really hot "even in the greatest rigors of winter."[11]

Though the house was windowless, the smoke hole and the doorways when open served to light it in the daytime. At night, besides the fire burning, pine knots and split sticks of pitch pine would give light if needed. The whole was "so defensive that rain, though never so bad and long, nor yet the wind, never so strong can enter." So adequate were the wigwams of the Cape Cod Indians that some continued in use at Bass River as late as 1778.[12]

Temporary wigwams, set up at the beach or at fishing and hunting grounds for a stay of only a night or a week or two, were a good deal less elaborate, and light enough to be struck and carried off within a few hours, though the pole frame might be left for another occasion. Captain Christopher Levett, who visited the New England coast in 1623/24, in 1628 first used the word "wigwam" in print. He put one up, Indian fashion, in an hour, and gave it the native name as he heard the phrase for "at home" or "my house" in Algonquian.[13] The houses of the less favored inhabitants who, perhaps, were not even members of the tribe, would be cruder than those of the chief or tribal members and scantily furnished. The quality of construction and workmanship would also vary with the status of the tribe and the materials available in the neighborhood. Indeed, accounts of some white observers speak scornfully of all the cabins—and of their occupants: Roger Williams, a not unfriendly observer, once called them "smoaky holes." Yet for the winter villages the type of construction was substantial.

The interior equipment was designed to carry the family through the season. Baskets, ranged about the room under the bed frames and hanging from the rafters, held household supplies. Utensils included symmetrical pots of baked clay for cooking; also bottles, bowls, pails, dishes and wooden dippers, ladles, spoons, and measuring cups. Pitchers and bowls might be made from gourds or turtle or crab shells; the hand utensils would be shell or wood. In the colder regions where the white birch grew, the vessels would be of bark. As Ruth Underhill describes the process, after bark had been painstakingly stripped from the birch tree, it was heated above the fire or by steam, then shaped for the desired vessel. Slender shoots of willow were bent to form the rim and also a handle by which the container could be hung above a fire. A large bark pail might hold as much as two to three gallons. Knives and skin scrapers would be made from chipped or sharpened stones, some with wood handles, others without.[14]

Among the necessaries would be thread and sewing baskets, perhaps decorated, holding needles—sharp bones from animals and fowl, or slivers of shell, each with an eye drilled in one end. Fine thread came from basswood inner fibers twisted hard, or the split roots of evergreen trees. One basket would hold parched acorns for food, another such medicines as dried herbs and household remedies for cuts, bruises, fevers, or diarrhea. One bag hanging from the roof might contain the soft fluff of cattails from the swamp for the baby's tender skin. Some would enclose coarse dried hemp fiber for weaving bags to hold heavy supplies, or to braid into ropes, fish lines, or cords for lacing together fish weirs of brush.

For the never-ending task of grinding corn, every household would have at hand a two- or three-foot section of tough hornbeam trunk, hollowed out. In this the cook ordinarily pounded her kernels, using a slender stone pestle shaped like an elongated cucumber. Alongside might be one or more low, bowl-shaped stone mortars, each also with a stone pestle shaped like a ball. In these, cornmeal could be ground into flour; or nutmeats, seeds, and herbs could be ground fine. All such operations involved need for well crafted implements as well as skill and patience.[15]

Our view of the Indian household would be incomplete unless it included dogs—perhaps a half-dozen to the family, in proportion to the master's standing. They were likely to be slim, with foxlike heads and the look of a wolf; in Maine they were black, white, red, or grisled, some small, some large, but not big by European standards. Indian dogs were extremely sagacious, so a traveler in the Niagara country said.

They would obey a low-voiced command—even a sign from the master's hand—and could be trained to lie quiet in the bow of a canoe, then leap into the water to retrieve a duck or goose that the master had brought down. So light in weight that a good crust on snow would support them, they were especially useful in running down moose or deer. They did not yelp, but howled, though "not with a great sound." If the hunt was successful and a deer, say, was brought home, the dogs received only the scraps; gnawing the bones might dull their teeth. If no game was killed, the dogs might go hungry for a week unless they hunted on their own. In other ways, too, they were treated as part of the family. According to Denys, if a dog mother could not suckle her litter or could feed only part of them, the Indian mother might act as a substitute until they could be fed soup. Dog meat—said to be good eating—was not normal fare, though on a great occasion a favorite dog might be sacrificed as a singular honor to a guest.[16]

The sole other domesticated creature was the hawk, trained to clear thievish birds from the maturing corn.

8.

Household and Personal Equipment

Indian household equipment, designed for peace and daily use rather than war or hunting, was made from the materials that nature furnished. It is notable that although eventually, after English settlement, the native woman took to the metal pot for boiling liquids, she long continued to use her mortar and pestle for bread.

Mortars were of several types. Two have already been mentioned: the stone bowl, in which a round stone held in the hand did the grinding, and the hollowed-out section of a tree trunk, in which a long stone pestle pulverized the grain. In addition, mortars made from large boulders, for community use, were common. These are found today at many native village sites and along all principal Indian routes of travel, more or less at intervals of a day's journey, tradition says. Judging from the shape of the grinding areas and their location on the boulders, they were often developed from natural depressions in the rock, sometimes more than one in a single boulder. The depression was likely to be a foot or two long and half as wide. The bottom would be slanted and open at the lower end, and pitched so that meal could be brushed from it into a vessel. Occasionally the depth of the depression in the boulder was broader and shallower, and it was flat on the bottom. This type may have been planned for rolling a rounded or egg-shaped pestle over the grain in the way tribes of the Southwest still prepare meal.[1]

Stone mortars of much smaller size are found, round or nearly so, with deep bowl-shaped hollows in which the grinding took place. In these, smaller round stones guided by the hand were the pulverizers. Such mortars, often not too heavy to hold in the lap, could be moved with the family from place to place, or into and out of the dwelling. They were useful for crushing small nuts, cherries, berries, herbs, vegetables, and dried fish or flesh.[2]

The large vertical wood mortar designed for pounding, was hollowed out to a depth of a foot or two from the center of a section of tree trunk. Sometimes the trunk was left where it grew, cut off at the proper height, and its interior would be excavated with hot coals and scraper. Usually, however, a convenient section was cut from a hornbeam, oak, or elm—all tough woods—and the center was gouged out with the help of fire applied direct or in the form of red hot stones. The mortar stood erect on its horizontal base. Its outer surface might be carved and decorated to the owner's taste, and the utensil passed down in the family. For this type of mortar, the pestle that did the pounding was usually a cylinder of hard stone, as much as two feet in length, painstakingly rounded and smooth on the ends and circumference. It was long enough above the mortar top to provide a solid hand grip. Stone suitable for the purpose was tough to work, yet a craftsman of artistic bent might occasionally shape the part held in the hand into the form of a bird, a beast, or a human body.[3]

The women of the family provided the power for grinding. Lafitau shows a Canadian scene where a pestle is tied to the top of a sapling. Each time the squaw brings it down hard for a blow, the trunk's resilience lifts it for the next. No such device is mentioned by early New England observers.[4] A different type of operation is indicated by a

14. Sachem Tantaquidgeon, a Mohegan of Uncasville, Connecticut; about 1930. He is displaying a mortar and pestle which, to his knowledge, were over two centuries old and still in use. Photograph by Howard S. Russell.

traditional mill reported from Pokanoket, the Rhode Island headquarters of the Wampanoags. Here a hole had been drilled deep in a boulder to hold a shaft. Stones were attached to arms extending horizontally from this shaft, which thus acted as a fulcrum. As the women continually pushed, the stones revolved in a circle and pulverized the grain. (Whether this is correctly ascribed to the Indians is uncertain.)[5] Whatever the method, the particles of grain became finer as grinding proceeded, and a light flour jolted to the surface. The squaw could spoon this off little by little, until a considerable proportion of the grist became fine enough to bolt through a sieve. Such methods for making meal and flour must have proved effective, for the colonists adopted them to prepare not only maize meal but wheat and rye, until such time as a miller could be induced to settle in their neighborhood and set up a wind or water mill.

Certain of these household supplies evidence not simply ingenuity but artistry as well. In basket-making Indian women were especially skilled. They plaited small baskets that were hung from the waist to hold seeds for planting or to carry a lunch when they went fishing; from wild hemp they wove large baskets that would hold maize or beans brought in from the field; and many a useful size between. Certain baskets were fine enough, yet loose enough, to sift flour; others when wet would seal tight as a drum. Some were "curiously wrought in blacke and white in pretie works"; others were decorated in colors. Their green came from swamp scum, brown from walnut, red from ochre.[6]

For coarse splint baskets like the ones farmers and gardeners use today, the method was to pick an erect, straight-grained black ash or oak, cut a section, pound it until the annual rings separated, then split these splints into the widths desired. Kept dry and properly used, a well-made splint basket lasts a very long time.

"Some of their baskets," says Josselyn, "are made of rushes, some of bents [a grass-like reed], others of a kind of silk grass, others of a kind of wild hemp; others of the barks of trees, many very neat and artificial [artistic] with the portraitures of birds, beasts, fishes and flowers in colours" which could include black, blue, red, and yellow. Winthrop saw women weaving baskets from cornhusks split into narrow strips. Porcupine quills were interwoven into fancy containers. At the shore, baskets might be plaited from "crab shells wrought together." On Block Island, in Long Island Sound, Captain Underhill and his soldiers wondered at the "many well wrought mats and several delightful baskets" they came upon, and that is generous praise from a Puritan soldier and an enemy. The interior Nipmucks of northern Connecticut and central Massachusetts are said to have been exceptionally skillful at basketry. Wood tells us that the women gathered the materials in summer,

15. Museum collection of garden and household tools: grinders, pestles, hoes, baskets, knives. Photograph by Wayland-Weston *Town Crier*.

seeming to imply that the less work-filled winter was the time of manufacture.[7]

"In their houses," Governor Bradford of Plymouth records, "they have several baskets wherein they put all their household stuff. Also they have some great bags or sacks made of hemp, which will hold five or six bushels." This type of hamper was woven of *Apocynum cannabinum*, the native hemp. (Lescarbot implies that the Indians may on occasion have planted this) or at least encouraged it to grow near their villages, though Champlain on Cape Cod was told that there the natural growth was plentiful enough. In 1633 John Oldham brought a supply of such fibers back to Boston from the Connecticut Valley: Governor Winthrop thought them superior to English hemp. Peter Kalm reports the plant plentiful in old corn grounds, and in the woods also. Thread from this hemp was thought finer and stronger than cotton thread. The English, after their arrival, made it into string and rope. Another fiber was derived from the inner bark of basswood. Rolled and skillfully twisted into string against the maker's leg, it furnished strong twine for making sacks, baskets, fish nets, and seines that could be held under water by stone sinkers, and strong enough to enmesh powerful sixteen-foot sturgeon. Even rope could be woven.[8]

Where sewing was needed, whether for baskets or for stitching together sheets of bark for canoes, New England's Indian women found excellent thread in the fine roots of cedar and other evergreens, or of hackmatack.

In upland and northern New England, birch bark made practical pots and pails, and household containers also. Skilled hands could turn sheets of bark into two-gallon pails, or into "delicate sweet dishes, furnished on the outside with flourisht works and on the brim with glistening quills taken from the porcupine and dyed some black and others red, the white being natural." Captain Waymouth, one of New England's earliest visitors, even mentions the forerunner of the modern strawberry and raspberry box. It was a square box of bark in which the natives brought berries to the English. All such basketwork and artistry in color was the accomplishment of the women.[9]

Burnt clay pottery is thought to have come into use among New England aborigines about the time agriculture began, perhaps a little earlier. That would be about a thousand years before the English arrived. Pots were fashioned to hold liquids and dry supplies, as well as for cooking.

Before they learned to make clay pots, earlier natives had chipped and ground their cooking vessels out of soapstone (steatite), a rather soft mineral that withstands fire without cracking or spalling. It is found in ledge outcroppings in such New England locations as Providence, Rhode Island; Bristol, Connecticut; Millbury, North Wilbraham, and Westfield, Massachusetts; and many places in Vermont. Primitive man quarried the comparatively soft stone and ground and shaped it into bowls, as well as vessels that could be safely set in the midst of hot coals.[10]

Once the women had acquired the art of making clay pottery that would withstand the heat of fire, the laboriously quarried and heavier soapstone vessels were superseded. By the time the first European observers arrived, cooking pots of the Algonquians had for centuries been of clay. They were generally tall, well proportioned, and shaped somewhat like a Grecian urn. Gookin calls them egg-shaped. The base was often curved to a point like an inverted cone, so that the pot might be set upright amid glowing coals or pushed into soft earth, supported by stones, and a fire built around it. Lescarbot compared the pots to French nightcaps. An English ranger thought they looked like the pots at home, but with rounded bases. Also reported, but perhaps of later origin, was a shape like a beehive.[11]

As in most parts of America, women more than men were the ceramic makers. The outline of the pots was graceful and was often enhanced, especially at the neck, with simple, incised designs. Though as thin as European pots, they were strong and might remain unbroken even if the contents boiled away. Champlain saw ears of corn boiling in them.

The potter gained the height desired by mingling wet clay with grit, powdered rock or shell, rolling the mixture into strips with her

16. Quarrying soapstone—a museum simulation. The hammer in the quarryman's upraised hand is copied from an actual quarry tool. *Town Crier* photo, Bronson Museum, Attleboro, Mass.

hands and adding one strip above another, rounding and shaping the vessel as she worked. Continuous patting with a stick wrapped with wet fabric made the whole solid. Everything in order, the final step was to apply heat. With firing, the clay solidified to the point where the vessel was capable of bearing the strains of cooking food and boiling water. A pot might also be produced by beginning with a large lump of clay and gradually hollowing it from the center with the fist.

In New England suitable clay was not always easy to find, and well-made pots were valuable. The women of the Narragansetts in what is now Rhode Island, as well as others in the Connecticut Valley, were especially skilled. (Pots of the Plymouth tribe are reported inferior.) They made all sizes, to hold a quart or up to several gallons.[12]

For centuries ornamentation was lacking or meager; but by the time Europeans arrived, New England Indian women were decorating their earthenware with a variety of simple incised designs. The color of the pot would be yellow, gray, black, red, or light tan. At the top a circular lip might reach outward. The lip could even be square and with both horizontal and vertical surfaces. Designs could be worked into either or both.

Though making pottery and weaving baskets and mats was women's work, it was likely to be men who made the wood dishes. The bowl-maker chopped a circle into a block of wood with a stone hatchet, then charred it with fire, or perhaps with heated pebbles laid on the part to be hollowed out. Next he scraped out the charred portion. He kept this up repeatedly until the vessel reached the shape, depth, and thinness he wanted. During the process, to prevent fire from burning through the wood, the bowl-maker kept the outside of the block soaked with water. The dish that resulted was sometimes surprisingly handsome and often of remarkable thinness. Made of grainless hardwood and well impregnated with the food fats that Indian housewives never washed off, it would be tough enough to last through years of use. Such a method is said to be still in use by natives in the interior of Venezuela to make dugout canoes.[13]

Among tough woods not subject to splitting and preferred for bowl-making were hornbeam, elm, white oak, and hard maple. Basswood was used, too. The woods varied with the locality. Henry Hudson's *Half Moon* officers were served food in well-made bowls of a red wood, which seems to indicate red cedar. The tough roots of the mountain laurel received from the English the name of spoon wood, perhaps from Indian practices. Burls and knots the Indian bowl-maker especially valued. To hollow out a maple burl with a modern steel chisel is not simple. The aborigine accomplished it solely with stone tools plus fire, or on the coast with a clam or oyster shell as scraper. Then he polished the vessel with the tooth of a beaver or other animal. Preserved wooden bowls and dishes of Indian origin are sometimes beautifully crafted. Besides serving a meal, a bowl might be helpful in drying and winnowing seed, even for roasting grain.[14]

If, in the New World, males shaped dishes, bowls, and spoons, this had its parallel in England at the time the English settled New England. There, in country districts, husbandmen fashioned the wooden bowls, spoons, and platters needed by their households. The colonists of New England brought the practice with them.

Beyond the provision of food and clothing and a wealth of implements, intensive, imaginative study of their environment enabled New England's natives to discover or adapt available materials to make tools and utensils for a wide variety of needs. From the animal world, besides the products already described, came raccoon fat to render a pail or a canoe watertight, and bear, seal, or porpoise oil, not solely for personal use but to be combined with a deer's brain for softening hides. A snakeskin might become a girdle, a turtle shell a handsome serving dish or, if small, a shining ladle. For sewing, needles—single and double pointed—and pins too had their source in ribs or tiny bones of bear, coon, mink, sable, and otter. Some of these were already provided with natural eyelets. Pointed fragments of shell served also, and goose bones provided awls for basketry. From bones, strangely, were derived the means of making edged tools. Held tightly in the hand, the bone or antler flaked off tiny chips from thin stones to leave a cutting edge on arrowheads, spear points, and chisels. A chisel might afterward be ground sharper by use of sand and water. Harpoons for the occasional whale hunt had their source in the pointed antlers of deer and moose, or eight inches of the deer's leg bone, with several side notches to form teeth. Beaver teeth, designed by nature for cutting wood, could be hafted to become efficient edged hand tools. A fowl's wishbone seemed naturally shaped to serve as a hook for fishing.[15]

The Indian had invented numerous other means to get fish for food. Besides the weirs mentioned elsewhere, which concentrated migrating or tide-borne schools of fish so that they might easily be taken, ingeniously arranged nets of hemp, held below the surface by stones, trapped the unwary in ponds and streams. Or the fisherman dropped in lines fitted with small slender gouges of bone sharpened at each end, hung by a hole at the center and baited. When a fish swallowed the bait, the gouge swung to horizontal in its stomach and could not be disgorged. For hook and line fishing a curved hook could be

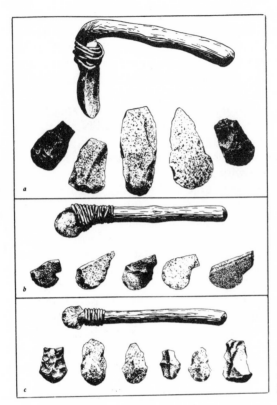

17A. Hafting scrapers (three probable methods), Connecticut Valley of Massachusetts.

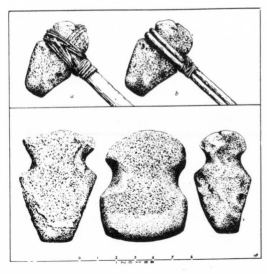

17C. Grooved axes, Connecticut River Valley of Massachusetts.

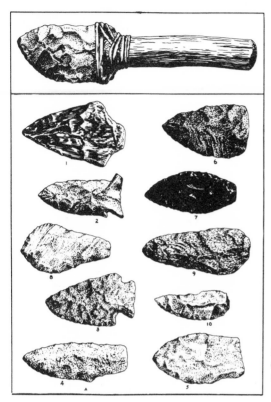

17B. Hafting stem and stemless knives: *1-5*, stem; *6-10*, stemless. Massachusetts and Rhode Island.

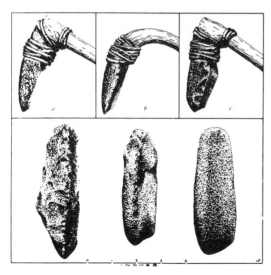

17D. Hafting adze and gouge blades, Connecticut River Valley of Massachusetts. *BMAS*, 23 (1962), 36-40.

carved from a flat piece of bone; or the fisherman could devise a sharply angled V-shaped hook held together by a cord.

For fashioning tools and implements a variety of stones provided the raw material. Anvil, hammer, abrader, and drill were of stone. Sometimes the workman held the hammer clutched in his hand, or he might attach a handle bound to it by thongs. Cutlery also might be of stone, but bones, shell, bear and beaver teeth, sharpened wood, and reeds also had their uses. As in cultivating corn or trapping a bear, ingenuity in adapting materials at hand solved the problems.

Clothing came from two main sources, skins of animals and woven plant fibers. The single universal garment of all except young children was a strip covering the genitals hung from the waist belt and fastened before and behind.

Covering was light in summer. In winter, to Europeans, the natives seemed strangely indifferent to chill. In southern New England men wore over the left shoulder, and caught together there, a supple tanned skin from moose, deer, or bear (perhaps more than one), hair side in, sewed or caught together under the right arm, and perhaps ornamented with colored designs: if a deerskin, its tail was wound about the waist. To shield the exposed right arm, they wore the pelt of a smaller animal, perhaps a deep-furred wildcat splotched with white, or a beaver or otter. This hung from the shoulder, leaving the arm free. Raccoon skins, the tails hanging loose, were especially popular. "A girdle set with formes of birds or beasts Begirts their waste which gentle gives them ease."[16] Among Western Abenaki of the north the coat might be of two skins, front and back with both arms free. A separate pelt protected each arm, caught together front and back by a cord.

Women wore knee-length skirts of skin and, in winter, a cloak formed of two deerskins, dropping from the shoulders and sometimes dragging behind. Leather leggings, supported also by the waist belt, protected the calves and ankles against injury from sticks and briars; they were longer for men and boys than for women. For travel, moccasins of moose or deer skin completed the clothing.[17] Girls might enhance theirs with a dye of flame color obtained from a root and with shining designs wrought from porcupine quills.

On Cape Cod in summer Champlain noted both men and women wearing light capes or shawls of woven textiles. Willoughby speculated that these may have been more for protection against mosquitoes than for warmth. (The women of eastern Maine, according to Mrs. Eckstorm, were not weavers of clothing.) Children ran about naked in summer.

To serve as garments and for similar uses animal skins had to be suitably processed, the method varying with the type of skin and the purpose—often a long, complicated job. To prepare a deer hide, for example, the usual practice was to place the skin under water in a running brook, one with a clay bottom preferred. This loosened the hair so that it could be readily removed. Next, a paste, perhaps of liver and brains, was spread on the flesh side to soften the hide. A stone gouge, followed by a piece of polished wood, was worked back and forth by hand to break the fibers, making the skin flexible. If a dark color was preferred, the hide was smoked in a damp fire fed with oak bark. One skin could be waterproofed and left pliable, another dried hard as a board, and a third worked as soft as chamois. If the hair was to remain, oil and hand manipulation of the skin were the means for making it supple. Where more than a single skin was needed for a garment, a bone awl and bone needle did the sewing. Soft, long-used skins went into moccasins for girls, embroidered in red, blue, and violet. Robes for special gala use might be white, and elaborately embroidered. Williams tells of moose and deer skins for summer wearing, painted in a variety of forms and colors.[18]

In Maine a man would wear furs in winter—beaver, otter, lynx, martin, squirrel—and sport a few eagle or turkey feathers in his topknot. A kind of feather coronet might bind the forehead. The long vertical strings of colored feathers for the brave which have come to be considered typically Indian are not local but of western origin and used in modern times. Colonial New England writers could hardly have failed to describe them had they been in use; they report that the natives spent hours dressing their hair, its style varying from tribe to tribe. Boys' hair was kept short until they reached sixteen. The girls and women let it grow full length, tied behind and gleaming with porcupine quills.[19]

Other ornaments included jewels (in the ears), necklaces, bracelets, pendants, and belts (of bright colored or shining stones, shells, and beads). Brereton at Martha's Vineyard met Indians wearing strings of beads made of copper tubing, from copper that they indicated was mined on the mainland. For weddings and feasts among the eastern Indians the male's summer costume was a mooseskin robe dressed white, embroidered top to bottom a finger's breadth wide, with closed or open-work figures of animals, in red, violet, and blue.[20]

Feathers were valuable, and not solely for headdress or ornament. Soft breast feathers might be matched and woven into coats for little girls, capes for their mothers, or colorful skirts for mother and daughter. Shoulder capes "quilled artificially," as Gookin puts it, were handsome. Traps for turkeys were carefully designed to avoid injury to the plumage.[21]

Glue might be an animal product, say from the hooves of deer, or be derived from the backbones of such large fish as sturgeon. From the bayberry the wife extracted wax (there were no bees of the European type). For dyes she turned to roots, berries, grapes, and leaves, and to

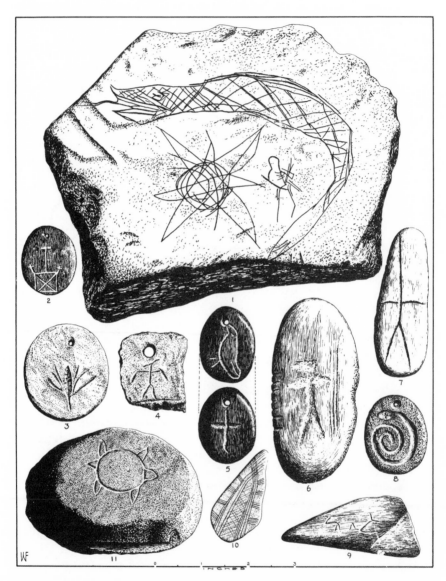

18. Moveable pictographs: *1, 2, 5, 6, 8, 11*, Narragansett Bay drainage. *3*, Maine. *4*, Duxbury, Massachusetts. *7*, Wareham, Massachusetts. *9*, Brookfield, Massachusetts. *10*, New Brunswick, Canada. *BMAS*, 27 (1966), 50.

such plants as alders, bloodroot, sumac, and lichens. Ingenuity continually surmounted difficulty.

In place of the colonial's flint and steel to produce fire, each Indian carried, in a leather case at his wrist or in a woodchuck skin hung from his belt "a Minerall stone . . . and with a flat Emeris stone tied fast to the end of a little stick, gently he striketh upon the minerall stone awel, within a stroke or two a spark falleth upon a piece of Touchwood . . . and he maketh fire presently" (Brereton). This practice goes back to ancient times. Indian sources of a later period, however, describe other methods. In addition to the legendary practice of rubbing two dry sticks together or twirling a hardwood rod on a base of soft wood until friction generated the needed spark, some Algonquians developed an ingenious apparatus to bring flame more swiftly. A white boy who went fishing with an old Indian tells of the Indian's making fire with basswood, birch bark, and a bowstring, apparently referring to the method that Nicolas Tenesles and others picture. He describes the machine as having a vertical wooden spindle, a crossarm, and a cord. The cord was attached at its center to the top of the spindle, wound about the mast, and fastened to the two ends of the crossarm. Swift raising and lowering of the crossarm with the hand kept the spindle flying. Pressing the spindle's lower end against a dry wood surface soon brought the hoped-for glow, and once this spark started, it was fed to the punk of decaying gray birch. Such a spark could be kept alive in the birch punk for hours; enclosed in shells or other incombustible material, it could even be attached to a waist belt and readily borne from place to place.[22]

9.

The Family Meals

From the game proudly turned over to her by her husband, from the fish of pond and sea, from the maize and vegetables she had grown in her garden, from the berries the children had gathered, the wild herbs and roots she had herself sought out and the store of supplies in her underground cupboard, what dishes would the wife concoct for her family? How accomplished a cook was she?[1]

The cooking arts of the Algonquian woman were simple, but her menu was nonetheless nourishing and satisfying. Even though her methods might appear to the modern housewife less than sanitary, the result contributed to the good health of her family.

Indian food was savory and at times varied. Of the southeastern Indians Adair commented that they could diversify their courses as much as the English or perhaps the French cooks. Below are listed some of the dishes and ingredients that colonial cooks, when they arrived, adopted or adapted from the Indians. In addition, a considerable catalogue of foods might be added which originated elsewhere in Indian America.

Changes have occurred in certain of these dishes in the last three centuries. Boston baked beans, for example, awaited the importation of West Indian molasses before assuming their modern form. Indian clam and fish chowder would have contained artichokes or groundnuts, instead of today's potatoes. Potatoes, though of American origin, did not appear in New England, except as rare imports, until the eighteenth century.[2] Indian menus, however, included numerous ingredients that the new-come English never thought of using.

The Cooking Pot

The natives ordinarily cooked flesh and fish by boiling in vessels of wood, stone, clay, or bark—sometimes by broiling over hot coals or roasting and baking in hot ashes. They also on occasion barbecued meat or fowl by hanging it on sticks close to the fire.

The favorite means of cooking in New England was boiling in clay pots with pointed bottoms set in the midst of the embers, or in vessels of green bark suspended over hot coals. Surprisingly, water will boil and food will cook in a pot made solely of the fresh bark of the birch or a few

Modern Foods Inherited from the Indians

Cereal Foods	Fruits and Nuts	Vegetables
Berry cake	Beach plums	Beans, baked or boiled
Corn bread	Blackberries	Bean soup
Corn chowder	Blueberries	Green corn
Corn fritters	Cranberries	Pumpkin, baked, boiled
Hominy	Elderberries	Squash, baked, boiled
Hulled corn	Gooseberries	Succotash
Johnnycake	Grapes	
Nut bread	Raspberries	
Squash bread	(black & red)	*Sea Food*
	Strawberries	Baked bluefish
	Watermelon	Clams, baked, steamed
	Beechnuts	Clam chowder
	Chestnuts	Cod
	Hickorynuts	Crabs
Fowl and Flesh		Fish chowder
Roast turkey and		Halibut
other local wild		Herring
game birds and		Lobsters, baked, boiled, broiled
animals of wide		Oysters, raw, escalloped, stewed
variety		Salmon, boiled, broiled, planked,
		smoked
		Shad
		Smelts
		Swordfish
		and many local varieties

other trees and suspended above a fire. This was a common Indian way of cooking up to historic times.[3]

An even more ancient method of boiling was to heat stones red hot and drop them at intervals into the liquid to be heated. The container might be stone, wood, or hide; anything that would hold water. This method was common in some parts of America, but only in Maine is credible evidence available that this was at the end of prehistoric time a usual practice of New England natives.[4]

Baking and boiling cereal foods were universal practices wherever maize or wild rice grew. As for flesh, once the use of pottery began, broiling and roasting meat were less favored than boiling it, for the juices were regarded as too important to waste. A fish might be cooked on a flat stone set above a bed of coals, or on the coals themselves. Planking steak and fish is said to be adapted from the Indians. A Rhode Island archaeological recovery appears to indicate clams set on edge about a hearth to roast until their shells opened. Native cooks are not recorded as frying either fish or flesh; but Morton says they delighted in roasting fish, and he apparently meant to include oysters.[5]

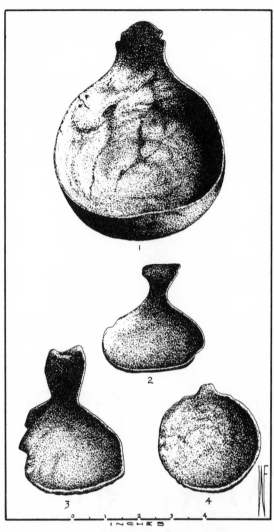

19. Wooden utensils. Deerfield, Massachusetts, Museum. *BMAS*, 36 (1975), 26.

Hungry Indians were not always particular about meat being fully cooked (in Maine Father Ralé said three-quarters of an hour was considered enough boiling), though in general they liked food thoroughly done. "They eat any sort of meat they can get." The only creatures not ordinarily eaten were carnivores. De Bry's engravings of the southern Indians, for example, show a snake being smoked on a frame over the fire, and Mrs. Rowlandson saw King Philip's warriors dine on rattlesnakes. Mother Ann, a colonial matron of Byfield, Massachusetts, had a black snake added to her pot of beef and turnips by a

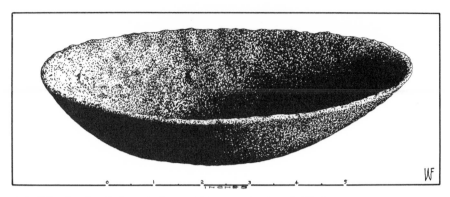

20. Wooden bowl, from before 1000 B.C., plastic solidified recovery. *BMAS*, 28 (1967), 26.

generous Indian guest. An Indian party is reported as dining on boiled mudturtles.[6]

They ate nearly every part of the animal, bird, or fish. Early writers often mention the cooking of "entrails." In the West, later, Harmon found Indians eating buffalo "entrails" raw, and liked them himself. Whether beyond the tripe, liver, heart and kidneys, the word also included intestines is not always clear. Birds were sometimes roasted whole, with bear oil to baste them. Perhaps the Indian had a clearer conception than moderns of the value of the vitamin-rich portions of beast and fish.[7]

Clams the Maine Indians baked in piles over heated rocks covered and interlaced with seaweed, with succulent ears of green corn and slices of fish added to the steaming pile; either clams or fish could also be the basis for a chowder. Fresh fish of all sorts were relied upon in warm weather. Excavation by William Ritchie on Martha's Vineyard and Long Island of shallow round pits containing clamshells led him to believe that over a base of stones heated from a fire, the natives had once in these pits baked or roasted shell and other fish—perhaps game also.[8]

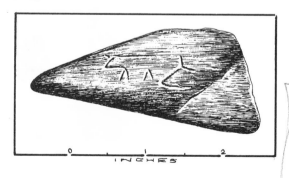

21. Slate knife, with incised effigy, probably from before 1000 B.C. *BMAS*, 28 (1967), 27.

Maize

All over southern New England and as far northeast as the Penobscot, maize and beans furnished two of the native cook's most important ingredients. How many ways the local natives had for cooking them is not recorded, but New York's Iroquois cooks knew up to forty methods for maize alone, each with its own name. A squaw in one western tribe detailed to an inquiring anthropologist a hundred and fifty recipes of various kinds without exhausting her mental cookbook of maize dishes.[9]

The Algonquians of New England cooked maize by itself and in a variety of combinations with fruits, vegetables, nuts, flesh, and fish. Green corn "in the milk" was roasted or boiled on the cob. They also scraped off and dried young kernels for future use. These—and later the hard, ripe corn of harvest time—were the family mainstay until green corn came again. For many dishes the kernels had to be ground to meal or flour, so grinding went on daily. Wood says it was also regular practice to put corn kernels into the soup pot entire, like beans.[10]

The most common ground maize dish, the true staff of life, was samp, or newsamp, a kind of porridge, which Roger Williams says "is the wholesomest diet they have." "From this," he continues, "the English call their samp which is Indian corn beaten and boiled and eaten hot or cold with milk and butter ... A diet exceeding wholesome for English bodies." A Dutch explorer called it very easily digested. The Indians ate theirs without benefit of milk or butter: even after the whites introduced cattle, the natives never learned to like either one. "Samp was ripe corn," says Carr, "either whole or pounded in a mortar or between stones, and boiled with any kind of meat or fish." Some tribes added grease. The Great Lakes Indians, for example, added oil or fat. In season, pumpkins or squash, fresh or dried and chopped fine, might be mixed in. In the spring the cook might drop in milkweed shoots. If the corn was dry and excessively hard, steeping it for half a day before grinding would make it suitable.[11]

The next most popular Indian maize dish was pone, which in numerous variations appears to have been the ancestor of what is today called johnnycake. In summer when the ears were in the milk it was especially toothsome. Timothy Alden, writing in 1795 about fond memories of elderly Cape Cod folks, tells how the Indians of Yarmouth used to prepare a delicious food composed of maize and other ingredients, which they called appoon.[12] For most of the year the method of cooking pone or bread was baking. One recipe was as follows: pound mature corn fine, sift it, make it into a dough with water or bear oil, cover the dough with leaves or pat it into little inch-thick cakes, and bake it in hot ashes. Good bread, but heavy, De Rasieres rated it in 1628. If preferred, the baking might take place on thin broad stones (probably soapstone) placed over the fire, or on broad earthen bottoms.[13]

John Winthrop, Jr., saw Connecticut Indians boiling the meal before baking, and Carr mentions steeping the dough. Delaware Indians (Algonquian) rounded dough into six-inch cakes and baked them in ashes, preferably those of dry oak bark, which did not cling to the bread. Some put a "bason" over the dough to protect it, then covered the whole with charcoal and embers. Carver calls the product very wholesome and well tasted, especially when served with purified bear's fat. Samuel Sewall, the old Salem judge, warned that "it must be alwaies new, never holds daies together."[14]

Berry cake and nut bread are also direct descendants of favorite Indian dishes. Strawberry bread in late spring turned into raspberry and cherry bread in early summer, then into blackberry, blueberry, and elderberry bread as later fruits ripened. Berry cake season did not end with frost but could continue with fruit dried and stored. Indians also boiled chestnuts (today almost extinct, from disease, but formerly from one of the most common and fruitful of New England forest trees). They were "very sweet, as if mixt with Sugar," and were eaten separately or stirred into bread dough. It would be strange if the natives had not also crushed butternuts, hickorynuts, and beechnuts and mixed these in, as Indians did elsewhere, not only for the flavor but to improve the quality of the bread mixture.[15]

To baked bread some Indians added a boiled variety. Nobody wrote down how New England Indians made it, but near the Great Lakes the dough was mixed with berries, nuts, and other ingredients as usual, plus boiling water. Then with hands kept cool by continual dipping into cold water, the squaw kneaded the mixture into flat cakes or dumplings. She slid them into water brought to a boil and cooked them for an hour, or until they floated. Dumplings added to a pot of fowl or other meat was a favorite combination. When made of new soft corn, the cook might add boiled beans: "lapped up in new corn leaves," says Parker, writing of the Iroquois.

Sometimes Indian cooks avoided grinding the maize into meal. Instead, they boiled the kernels whole (evidently dried kernels) "till it swell, and breake, and become tender and then eat it with their Fish or Venison instead of Breade." This is rather like what is today called hominy, though Nicola Tenesles claims that hominy in Algonquian meant "beaten berry."[16]

Heckewelder speaks of the addition of pounded dried meat,

beans, and chestnuts to a dish of boiling cornmeal, and Lechford adds oysters, clams, lobsters and other fish. Gookin puts in shad, eels, herring (bones and all), and any meat taken. The Indians never threw out water in which pumpkins or other vegetables were boiled, or broth in which they had cooked flesh or fish. The family either drank the liquor as a beverage or bouillon, or the cook made it the base for a stew, often thin enough so that no beverage was needed. Maine Indians boiled bass heads for soup stock. (An experienced cook today includes parts of the head in a fish chowder.)[17]

Indians in Rhode Island in the 1660's had a dish similar to escalloped oysters: "They bake bread of Indian corn which they call pagataw: with this and austres, a kind of snail, they make a dish which is widely used." Nicola in Maine tells of pounded acorns being added to boiled oysters.[18]

For such purposes corn picked when filled out but still in the milk was best (as earlier noted); then it was boiled, dried, and stored. When they wanted a stew, they boiled it again, and ate it that way "or amongst their Fish, or Venison or Beaver's Flesh" as "a principall Dish, either at their ordinary Meals or Festivale times." Corn in the milk the English denominated "sweete Corne," the Indians "Pondoncmast" (though it was not what we call sweet corn today).

John Gyles, a colonist held captive in the Penobscot and St. John's valleys in 1689, helped prepare for a "principall" dish. He and his captors boiled ripe green corn, cut the kernels off with clamshells, and dried them in the sun till they were no larger than a pea. They would keep for years, he says. Boiled again, the grain swelled to natural size, but "tastes incomparably sweeter than the other corn." Gyles and the Indians cached this in underground storages, except for what they took up the St. John's River for the fall hunting season. Sharp shells broke the kernels sufficiently so that after drying, the grain might be crumbled by the hand. For one inland tribe (the Wyandottes), a knife or a deer jaw instead of the sharp shell was the tool used.[19]

In his account Gyles appears to refer to the favorite light lunch of the New England Indians—Nokehick, or parched cornmeal. The parching is said to have turned the corn's starch into sugar. Methods of preparing parched cornmeal varied from tribe to tribe. The Delawares preferred a blue sweetish variety of corn parched in hot ashes until it burst like popcorn. They pounded this to flour, then sifted and cleaned it. Winthrop tells how the Connecticut natives likewise put the corn among hot embers, stirring it without letting it burn, until it was "turned almost the inside outward, which will be almost white and flowery," then pounding it into fine meal in a wooden mortar.[20]

All the old chroniclers agree that the resulting meal was sweet and "toothsome," so hearty that, eating it as he felt need, with a little water, an Indian could travel many days with no other food. Put in a long leather bag trussed at his back like a knapsack, so Wood records, the traveler needed to take only "thrice three spoonsful per day, dividing it into three meals." Bartram considered a quarter pound of this travel food, with a pint of water, a hearty meal. (Eating too much could be dangerous.) Lahontan tells of a long expedition where each man bore a bag containing ten pounds. Nailer Tom Hazard, the sage of South County, Rhode Island, at a later time remarks that the powder was filled "with sweetness and life sustaining power."[21] Some tribes (not in New England) combined powdered dry maple sugar and parched corn meal to form this travel food. A small sack of the combination, carried under a man's arm, according to Kalm, would provide his food for one or two months.

Roasting fresh corn (as distinct from parching) is mentioned as an early practice among tribes in other parts of the country, but Winthrop's appears to be one of only a few Puritan accounts. He tells how the Indians roasted the ears before the fire, or, covering them with embers, picked off the roasted kernels and ate them.

Sweet corn, roasting ears, and boiling green corn having been mentioned, it should be pointed out that modern varieties with exceptionally high sugar content appear not to have been known in New England in prehistoric times. A Revolutionary soldier, Captain Richard Bagnall, brought the seed of the first sweet variety (white, not yellow) home to Plymouth after he had served in the Clinton-Sullivan campaign in western New York.[22]

If New England Indians had any variety of popcorn, colonial observers made little mention of it. That so spectacular a characteristic as the popping of the kernels should have escaped notice by white chroniclers would be remarkable. The nearest approach is in the language of Winthrop, "almost white and flowery." This sounds like a true popcorn, but if so, it failed to catch the attention of Williams and other white observers. A French writer saw Iroquois Indians pour hot maple syrup over popcorn and poetically named it snow food, but I have found no such record in New England.

Beans, Squashes, and Pumpkins

Almost as valuable as maize to the aboriginal cook were beans. At their tender stage the two were "seethed" together to form "sutsgut-tahhash." Dieticians find both corn and beans excellent sources of protein; and beans, which contain albumin and amino acids, in both of which maize is deficient, supplement it by adding nutritional value. The natives discovered their nutritious properties only through long experience.[23]

The Indians ate beans both in their tender early state and dried and stored. They cooked them by themselves, mixed them whole into bread batter for baking, and put them in dumplings, stews, and chowder. Tribes everywhere enjoyed such combinations. Carver calls "beyond comparison delicious" a dish of young corn and young beans "boiled together with bear's flesh, the fat of which moistens the pulse."

Beans were especially welcome before other crops matured. Hubbard, historian of the earliest Indian wars, as earlier noted, tells of the discouragement of uprooted Indian villagers, who feared they would be in great want of such summer fruits as beans and squashes, which they could live on until corn came. As the season advanced, beans appeared with corn cut from the cob in many combinations and with every kind of berry. Some were made into chowder by boiling them with fish cut into small pieces, with maize and other ingredients. A good chowder needs a dash of onion, and Josselyn remarks that "Wild leekes . . . the Indians use much to eat with their fish." Beans not needed for summer meals were dried for winter, to be boiled soft with fresh meat. It will be recalled that in November of 1620 a Mayflower party landing on Cape Cod found a bag of beans along with parched acorns in a pit with corn. Indians living near the shore are also said to have eaten the beach-pea.

The earliest writers made no mention of baking beans in earthen pots, or in beanholes in the ground—practices traditionally considered to have been learned from the Indians. Beanholes are reported among Maine Indians, however, whence the beanhole tradition may come. They were also common in Iroquois country. Cooking holes discovered by archaeologists in coastal southern New England could have been put to this purpose.[24]

Squashes and pumpkins, as we have seen, had a valued place in Indian diet: young or mature, fresh or dried, as a main dish or mixed into bread or added to pottage. Pastorius observed an Indian pumpkin picnic in Pennsylvania in 1700. "I saw four of them dining together in great enjoyment of their feast . . . a pumpkin, simply boiled in water, without salt, butter, or spice of any kind. Their seat and table was the bare ground, their spoons seashells, wherewith they supped the warm water, and their plates the leaves of the nearest tree, which . . . they had no need of washing or preserving."[25]

On Cape Cod in July, Champlain enjoyed as a salad squashes the size of a fist. They must have been what Roger Williams heard called "Askutasquash"—meaning green, or to be eaten green, according to

Stoutenburgh's Indian Dictionary. "Their vine apples," Williams dubbed them, "which the English settlers from them call squashes; about the bigness of apples, of several colours . . . sweet, light, wholesome, refreshing." Josselyn, too, deemed them "pleasant food, boyled and buttered and seasoned with spice. But the yellow squash, called the apple squash (because like an apple) and about the size and bigness of a pomewater [a large, sweet English apple or quince] is the best kind."[26]

Delaware women (Algonquian) were particular in their choice of pumpkins and squash and in cooking them. The less water, the better the dish, the women said. They were best of all stewed solely in their own steam in pots covered with large pumpkin leaves. For winter use all eastern tribes dried squash and pumpkins in great quantities and later ground or soaked the flesh as needed for bread and puddings. Sometimes, not taking time to boil, they ate the dried flesh with dried meat.

Squash seeds were a delicacy too. Roasted like peanuts, or merely split with the thumbnail, the germ was a tasty treat. Pumpkin and squash seeds also had a medicinal role. Dried, powdered, and mixed with water, they were thought to help urinary troubles. Among the colonists, pumpkin seeds became a well-known country vermifuge, probably from Indian example. Like the pumpkin, the watermelon was a tasty and healthful summer food.

Roots and Nuts

The tubers of the Jerusalem artichoke were eaten either raw or cooked. Growing three or more to a plant, nutritious and heavy in starch, they added sweetness, body, and their special flavor to pottages of flesh or fish. The roots could also be roasted. Unlike modern refined cane sugars, the levulose of the artichoke is considered harmless to diabetics.[27]

As for the groundnut, Henry Thoreau, a close student of things Indian, tells how he dug some one afternoon, nearly as large as a hen's egg, from six inches to a foot down. Roasted, he reports, they have an agreeable taste much like a potato, though somewhat more fibrous in texture. Boiled, they were unexpectedly dry, with a more nutty flavor. Captain Gosnold, who in 1602 found great quantities of them—"fortie together"—on the offshore islands, thought them as good as potatoes, which had been introduced into Europe from South America in the preceding century. In recent times the Menomini (Algonquian) are reported to have cooked dried sliced tubers with maple syrup. A visitor considered the result superior to candied yams. Other Indians ate raccoon's fat with them. The seeds also were good food, and compared favorably to cultivated peas. Mrs. Rowlandson remembered how, when she was a captive ravenous with hunger, "the Lord upheld my spirit"

22. Soapstone kettle, from Fort Hill, East Providence, Rhode Island. A kettle like this, ground from solid soapstone, could be set among hot coals. *BMAS*, 17 (1955), 8.

with a bit of bear meat and groundnuts boiled together for her by a kind squaw. Another time she ate them in broth thickened with meal ground from the bark of a tree, plus a handful of "pease," perhaps groundnut seeds. Once, merely cooked as a little cake, they sufficed her.[28]

Mushrooms get little or no mention as a native food, perhaps because of the fatal results of eating certain types.

Nut bread has been cited as a favorite food. Walnuts, hickorynuts, beechnuts, and chestnuts, dried and pounded to flour, were used to thicken breads, stews, and pottage. Johnson in his "Wonder-Working Providence" was enthusiastic about the sweetness that boiled chestnuts add to bread. The bread he so enjoyed may have been like that described by Adair in the South, where the nuts were picked green and parboiled, and the shells removed; they were then pounded in a mortar with corn in the milk, and the resulting paste was boiled in corn leaves. "Boiled chestnuts is their white bread," Johnson avers, speaking of the Narragansetts of New England. Partly because of their flavors (though this is seldom mentioned by New England writers), nuts were also a favorite ingredient in cooking.[29]

The walnut had a special use. When the mother's breast milk failed, she had a substitute. Mrs. Elizabeth Hanson, of Dover, New Hampshire, with a newborn baby at her breast, was captured by Indians in 1724. Her milk dried up, and the babe's bones showed. A squaw taught her to beat walnut kernels and water to a milk and boil it with very fine ground cornmeal. "My babe . . . quickly began to thrive and look well, which gave me great comfort." The Iroquois of New York had a similar formula. They dried and ground hickorynuts or butternuts and added ground dried bear or deer meat. The resulting powder, dropped into boiling water, made a liquid baby food. Peter Kalm, the Swedish botanist, called the powder nut "flour"; and when mixed with water the liquid was as white and sweet as milk. In southern New England a mother, to nourish her infant, would add boiled squash to this walnut milk. John Long saw wild rice pulverized and boiled in water with maple sugar for the same purpose.[30]

Acorns were less easy to handle. Some varieties, those of the red oak, for example, are high in tannic acid, hence had to be boiled with the ashes of rotten maple wood to remove it. On the other hand, boiling white oak acorns (the preferred variety) brought a clear, sweet oil to the surface to serve as lard or butter. Acorn flour was mingled with many sorts of meat, fish, clams, lobsters, oysters, and other ingredients in Indian cooking. Williams thought that the Indians preferred maize meal to acorn meal; they did dry a supply of the latter, however, "and in case of want of corne, by much boyling they make a good dish of them; yea sometimes in plentie of corne doe they eat these akornes for a dayntie."[31]

Wild rice, the grain staple of many western and Canadian tribes, is found in northern New England waters, less often in southern New England. Chemists report it one of the most nutritious of Indian foods, high in protein and vitamin B, low in fat.

New England natives were fond of the sweet, gelatinous roots of the common yellow pond lily, *Nuphar advena,* and often dried them for winter. "Long aboiling they taste like the Liver of a Sheepe," Johnson wrote. They were eaten boiled or roasted, sometimes with fowl. Since muskrats are also fond of the roots, the natives let these busy creatures collect and store them, then raided their storehouses, being careful, as noted earlier, to leave the animals a supply for their own use. They valued also, for eating raw and for cooking, the roots of the cattail, rich in protein, and the spring shoots of the marsh marigold, or cowslip, found in the mud of shallow ponds and backwaters.

How such roots were preserved locally is not clear. The Meskwaki of Wisconsin cut the roots of the yellow lotus into sections, strung them on basswood fibers, and hung them to dry on the rafters, to be soaked later for cooking with meat, corn, or beans.

Among the "other roots" that Roger Williams speaks of as Indian food might easily have been sweet flag; the tubers of the arrowhead, common in New England shallow waters and used by other American tribes; and, from the upland, Solomon's seal, Jack-in-the-pulpit, and Turks Cap lily.[32]

Fruits

Strawberries were highly valued and very popular in season as well
as for winter fruitcake. When the strawberries had gone, the children
picked the juicy black thimbleberries, red raspberries, and blackberries
that followed. Next in ripening came the sweet, powder-blue lowbush
blueberries, then the taller varieties, and later, in the swamps, the more
acid highbush berries. All were eaten fresh, added to breads, or dried
for future use. On gravel knolls children gathered seedy huckleberries,
and in the woods the fruit of gooseberry bushes red and green, described as "naturally growing." In most years all yielded bountifully for
both bears and men. Elderberries, the last of the summer bush fruits,
hung in rich bunches over the marshes, except where children had
earlier picked the sweet-scented blossom clusters to dry for flavoring.
Probably it was these "blackberryes, somewhat like Currants" of which
Josselyn saw "great store going into Indian boyling Puddings, for
variety in the English manner."[33]

With September, bogs and meadows, both inland and near the
shore, reddened with tart cranberries on their bronze vines. "Certain
small fruits like to small apples," Lescarbot describes them, "whereof we
made marmalade for to eate after meat." The natives did not know that
cranberries contain iodine and iron essential to the human body; but
they found them healthful.

Champlain recorded on islands near Cape Porpoise, Maine, "so
many red currants that one sees for the most part nothing else." Perhaps
they were red raspberries, common there, or the delicious little vine
cranberries of the Maine coast, far tastier than the modern cultivated
cranberry. Other wild berries must have been used, for Thoreau writes
in the 19th century: "I have added a few to my number of edible berries
by walking behind an Indian in Maine, who ate such as I never thought
of testing before."[34]

Not to be overlooked is the bitter but pleasant tang imparted to
food by the beach plum, native to sandy Cape Cod, Narragansett Bay,
and the islands. These plums the Long Island natives valued so highly
that when a chief there sold his lands to the whites, he carefully reserved
"all liberty and privileges of plumming." At Plymouth in 1621 Winslow
lists three colors: white, black, and red, "and almost as good as Dam-
sons." Josselyn adds yellow. "Delicate" is the word Pory uses to describe
the Plymouth plums, doubtless *Prunus maratima,* today's beach plum, a
favorite for jelly.

Of the plum Wood makes a rhyme: "Within this Indian Orchard
fruites be some / The ruddie Cherrie and the jettie Plumme," and
Verrazano had listed it in the preceding century. Hedrick states that

Prunus nigra (the Indians' single fruit, he calls it) grows sparingly along the New England rivers. In the early days of Sudbury, Rev. Edmund Brown speaks of native plum trees as distinct from cultivated plums. In a 1789 diary Rev. Nathan Perkins, traveling into newly settled western Vermont, calls plum trees natural to the country.

Returning to Wood's rhyme, the red wild cherry that he mentions had black and purple relatives: Colonial herbalist Manasseh Cutler counted seven in all, some with less of the chokecherry aspect than others.[35]

Besides plums and cherries, the natives were fond of the shadbush fruit, ripening in midsummer, and dried them for later use. Among tree fruits, they gathered the blue-gray berry of the red cedar, which grows thriftily on even the driest, poorest New England hillside, and is high in sugar and starch.

Verrazano mentions apples, and Van der Donck, who sailed along the Connecticut shore as well as up the Hudson, says he saw several kinds. He omits them from his list of fruits in Indian orchards, as does Pory. Although the wild crabapple is a New England native, it was not plentiful along the coast.

To European sailors and explorers accustomed to the vineyards and wine of the Old World, grapes were the most attractive native fruit. A Plymouth chronicler in 1622 rated native grapes as of only tolerable flavor, but another called them very sweet and strong. The Indian ate grapes in their natural and dried state but never made them into wine, as the English soon tried to do. No New England Indian made or used intoxicants until the Europeans demoralized him, but natives whom Van der Donck met in New York pressed out and drank fresh grape juice. Early New England and Virginia observers often write that the Indian's regular drink was water. Mrs. Rowlandson watched Indian dancers "hopping up and down one after another with a Kettle of water in the midst, standing warm upon some embers, to drink of when they were dry."[36]

Yet some Indians enjoyed flavored drinks. The late H. E. Pulling, who grew up among Middle Western Algonquian forest tribes, writes that there were at least two substitutes for coffee, and four kinds of tea were made by dipping elderberry blossoms in very hot water. They liked pleasant drinks on hot days, he says, and made them from wild fruits, including those of the smooth sumac, from strawberry and raspberry leaves, and from chokecherry bark. They tapped large grape vines in spring and obtained a drink tasting much like grape juice; they even dug the roots of the black raspberry and made a drink from the bark. Boiled water was made tasty also with wintergreen, spruce, and wild cherry twigs. The Hurons used the juice of corn and squash as a beverage. With their deep knowledge of the properties of plants, it seems scarcely possible, despite a paucity of local evidence, that New England Indians did not use some of the pleasant mixtures of fruit juices and water known to other Algonquian tribes.[37]

The soft inner bark of certain trees and many of the lichens that cling to rocks have nutritive value. Indeed, as earlier noted, the name of the Adirondack Indians is said to be translated Tree Eaters. Mrs. Rowlandson mentions how her captors used bark when living off the country in winter, and other observers have left similar records. Usually, however, bark was a last resort. And eating lichens might result in severe digestive disturbances.

Sugar and Salt

Neither sugar nor salt was a factor in the diet of most southern New England tribes when Europeans first met them. Maple sugar is generally considered a native product of aboriginal origin. Yet in marked contrast to the many accounts of maple sugar by French colonists in Canada, none of the earliest white observers of New England native life mention it. This was not because maple trees of certain types were not plentiful, for Josselyn carefully notes how maple wood ashes make lye to force out oil from oak acorns, and many early writers speak of the maple in one way or another.

Perhaps maple sugar is not mentioned because early records relate almost altogether to the seacoast tribes, especially those of southern New England. The rock maple is found all over highland New England, less often near the coast; Thoreau in a later century mentions a rock maple in the Concord woods; but few sugar maples grow naturally east of the Berkshires and the Taconic Range, or south of the hills of Vermont, New Hampshire, and Maine. Seldom are they self-propagated within reach of the sea winds, where most Indian tribes had their seats when the first whites arrived. There is, in fact, evidence regarding non-use of sugar. Thomas Lechford states specifically of the Massachusetts Bay Indians: "They will not eat sweet things, nor alter their habits willingly."[38] Near the end of King Philip's War, Connecticut troops captured scores of Narragansett prisoners, one of whom they allowed their Mohegan allies to torture. The Mohegans cut around the joints of his fingers and toes and broke them off. The captive never flinched. To the taunts of his tormentors he answered "that he liked the war well, and found it as sweet as the Englishmen do their sugar." Some doubt is cast on Lechford's categorical statement by a request of Roger Williams to Governor Winthrop in a late 1636 or early 1637 letter of diplomatic counsel: "Sir, if anything be sent to the [Indian] princes, I find that Canonicus would gladly accept of a box of eight or ten pounds of sugar, and indeed he told me he would thank Mr. Governor for a box full . . . ," but this may have been an acquired taste on the part of the Narragansett prince. Dorr, a Rhode Island historian, suggests that it resulted from twenty years of trading with the Dutch.[39] A Department of Agriculture writer of 1866 says that New England Indians combined coarse-grained sugar with fresh pounded "suppasoin seasoned with dry whortleberries," a custom of tribes elsewhere; but no word for sugar appears in either Williams' "Key" or Cotton's dictionary of the Indian language.[40]

The first reference by an English writer to the use of maple sugar in what is now New England appears in a book by Hon. Robert Boyle, published at Oxford in 1664. Boyle says he has been assured of the existence in some parts of New England of a tree that exudes a saccharine sap.[41] The earliest comprehensive description of the making of maple sugar in New England seems to be the paper Paul Dudley of Massachusetts in 1720 contributed to the Royal Society, of which he was a member, though sugar making in Canada had previously appeared in the Society's records in 1684. Dudley states that "maple sugar is made from the juice of the upland maple or maple trees that grow in the highlands."[42]

The Housatonics, a group composed of Mahicans from Hudson Valley with remnants of various Connecticut tribes who settled on the Housatonic River in the southern Berkshires in the early eighteenth century, certainly boiled maple sap, for the whole process of sugar making is carefully described in 1753 by Rev. Samuel Hopkins, a resident white missionary who yearned for their souls. "The molasses that is made of this Sap is exceedingly good," he comments, "and considerably resembles honey." The Mahicans may have brought the maple sugar habit to the Berkshires from New York, or it may have come from Canada, to which some Connecticut Indians had fled when the English drove them out of their homes along Long Island Sound.[43]

The Penobscots of Maine made maple sugar, perhaps even from aboriginal times. Speck says that maple groves up river were family possessions generation after generation, carefully demarcated like hunting territories. The historian of Brattleboro, Vermont, states that the Squakheags, a Connecticut Valley tribe whose territory extended south to take in Northfield, Massachusetts, made maple syrup. Maple sugar was and is a highly popular food with Algonquian tribes of the Middle West and Canada. Lafitau shows an engraving of the process as he observed it in Canada. The Ojibways especially claim the sugar maple as Min-an-tik, "Our Own Tree." In some tribes sugar huts descended from mother to daughter. So perhaps it was from lack of sugar maple trees that sugar was not a factor in the diet of the populous tribes of coastal southern New England. The subject of maple sugar deserves attention, however, since the making of it today is generally classed as an agricultural enterprise derived from the Indians, and since the Penobscots, Squakheags, and Housatonics, at least, made sugar in New England in historic times.[44]

The processes of producing syrup and sugar have changed little until recently. Now metal spouts and pails and plastic piping have replaced the forefathers' wooden pails and the earlier stone, wood, and bark utensils of the Indians, and oil often replaces wood for fuel. The colonists' metal kettles for boiling down probably improved quality, for one of the French fathers complained of a burnt taste in the native product. His own people, he remarked, made it better than the Indian women who had taught them. At any rate, among tribes that used it, everyone agreed that maple syrup and sugar added zest to any menu.

To make the syrup, a first step might be to hollow out a log as if for a canoe, to gather sap in.[45] Speck never heard of this among Maine Indians, however. Penobscot families there, and others where the white birch grew, prepared birch bark vessels to receive the drippings from the trees. These were seamless or stitched at the corners with slender basswood fibers or spruce roots, and sealed at the seams with resin. Some tribes made them of elm bark. Next, with an axe, the men cut gashes in the trees and fitted elderberry twigs in the gashes, or sap runners of hardwood beveled to fit. The sap ran down these and dripped into pails.[46]

The sugar maple, silver maple, wild cherry, black maple, and box elder are all recorded as being tapped somewhere, as well as birch and ash (the sugar of the last two being bitter). The box elder yields beautiful white sugar, but not enough. One traveler who tried it thought its sugar less sweet than that of the rock maple.[47]

After collecting the buckets, the family boiled the sap over the fire. Eastman tells how, in his Minnesota boyhood, the grandmother would pour part of the thickened molasses into birch molds of various shapes to harden, or into hollow reeds and canes, even into the shells of duck and goose eggs saved for the purpose. Small candies might be set aside as a treat for little folks. Boys had a special duty in sugar making, Eastman states: to shoot pilfering rabbits and squirrels before the animals could gnaw holes in the birch bark pans or upset them. In some tribes sugaring off was so much a family frolic that in addition to making the hollowed-log containers, men helped also with boiling the sap.

A family might pulverize some of the hardened sugar and pack it away in rawhide or birch bark cases. If the supply was limited, it was a delicacy kept for feasts. In the north, sugar might be served with wild rice, parched corn, groundnuts, or dried meats. Hardened in egg shells, it made a handy lunch for travel.

Rev. Samuel Hopkins gives details on how sugar was made in the Berkshires, where maples abounded: "After it is boil'd, they take it off the Fire and stir it till it is cold, which is their way of graining it." In Maine in historic times the Penobscots poured syrup into birch bark cones about nine inches long and often gave these away as presents. Thick maple molasses might be poured onto sheets of birch bark to harden. Canadian Indians and others sometimes boiled sap in clay pots, poured the molasses into shallow basins, froze it, and then threw the ice away, leaving the sugar pure. Wisconsin tribes celebrated the sugar season with a votive offering and a great dance and feast.[48]

In Acadia, Sieur de Dieuville ate maple sugar on wild strawberries, but he does not say whether this had been an Indian custom.[49] The Menomini enjoyed it with cranberries and blueberries, and even cooked groundnuts with it to eat like candied yams. The Penobscots of Maine combined syrup with both artichokes and groundnuts. They also melted rock sugar in water for a beverage.

The nourishing qualities of maple sugar impressed the Swedish traveler Peter Kalm as he journeyed through the middle Atlantic highlands in the 1700's. "I have, in my trips through the lands of the

23. Canadian Hurons making maple syrup, historic period. J. F. Lafitau, *Moeurs des Sauvages Ameriquains* (Paris, 1724) II : 125.

savages had many good meals of just sugar and bread when no other food was available," he tells us. "When we reached the villages of the savages we received more than anything else gifts of large pieces of sugar, which stood us well in hand on our trips into the wilderness. When the savages cooked gruel or mush for us from cornmeal they added lumps of sugar to make up for the lack of milk."[50]

For Indians of the interior, maple sugar took the place of white man's salt, for which many tribes had no taste. "It is singular," a Canadian observer reports, "how soon one may acquire the taste for this substitute for salt, even on meats." The quantity a family could make and consume was astonishing. Thomas McKenney in his "Tour To The Lakes," speaks of three families making four tons of sugar in a season, "some of it very beautiful . . . as white as Havana sugar and richer."[51]

Salt, the early New England tribes never used. Neither Eliot's Bible nor Williams' dictionary had a word for it. Wood and Hutchinson both say the Indians ate without it. When in King Philip's War, Queen Awashonks entertained Captain Benjamin Church with a fish dinner of sea bass, flounders, and eels, no salt was to be seen. Even after a half century of influence by English habits, salt was apparently superfluous. Nicolar of the Penobscots gives the word for salt as Sur-lur-waia (an adaptation from the French, apparently), but says the tribe did not eat it. Cartier affirms of the Canadian tribes he met, "Their whole subsistence [vivre] is without any taste of salt." Carver, much later, says that many Indian natives had never seen it. Hennepin saw none among the Hurons. New Jersey Algonquians boiled beans without it. Even in this century, many Menomini (Algonquian) used no salt.[52]

A people as intelligent as the New England Algonquians, who had discovered the properties and value of a multitude of herbs, animals, and fishes, and who were bordered by the sea, could hardly have been ignorant of the possibilities of salt. A logical conclusion is that with a wealth of saltwater fish available to all tribes—even those dependent on interior rivers and ponds—they felt no need for a salt supplement. Speaking of clams, Williams writes: "These they boil, and it makes their broth and their bread seasonable and savory instead of salt." Moreover, as already noted, Indians found roots from low places especially attractive, and ate the digestive parts of animals; both are likely to contain concentrated food salts.

Drying or smoking flesh and fish, the Indians did not need salt as a preservative. By mixing sassafras and other herbs with such fats as bear oil, they could keep the oil sweet even in hot weather.

Yet practices change. Morton observed that some Indians were beginning to use salt. Once they had seen how helpful it could be in preserving meat, they would beg for it. By 1745 Nehemiah How's Indian captors had refreshed him with meat cooked in salt, which they had left in a cache with other foods against their return journey through the Vermont mountains to Canada.[53]

Game, Fish, and Seafood

Native cooks used whatever food was at hand. Indians enjoyed venison as one of their staples and planned to get a supply of it each fall, as well as of moose meat in the north and east where this was available. Bear furnished juicy steaks (the meat of a young bear was a special delicacy), also fat to butter corn cakes, grease bodies, and oil hair. In Canada Le Jeune saw solid bear fat eaten as a person might bite an apple today. The natives stored it in jars, with sassafras or slippery elm bark slipped in to keep it sweet. Near the sea, seal and whale oil were prized. Raccoon, beaver, otter, turtle, skunk, rabbit, woodchuck, rattlesnake, seal, whale, frog—the meat of every kind of mammal except flesh eaters like the wolf—the natives cooked and ate. Thoreau in a later time found agreeable the woodchuck meat quarried by a dog belonging to a French Canadian woodsman friend. Even the faithful and valued dog, as noted, might be slaughtered when needed.[54] The Indian was skilled at devising ingenious traps and deadfalls, designing them not solely to catch the animal desired for food but so as to prevent damage to skin or fur, and so constructed that a beaver or other sharp-toothed animal could not gnaw his way out.

Roast turkey graced the first Plymouth Thanksgiving, and ordinary native meals as well. From river and salt marsh came ducks and geese which in their season furnished both meat and abundant oil. From the woods came partridge, woodcock, and quail. Tremendous flights of wild pigeons, a breed of beautiful birds now extinct, provided an important source of food during their brief spring and fall migrations. So immense were the flocks of these birds that they are said to have completely shut out the sun as they flew. Where at night they roosted on branches of trees, it was easy to knock them off with sticks. Says a 1648 colonial record: "It is incredible what multitudes of them are killed daily. It was ordinary for one man to kill eight or ten dozen in half a day, yea five or six dozen at one shot."[55]

In New England, should game be scarce, there was always fish. No Indian would think of locating a wigwam or a settlement except within easy reach of fresh or salt water or, better, both. Great runs of herring or shad, abundant salmon, and occasional sturgeon migrated up rivers and brooks in spring, the herring easy to dip out at weirs by the basketful. Even tribes hostile to each other gathered at the great falls to spear and smoke the larger fish. Bass, pickerel, trout, eels, and a store of other tasty fish were native to the fresh waters.[56]

Most of New England's Algonquians, more fortunate than tribes far inland, also had the sea as a resource, with oysters, scallops, crabs, and quahogs available at the shore itself and a wealth of fish not far distant. A meal might include several kinds. Tribes further removed could trade deer meat for dried shellfish. The clam bake is considered a modern heritage from the Algonquians. The immense shell heaps the English settlers found on Cape Cod and the Connecticut, Rhode Island, and Maine shores, even on an occasional inland river, testify to the native love for shellfish.

In fresh waters and on frozen ocean bays, fishing through the ice was a help to the larder in winter. The muddy bottoms of shallow swamps and sluggish rivers yielded fat eels, of which the Indians were especially fond, and hornpout or bullheads. From Cape Cod eastward, Indians from their canoes hunted seals and the mammoth whale, skillfully and dangerously. Whales and other large water dwellers sometimes cast ashore in storms were a perquisite of the chief sachem. The Indians scrupulously preserved fish, seal, and whale oil in skins, jars, and gourds, and buried it for future use.

A Diet for Superb Health

To sum up the features of Indian diet, if one measure of the status of any branch of the human family is the abundance and variety of its food and the skill used in its preparation, then to judge by such a standard, the prediscovery New England Indian cook would stand well. Moreover, she had learned to make use of a wide choice of edible vegetable, fruit, and medicinal plants; and of the animals, reptiles, and fishes with which a bountiful nature had blessed her environment, including many that moderns undervalue, dislike, or completely overlook.

The Indian methods of preparing and combining foods detailed here have been of considerable variety; they resulted in a diet diversified and balanced, contributing to a lithe and healthy body, vigorous and with stamina. All explorers who visited New England shores testify to this, and the English who associated with the natives after colonization comment on the great agility and endurance of the natives. An Indian runner could cover as many as a hundred miles in a single day, and on the second day afterward return in the same time. One reason lies in the native diet. Long journeys like this, as well as quick removes, required a lightweight but nourishing ration. "Nokehick" or "nokake," the meal from parched corn described above, was the answer.

Beans might almost have been invented to supplement maize. An acre of beans, it has been calculated, might feed a man for a whole year; but an acre and a half of land would be needed for a year's ration of wheat, the European staple. Beans fitted perfectly the intensive succession and cropping program of the Indian garden.[57]

The produce of cultivated fields—beans, maize, pumpkins, squash, artichokes—thus formed one sound foundation for the native diet of most of New England. Fish, flesh, and fowl, supplemented by roots, nuts, fruits, berries, and other foods provided largely by nature, in some cases with human assistance, formed the other.

Inland, swamps provided a great variety of edible roots and seeds. Dr. Joel E. Goldthwait, a bone specialist, told me that in his opinion these lowland contributions to Indian diet had much to do with their sound teeth, their firm, resilient bones, and their general good health. The marsh plants they ate were rich in minerals washed from higher lands. He believed that modern people rely too much on foods grown on upland soils from which the minerals have been leached, and as a result their health suffers. To test this view, at the Peabody Museum I examined the teeth in forty aboriginal human jawbones dug up in Massachusetts. Few showed signs of decay.

That the type of food the natives ate had much to do with the excellent physique and health of body to which early writers testify was also the opinion of H. E. Pulling, who grew up among the Indians of Minnesota.[58] Nineteenth-century Americans who have lived long with Indians have commented that while eating the native food, their bodies seemed buoyant, more responsive. Certain negative evidence appears to support this view. Palmer in 1870 recorded as common knowledge of army men stationed among Indians in the West that when confined to white men's diet, the natives pined away; sometimes, under such conditions, they would die one after another, as if visited by an epidemic. Among modern Menomini, Smith relates that the old men believed that their aboriginal diet acted as medicine, and that by eating white man's food they acquired his diseases.[59]

The wealth of nuts New England afforded made many another tasty and nourishing contribution to fall and winter diet. The quantity an Indian could consume appeared to some observers almost incredible. In deeds of land to the English, one privilege often reserved by the grantors was that of nutting.

All in all, from woods, waters, and his cultivated fields, the New England Indian usually ate well and with greater variety than did many

North American tribes. His ordinary food contained all essential calo-
ries, vitamins, minerals, acids, and trace elements necessary for healthy,
enduring bodies and active, ingenious minds. Yet when forced by
circumstance—such as the necessity for a swift removal—to go without
food, Indians could stoically endure fasting. For despite so many good
things to eat, both cultivated and wild and seemingly in abundance,
there might still be hungry times. On a visit to Chief Massasoit, two
Pilgrim emissaries from Plymouth and their Indian hosts for two or
three days had next to nothing to eat. Missing a few meals did not
disturb the natives, but the visitors, to keep body and soul together,
finally had to head for home.

The Jesuit fathers in Canada tell frequently of want, even starvation, in their long winters among the forest tribes along the Great River.
But those tribes depended on hunting and gathering, and woods deep
in snow were far from being filled with game, as Jesuit writers make
amply clear. The New England Indians, the agricultural tribes at least,
commonly had food enough and to spare. More than once their stores
were to save the hungry white newcomers from want. Even when cut
off from their base of supplies and forced to live off the country, Indians
could take care of themselves, as Mary Rowlandson's narrative clearly
shows. This minister's wife, dragged from her home in Lancaster in the
dead of winter amid snow and cold, traveled with her captors through
twenty-two "stages," into western Massachusetts and southern Vermont then back to the shadow of Mt. Wachusett in central Massachusetts, where she was ransomed.

It was thought by the English, she says, that "if their Corn were cut
down they would starve and die . . . yet how . . . strangely did the Lord
provide for them; that I did not see (all the time I was among them) one
man, woman, or child die with hunger . . . I can but stand in admiration
to see the wonderful power of God, in providing for such a vast number
of our Enemies in the Wilderness, where there was nothing to be seen
but from hand to mouth."

Some colonial accounts, nevertheless, mention the improvidence
of natives. This characteristic might better be termed open-handed
hospitality. Hunting tribes and peoples practicing noncommercial agriculture anywhere are likely to feel an obligation to share generously
with neighbor and stranger. Heckewelder, the sympathetic Christian
missionary to the Middle Atlantic Algonquian Leni-Lenapes, explains
their point of view: "They think that [the Great Spirit] made the earth
and all that it contains, that when he stocked the country, it was for all.
Whatever liveth on land, whatever groweth out of the earth, and all that
is in the rivers and waters, was given jointly to all." Roger Williams tells
how, when eating, they would offer a visitor what they had, though it

were little enough for themselves. If fish or flesh came in, he says, they made their neighbors partake with them. Many a time, he adds, even at night when nothing was ready, Indians and their wives had risen to prepare him refreshment. He terms them free as emperors with hospitality.

Summing up the Indian food situation as a whole, Lucien Carr declares that from the quantity and quality of the products of his fields and the many ways of cooking his food, the Indian had nothing to fear from a comparison with his new English neighbor.[60]

10.

The Roles of the Sexes

In considering the roles of the Indian man and his helpmeet, we need to discard present-day conceptions of the duties and contributions of the two sexes; to make allowance for the different but nevertheless prejudiced accounts of colonial observers; and to balance against both the conditions of native life that the Indians faced and their solutions for providing an adequate, satisfying existence.

To the new-come English the Indian division of duties between men and women appeared designed to make life easy for men while women shouldered the harder tasks. Among New England tribes, the male's attitude, were we to accept without examination the comments of numerous colonial observers, was "Let the woman do it!" "The men employ their time wholly in hunting and other exercises of the bow," said Governor Edward Winslow of Plymouth, "except that they sometimes take some pains at fishing. The women live a most slavish life: they carry all their burdens, set and dress their corn, gather it in, and seek out for much of their food, beat and make ready the corn to eat and have all household care lying upon them." It was their job, when the temporary shelter was to be moved, to take down the wigwam, roll up the covering mats which formed the walls, and carry these and the poles on which they had rested to the next location. In March and April before planting started, the women gathered firewood. Daily they brought water from the spring to boil above the flame. They dug clams, caught lobsters, fished, picked berries, and "curried and suppled," as Lescarbot says, the skins of the game their men shot or trapped—all in addition to cooking meals and making up clothing. They were the farmers, breaking the ground, planting the seed; cultivating, weeding, harvesting, storing the crops; and selecting seed for the season to follow. Young girls were helpers.[1]

"Industrious," Thomas Lechford called the squaws. "They doe most of the labour in planting and carrying of burdens; their husbands hold them in great slavery, yet never knowing other, it is less grievous upon them." Christopher Levett observed that "their wives are their slaves, and doe all their work: The men doe nothing but kill Beasts, Fish ec."[2] (The English classed hunting as recreation: to the Indian male it was work.)

George Catlin, two centuries later, used the same term, "slaves," to describe the squaws in certain western prairie tribes. No New England writer, however, goes to the point of the French Jesuits, who report that the women of less advanced nonagricultural Algonquian tribes were burdened with so much heavy work that they could not bear fully developed children; abortions were frequent, and the proportion of infant deaths extremely high. In general, testimony from New England is the opposite, although John Winthrop records that when requested by the neighboring Puritan authorities not to work on the Lord's Day, an Indian replied: "It is a small thing for us to rest on that day, for we have not much to do any day, and therefore will forbeare on that day."[3]

Yet the station of the woman, busy as she was, did not confine her wholly to drudgery in the field and by the fire. In the early seventeenth century several New England tribes had squaws at their head. If the sachem had no son, the queen ruled. It was the squaw sachem of the Mystic Indians, north of Boston, who signed the deed to the English of that fertile valley. One powerful head of a large clan was Awashonks, woman ruler of the tribe on the east side of Mt. Hope Bay, to whom in King Philip's War Captain Benjamin Church successfully appealed to prevent the tribe's joining the enemies of the English. A woman of high birth named Weatamoo became chief of the Pocasset tribe, not her husband, Petononowett. In Connecticut a squaw sachem, Shaum-pishuh, ruled the Quinnipiacs at Guilford. At Haddam in 1662 two "queens" as well as two chiefs signed the deed, a not infrequent case. Sir William Johnson, in New York, questioning an Indian of the Six Nations about land transactions, inquired if women had any rights in land disposal. "They were the properest owners," was the reply, "they being the persons who labored on their lands, and were therefore esteemed in that light." When important matters were afoot, the women were not ignored. Roger Williams tells how the squaws formed in a circle to learn the news and to hear the business of the tribe debated. Among the western Abenaki in the north both women and children took part. It can scarcely be doubted that they influenced decisions.[4]

As a person, a woman was the unquestioned mistress of her body. If unmarried, she might without shame accept a bed companion or withhold her favor as she preferred. Unmarried pregnancy was, however, a disgrace—to be avoided, if necessary, by the use of plant preventives. Menstruation did not usually begin until the late teens. Seclusion in a separate hut during the monthly period was the rule. Violation of the chastity of unconsenting girls is said to have been unknown, as was also the rape or abuse of a married woman. Incest incurred disgrace.[5]

Monogamy was the custom, but a chief or shaman might take other wives in addition to his principal wife. Marriage was by consent of the parents, with a dowry expected from those of the bride. Among Western Abenaki the suitor made his proposal through another person by offering a present which the young woman could accept or not as she chose. In some tribes, during a trial period the couple slept head to foot. Though usually permanent, marriage was by no means indissoluble. A husband could put away his wife, or, as was more likely, a wife who felt put upon by a mean husband could leave, taking her children, if any, and go to another tribe. They were never unwelcome, says Winslow, "for where most women are is most plenty": it was they who did not only the cooking and planting, but the tanning, basket-making, and weaving.

On the other hand, affection between husband and wife might run deep. One husband was known to travel forty miles and back, two days' journey, for cranberries as medicine for his ill wife. Love of a lost husband, Gookin says, might send the widow into deep mourning that could last for years. A widow seldom remarried. Williams tells also of the lamentations over a loved one's death.[6]

The married woman was complete mistress of her house and household. If the exterior of the wigwam was composed of mats, it was she who had made and fastened them. To her fell preparation of the meals, and she assigned positions for eating and sleeping. She worked up the skins of animals into clothing, shaped the clay pots, wove baskets and fashioned textiles, cared for and sang lullabys to her babe and the young, and with the help of her daughters did the household duties. She took on most of the growing and storage of the cultivated crops, and ground the corn she raised. All the pots, tools, and furnishings belonged to her. Clearly she was indispensable in field and household.[7]

Back in 1623 Rev. William Morrell, one of the English who tried to start a settlement at Wessagussett (later Weymouth) testified in verse to the worth of the Massachusett women:

> Their slender fingers in a grassie twyne
> Make well form'd baskets wrought with art and lyne
> A kind of Arras or Straw-hangings wrought
> With divers formes and colours, all about
> These gentle pleasures, their fine fingers fit
> Which Nature seem'd to frame rather to sit;
> Rare Stories, Princes, people, kingdomes, Towers,
> In curious finger-worke, or Parchment flowers
> And what so ere without doores give content
> Those hands doe digge the earth, and in it lay
> Their faire choyce Corne, and take the weeds away.

The young blood looking for a bride did not choose a girl from his own clan or gens. Invariably his suit would focus on a suitable female of different descent. A Deer would not marry a Deer, but if well favored and providing proof that he was an accomplished hunter, he might be welcome among the Partridges or the Fox family. In southern New England he would go to live with his bride's people and descent was reckoned through the mother. But in the north, among the Western Abenaki, the father's line prevailed, though the young couple would be welcome in the longhouse of whichever family had room.

For the assertion that the Algonquian squaw in New England was overburdened or ill-treated, or that her health was ruined by labor, little direct evidence can be found. The excellent physical health attributed to women of the agricultural tribes is testimony to the contrary. Among the Rhode Island Indians whom Roger Williams knew so well, work can hardly have injured them physically, for he remarks that their very "labour is questionless one cause of their extraordinary ease of childbirth [and the] women nurse all the children themselves." Many observers corroborate this, and some contrast it specifically with the difficulties of colonial women in childbearing. Morton and others comment on the excellent condition of the Indian infants and on the length of time during which the mothers continue to suckle them. Champlain notices the number of Algonquian and Huron women who, though they performed onerous duties, are powerful women of extraordinary height, and certain Narragansett burial sites offer supporting evidence.[8]

Life could not have been a round of drudgery, for there were plenty of women's games. Wood called the Indian woman's voice a well-tuned instrument. Williams comments on the pleasant sociable way the women had of despatching their field work. Says Adair (in the South), "They fall to work with great cheerfulness: sometimes one of their orators cheers them with humorous old tales and . . . agreeable wild tunes." It was much like the bees or quilting parties of the later colonial women.[9]

To both woman and maize the Wabanaki, the tribes of northern and eastern New England, New Brunswick, and Nova Scotia, gave the honored name "Mother," calling woman the first mother, hence— properly—the one who plants, and maize with its milk the second mother. The missionary John Heckewelder, who lived for many years with the Algonquian Delawares, thought the work assigned to women no more than their fair share of what was at best an arduous life for both sexes.[10] The lot of the squaw among the agricultural tribes should be compared not with the modern American woman's but with that of the English farm or frontier wife to whom the Indian woman resigned her fields. The farm woman of the sixteenth and seventeenth centuries in England, and of the seventeenth in New England, also lived by labor.

She fed and cared for her household. She spun and wove the cloth and made the clothing. She manufactured soap and candles, churned butter, and pressed cheese. She hatched the chicks, fed the poultry, and tended the bees, the herb garden, and the vegetable garden. She often milked, and in extremity might help with haying and field tasks. In England (and sometimes in early New England), if near a market town, very likely she sold the farm produce in the market. Her burden was heavy.

Mary Jameson, a white woman, lived for many years in the Indian manner among the Iroquois, an agricultural nation in many respects comparable to the tribes of southern New England. She regarded the lot of the Indian wife as not overburdensome: "Their task is probably not harder than that of white women, and their cares are certainly not half as numerous or so great."[11]

Of the man's duties the most important was to acquire the skill and maintain the physique necessary to defend the tribe, and to obtain the essential meat and skins for his household by hunting, trapping, and fishing.

His first obligation was to safeguard his family's life and their home in case of war. Though warfare was not frequent among New England tribes, a raid by an enemy was always a possibility. As to hunting, in long-settled country like southern New England game was often scarce and found only at a distance. When the brave was not actually hunting, his skills nevertheless had to be maintained: his limbs kept supple, his wind sound, his lungs capacious for swift and distant travel. The teenage boy emulated his elders.

Hunting and trapping were emphatically not sports but often exhausting body-wracking, tedious tasks and deadly earnest. "The fatigues of hunting wear out the body and the constitution more than manual labor" (Heckewelder). In Maine the fleetest young men were even trained to run down a deer or moose, a feat that might take more than a single day. A bow and arrows require far more skill and strength, as well as a closer approach to game, than does a high-powered modern rifle. Yet an Indian had to be so dexterous that he could strike a deer or wing a goose without pausing. The hunter's legs had to carry him to the deer run perhaps twenty miles distant; and he might return after several days with only a paltry bag of game, and half famished. Carefully prepared traps might be found empty. Yet on the brave's skills, wind, and endurance might depend both food, if the harvest had been poor, and clothing for his whole family. The notion that in early times the woods were full of animals and birds waiting patiently for the hunter is a myth. The Indians, says Wood, leave no place unsearched for deer.

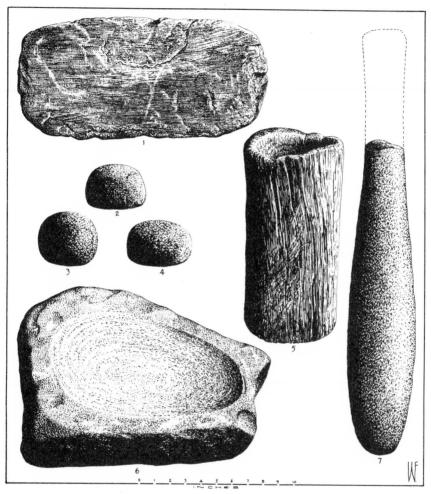

24. Ochre- and maize-grinding equipment: *1,* honing stone blocks for grinding red ochre: *2–4,* stones for grinding maize. *5,* log mortar. *6,* shallow stone mortar. *7,* corn-mill pestle. *BMAS*, 31 (1970), 21.

Aside from hunting and fishing, the Indian male had certain family duties and obligations. When new fields were needed for planting, it was the men who brought down the big trees. When a field was to be broken up, however, all the neighbors, both men and women, came in to help.[12]

At the outset of family life the husband provided the frame and sometimes the bark roof for the wigwam. In southern New England the man felled the tree for the canoe and shaped and hollowed out the log.

Further north, where the canoe was of birch bark, he sought out a big birch perhaps at a far distance and peeled great strips of bark from the tree to cover the frame he made. Only then did the women take over, sewing, caulking, and pitching the bark and shaping it to the ribs. The man framed the family snowshoes. From his labor came bowls and spoons of wood for the household, stone hatchets and knives, and weapons of all types. On the coast it was the men who made spears and harpoons as well as the dugout for the whale or seal hunt. Inland, they constructed traps and deadfalls. In country where the rock maple grew, the males might take part in the sugar harvest along with the rest of the family.[13]

For advanced tribes of southern New England, division of labor was not solely according to sexes. The Narragansetts, at least, had gone further. Certain skilled males had a reputation for making bows and arrows, others for their prowess as hunters or fishermen. Women learned special skills in shaping earthen vessels or in manufacturing the highly prized wampum into strings and belts with unusual artistry.

On occasion, in some tribes, the brave would help the squaw with her field work and in harvesting the crops "either out of love for his wife," Williams says, "or care for his children, or being an old man, which by the custom of the country, they are not bound to do."

25. Traditional trailside boulder mortar, for travelers to grind corn. Sudbury, Massachusetts. *Town Crier* photograph.

Each sex, then, had its place, its duties, and its responsibilities—clear, well defined, and known to all. Women controlled the household and its resources, the stores of food, and the fields that produced much of it. Men shouldered the dangerous and exhausting duties, protecting tribe and family, providing meat and skins, and doing certain specific labors of strength and skill. The children picked fruit, watched on raised platforms against crows, blackbirds, and other marauders in the fields, helped their mothers plant and reap, and were encouraged to learn the innumerable details of woods, weather, animal, bird, and insect life. Day after day they acquired the arts and skills of the tribe, memorized its legends and signals, and built the physique that they would need later. Meanwhile, with the approval or forbearance of elders, they enjoyed childhood to the fullest. All had their work and their diversions. All knew the parts they were to play, and most played them willingly. It was a satisfactory and productive way of life, developed by an intelligent and observant people in accord with their particular conditions.

11.

The Day's Round

What might a day have been like for an Indian family in that rugged, richly watered landscape now called New England during the years before the Pilgrims arrived to change forever the Indian way of life?

The month is January. Yesterday the afternoon's pale sun struggled west into a gray cloud. This morning the wind howls in from the northeast. Already, as it lightens outside, two inches of fine snow cover the frozen soil between the rows of dead stalks in the Nipmuck family's acre of cornfield, and every hour adds depth.

In the wigwam it is cold. Last evening's fire at its center is white ashes except for a few live coals deep underneath. The mother throws off her bearskin cover and rouses the children. She sends her young son out to the carefully covered storage of dry wood to bring in a half dozen armfuls. His sister laces up her moccasins, ties a deerskin tight around her, and heads through the snow to uncover the spring and return with a pail of fresh water in each hand. The father sleeps late. Sensing that a storm was due, he had visited his line of traps the previous afternoon—but brought back nothing.

Nearer home, with his small bow and arrow, the brother had proudly brought in two red squirrels. The mother now skins these carefully, drops the waste to the two hungry dogs, and hangs the little pelts from a roof-pole, to be dressed later. The meat she cuts into the boiling pot that stands erect in the midst of the freshened fire. From bags stored under the bed frames that form a letter U about the sides of the wigwam, she adds handfuls of dried beans, some red, some blue; dried squash strips; and sliced dried groundnuts. From a bundle hanging overhead she crumbles in a small handful of dry wild onion for flavor. The fire glows and sparks around the pot and the contents begin to boil. With a wood paddle the sister stirs the soup. She lets it cook well: no one is going anywhere in this storm. The smoke lingers in the cabin as the wind swirls about the hole above its center.

The baby brother has already had his meal. He is hanging in his cradleboard from one of the roof supports, and crowing. By the time the soup in the pot is thick and ready, it has been three hours since the gray dawn. The family dip it out into wooden bowls and eat it from large clamshells they brought home from the beach last summer. Nobody worries about washing dishes afterward; they merely wipe them out. Indians harbor no infectious diseases. This big late breakfast is the sole set meal of the day. The pot will sit there all day, warm among coals, and anybody may dip in when he or she feels hungry.

The day is dismal. Only the partly open smokehole at the center of the roof lets in light to mingle with the glow from the fire: too little light for any fine work. So mother and daughter grind corn. Anticipating a storm, they had brought in enough the day before from the underground storage to last several days. The wigwam is noisy as they pound the kernels in the wooden mortar. They sift out the fine meal for cakes, then pound the rest.

Father and son also have their stormy day job. Father pulls out from under the bed boards two tough burls of white oak preserved for making wooden bowls. They prop these on the floor with stones, close to the fire and under the smokehole. They heat large pebbles among the coals, even lift live coals out of the blaze with shell tongs bound to wood handles, and lay them red hot on one of the chunks of oak. The solid surface burns a little, chars more. The draft from the storm outside draws the smoke upward through the wigwam roof. After the wood burl has charred well, then cooled, the boy, using sharp stones, scrapes out the burned part while his father chars the second burl. Charring and scraping then goes on all over again, reaching deeper inside the knots of wood. Each begins to take the shape of a bowl.

Slow work, but there is no hurry on this bad day. By afternoon the youngster has dug well down into each burl. The holes are bowl-shaped but still rough. The father shows him how to use sand to rub the inside down to an even surface, then smooth it with a beaver's tooth. At last each has in his hand a two-inch-deep round soup bowl, thin on the edge and flat on the bottom. The mother gives the boy a little lump of bear's fat from her stores. He rubs this in and polishes the wood with the beaver tooth. By night he proudly holds up a new soup bowl of his own making, its round edge no thicker than one of his lips.

Mother and daughter long ago finished grinding the corn. They sifted the meal and mixed in last summer's dried blueberries along with water and raccoon fat. The girl has patted the dough into little round flat cakes. After the bowl makers finish their work with the fire, the mother slips a flat stone over the coals and lets the cakes cook, first on one side then the other. When anyone is hungry, a cake will be eaten, along with a bowl of the morning's reheated soup.

What with the gray light from the continuing storm and the smoke from bowl-making, the afternoon has been too dark for weaving; so mother and daughter have settled down on the edge of the bed boards to prepare twine for next spring's fish lines and nets. They pull down from under the roof supports a bundle of wild hemp that had been tucked in there. They peel off the outside of each stalk, leaving the inner fibers. These they roll and twist against their legs to make a single endless cord. It is tough and, when they finish, strong enough to stand the pull of a big salmon or bass. On some brighter day the cord can be knotted into a fishnet, or braided into a rope.

As early night comes on, the deerskin doorflap of the wigwam is raised and promptly dropped back in place as Uncle Walking Deer and Aunt Mist-in-the-Sky come in. They have traveled across the field on their snowshoes and will share the newly baked blueberry cakes. While the father and uncle smoke their pipes, one of them tells stories about Glooscap, the ancient hero of the tribe: how he fooled Master Wolf, and how little Spider made a net of tiny strands strong enough to catch foolish Grasshopper. Brother sits absorbed; he plans some day to be a storyteller and to smoke a pipe like Uncle Walking Deer.

With the storm still driving snow against the wigwam's bark walls, the visitors start home early. The mother carefully banks the fire. Everybody lies down on the skins covering the benches, their feet toward the heat. They pull the warm bearskins over them and hope that tomorrow may be a brighter day.

On a bright July morning the wood thrushes have been up early, singing. The Nipmuck family wakes with them. The members eat hurriedly: before it gets too hot the father and the boy are going fishing while the mother hoes a dozen rows in the cornfield. The dogs have already rushed off and are furiously digging at a hole that a young woodchuck has opened during the night. It is under the pile of stones at the side of the cornfield, where the squash vines are beginning to run.

Nobody heads off alone. Father takes the birch canoe on his back and starts toward the big pond. Son trots along with the paddle, a willow fishpole, and worms. Father will fish for pickerel or bass from the canoe. The boy will try for hornpout and sunfish in the shallow water among the lily pads along the shore. The girl has a bark pail; she is going berrying.

"Look out for rattlesnakes," the mother warns the daughter as she leaves. "If you go swimming," the father tells the boy as he paddles off (all Indian boys learned to swim), "keep away from the spring; you might get a cramp"—and he points to a place where a cold stream of underground water boils up into the warm pond.

By mid-morning the mother has finished her hoeing. The girl returns with her boxes full of berries, her lips showing that as many have gone into her mouth as into the containers. The mother puts the almost full boxes out of reach. Everybody will be hungry later.

With the baby on the cradleboard hung on her back, the mother goes off with the daughter toward the meadow. At a cool spot under the trees by the brook they are going to mold clay into cooking pots. She takes along a basket full of bits of ground shell. Last month after the corn was planted, they brought these back from their trip to the shore, where they had eaten clams and lobsters and played games. The mother hangs cradleboard and baby on a branch.

To make a pot they must have clay. At the edge of the meadow the brook has cut its way down to a thick bed of clay left long ago by glacial waters. With a wooden scoop the mother digs out a gray pailful and brings it back under the trees. She takes a big lump in one hand, a little ground shell from the basket in the other, and kneads them together. Wetting her hands, with her thumbs she shapes the lump into a cone, round, and pointed at the bottom. Meanwhile, she has the daughter dig a round cone-shaped hole in the ground and line it with leaves and grass.

When the mother is satisfied with the clay mixture, she presses the inside of the V into a saucer shape, then rounds and smooths the edge. She sets the clay V in the hole the daughter has made, and firms the soil around it to hold it erect. She takes another handful of clay, mixes in shell and a bit of grease, and between her palms molds this into a slender rope. She lays this rope in a careful circle around and above the edge of the V base. Then she molds another rope, slightly longer, and deftly lays this on above the first. The clay begins to shape into a circle. It is going to be a pot. With a flat, wet paddle she pats and firms its surface inside and out until all is smooth and solid.

Each added ring of clay increases the pot's height, and causes it to bulge a little more. Yet the potter keeps it round and smooth and no thicker than her little finger. At length, as the pot grows tall, she begins to draw its circumference in and narrow it for a neck. She adds a flaring lip all around. Yet she has not finished until her earthenware has been decorated. With a bit of shell she gently scores the clay of the pot's lip and shoulder outside, forming a geometric design.

While the clay vessel dries, the hungry baby is nursed. Mother and daughter then gently lift the finished pot into a bed of leaves inside a carrying basket. Mother hangs cradleboard and baby on her shoulders once more, and picks up the basket. It is heavy, so the daughter takes one side. Together they carry basket and baby back to the wigwam. After the pot has dried for a few days, the mother will bake it slowly, gradually, among hot coals until the clay walls turn red and harden. It will then be able to stand upright in the midst of the fire without cracking, even though water or soup boils hard inside.

By late afternoon the whole family is home again. On flat stones by the outdoor fire the half dozen hornpout that brother has hooked are

ABORIGINAL NEW ENGLAND POTTERY

Rolled clay strip
start of coiling

1.   2.

Coiled constructi
in its finished state.

1. Before pressing together
2. After pressing together

COILING PROCESS OF CONSTRUCTION

Pot construction on
a basket used as a
form.

Process of modeling
upper portion of pot
with stone modeling
tools.

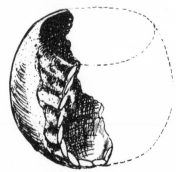

Coiled construction
obliterated by plaster-
ing clay over surface

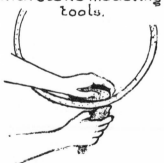

Method of reinforc-
ing while modeling
the walls of the pot.

26. Native pottery in the making. *BMAS*, 15 (1954), 31.

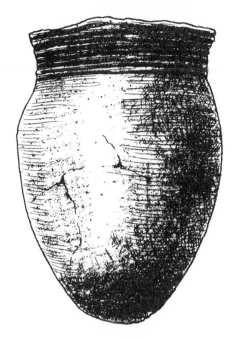

27. Algonquian pottery vessel (full size), South Windsor, Connecticut. *BMAS*, 17 (1956), 53.

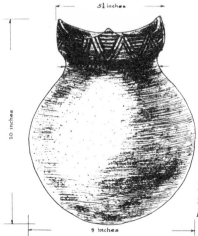

28. Pottery vessel showing Iroquoian influence. South Windsor, Connecticut. *BMAS*, 17 (1956), 54.

sizzling. The father from his canoe got two handsome pickerel that will make a tasty meal tomorrow. Daughter's berries and the mother's corncakes are just the right extras for a filling supper. While everyone eats, daughter tells how a fat, black bear was eating berries beyond her on the edge of the woods, and how the dogs finally dug out the woodchuck, but tore it to pieces and ate it before she could get to it to save the skin. The son had seen an enormous fat turtle from the pond go off into the woods to lay her eggs. He didn't bother her, for that would be wrong at this time of year when she is preparing for her coming family.

Uncle Walking Deer drops by. He has been hunting for a porcupine so that Aunt Mist-in-the-Sky can make a handsome cape for their little daughter. He looks at the sunset, forecasts a good day tomorrow, and leaves. It is growing dark.

12.

Beyond the Round

Native life was not solely labor and routine. Besides their never-failing feasts of thanksgiving, the Indians had a wide variety of amusements, from public exhibitions and contests to small, quiet games playable in or about the wigwam. Some of these would bring together scores, even hundreds, of contestants; others amused only a few. The gambling spirit in particular was very high.

The spring run of salmon, sturgeon, and herring up the freshwater streams to spawn was an occasion (to be described later) that brought together the members of many tribes and villages at the great falls, like those at Chelmsford and Amoskeag on the Merrimac. Any ill feeling was put aside while all participated in nature's bounty.

Then in summer such inland tribes as the Nipmucks left their corn to mature while they followed the paths to the Connecticut shore, say at Milford. A favorite spot in the Massachusetts Bay shore was Lynn Beach. There they could enjoy lobsters, oysters, and clams, smoke a supply for the cold months to come, and swap deer meat for fish with the shore tribes. All such gatherings offered occasion for sports, games, and contests for both youngsters and their elders in marksmanship, footracing, and swimming. At the last both boys and girls were adept.

Most spectacular of these was a ball game of which the modern descendant is Canadian lacrosse. The small ball (perhaps originally of wood) was likely to be of deerskin, four inches across and stuffed with that animal's hair. The field was some broad, clean, sandy beach or what Roger Williams calls a soft, smooth heather, where the naked feet of the players would suffer no harm. The distance between goals, varying with the terrain, might be as much as a mile, and the number of players run into the hundreds. "It is most delight to see them play in smaller companies," says Wood, "when men may view their swift footmanship, their curious tossings of the Ball, their flouncing into the water, their lubberlike wrestling." It might take as much as two days of struggle, town against town, to make a goal. In such physical competitions the contestants might paint their faces and distort them, to minimize the chance for personal animosity.[1]

The prize? Each town's goal post would be hung with strings of wampum and with beaver, otter, and other valuable skins. Private bets among the players would include clothing, skins, valuables, even to the extent that a losing player—and maybe his wife—would have to travel home all but naked. Meanwhile, according to Wood, "the boys pipe and the women dance and sing trophies of their husbands' conquests." It was all done in good spirit, and when the clams and oysters were dried and smoked, everybody joined in a feast before setting out for home with the supplies for winter.[2]

Another principal opportunity for merrymaking was Put-tuck-qua-quock, or arbor playing. The playhouse was a framework of poles from 16 to 20 feet tall, sunk in the ground. On these the rivals and their supporters, town against town, hung strings of wampum and other trophies to go to the winner. The game was played with a type of dice, "plumb stones painted," which the champions "cast in a Tray with a mighty noise and swearing." A similar noisy game was Hubbub. Two small bones or beans, black on one side, were put in a smooth wooden tray. When the player lifted the tray and then thumped it hard on the ground, the bones jumped and changed colors and positions. Meanwhile the players whipped their hands back and forth "smiting themselves on the Breast and Thigh, crying out Hub, Hub, Hub" so as to be heard for a quarter mile. Stakes included every kind of valuable.[3]

A scatter game rather like jackstraws called for throwing a handful of straw reeds or rushes into the air and swiftly calculating their number. There was a similar game called puum, played with short sticks, and a spear or javelin casting game. As the latter was played by Middle Atlantic Algonquians, two teams—each player with a light spear in his hand—faced each other perhaps twenty feet apart. A hoop was set rolling down between the lines. Each player in turn tried to strike and stop it. Once stopped, the opponent opposite must also strike it or lose his spear. The game went on until one side or the other was stripped of spears.[4]

Willoughby describes a somewhat similar New England contest. A flat stone, rounded to a disk, was spun off on its edge. The object of each player was to hurl an eight-foot pole to land as close as possible to the spot where the disk would come to rest. As with the hoop contest, the loser paid a forfeit. Hallett mentions shinny (still played by New England boys three centuries later), similar to modern hockey. Each with a stick in his hand, the players concentrated on sending a ball of wood, stone, or skin into his opponents' territory. Tugs-of-war and games of swift calculation were both popular.[5]

A feat of individual skill was the cap and pin game. A series of perforated bones were strung on a cord. As the player swung the cord, the feat was to slide a slender pin or dart of bone into one or more of the perforations; or with a dart to impale a tightly tied bunch of cedar twigs

29. Gaming stones: *2*, North River Sites, Massachusetts; *1, 3-9*, Narragansett Bay Drainage. *BMAS*, 27 (1966), 63.

as they swung; or to slide the dart into a hole in a swinging bit of deerskin.[6]

There were quiet games of dice for two or more, played with cherry stones, grains of corn, or woodchuck or beaver teeth. Some were similar to a modern game of cards, the score kept with sticks.

Toward autumn, according to Williams, important ceremonies with dances, carried on in a longhouse, would bring out "thousands" of people. A liberal distribution of gifts by one dancer after another made such gatherings popular.

There was fun for the youngsters, too, all year. All children learned to dog-paddle, and like their elders they had swimming matches. They slung stones underhand (or, in winter, on ice, they hurled sticks six to ten feet long) to see whose would go the farthest. They spun tops made of wood, bone, stone, or clay; played forfeits; and had a game similar to "Button, button, who's got the button?"

Men, women, and children, all ages, had their good times. When the games involved wagers and gambling and the unsuccessful had to return home stripped of everything except a breech-cover (while winners went back rejoicing), even the loser "appears as merry as though he had won all and everyone remains friends."[7]

For people who lack writing, memory becomes all important: the ancestry of the family on both sides for several generations; their deeds in hunting and war; the complicated habits of animals, birds, plants, and weather—these took no study lamp or pen to learn. Indian children absorbed them from their elders on the trail, around the wigwam fire.

Then there were tales like the modern "Paul Revere's Ride" and "The Wreck of the Hesperus," part fact, part imagination; and explication of morals and religion comparable to the choice by Adam and Eve in the Garden of Eden—all to be learned by heart. Many Indian tribes considered themselves descended from animals: the good-natured bear or the wise moose. Moreover, says Leland, "It is well known to all Indians who still keep the faith of the olden times that there are wonderous dwellers in the woods such as elves and fairies" who "Work great wonders, charm wild beasts."

In folklore and fable, early Puritan writers had little interest: merely scorn for the tales and their narrators. Only from the last century and from the memories of elderly Maine Indians have we learned much of this aspect of native culture.

The memory of an Indian of Oldtown, Maine—Nicolar— illuminates the world of the supernatural as it comes down by tradition to recent Indian generations from the unwritten past. The hero of the tales he tells is Glus-gahbe or Glooscap, the great teacher. He had a hand in creating all things; he could turn himself into an animal and skip and jump across the countryside. He enjoyed playing jokes, but also helping humans and animals who were in trouble with giants and sorcerers. The titles of some of these tales indicate their content and scope: "How Glooscap Made His Uncle Mikshish the Turtle into a

Great Man and Got Him a Wife"; "Of Turtles' Eggs, and How Glooscap Vanquished a Sorcerer by Smoking Tobacco"; "How Glooscap Changed Certain Saucy Indians into Rattlesnakes"; How the Great Glooscap Fought with Giant Sorcerers at Saco and Turned Them into Fish"; "The Merry Tales of Fox, the Mischief Maker."

Glooscap almost always comes out on top, but in one instance, the story of Wasis, from the Penobscot, his charm fails totally. The title of this story is "How the Lord of Men and Beasts Strove with the Mighty Wasis and Was Shamefully Defeated":

Now it came to pass when Glooscap had conquered all his enemies, even the kewahgy, who were giants and sorcerers, and the *m'téoulins* who were magicians, and the *Pamola*, who is the evil spirit of the night air, and all manner of ghosts, witches, devils, cannibals and goblins, that he thought upon what he had done, and wondered if his work was at an end.

And he said this to a certain woman. But she replied, "Not so fast, Master, for there yet remains one whom no one has ever conquered or got the better of in any way, and who will remain unconquered to the end of time."

And who is he? inquired the Master.

"It is the mighty Wasis," she replied, "and there he sits; and I warn you that if you meddle with him you will be in sore trouble."

Now Wasis was the Baby and he sat on the floor, sucking a piece of maple sugar, greatly contented, troubling no one.

As the Lord of Men and Beasts had never married or had a child, he knew nought of the way of managing children. Therefore he was quite certain, as is the wont of such people, that he knew all about it. So he turned to Baby with a bewitching smile and bade him come to him.

Then Baby smiled again, but did not budge. And the Master spake sweetly and made his voice like that of the summer bird, but it was of no avail, for Wasis sat still and sucked his maple sugar.

Then the Master frowned and spoke terribly, and ordered Wasis to come crawling to him immediately. And Baby burst out into crying and yelling, but did not move for all that.

Then, since he could do but one thing more, the master had recourse to magic. He used his most awful spells and sang the songs which raise the dead and scare the devils. And Wasis sat and looked admiringly, and seemed to find it very interesting, but all the same he never moved an inch.

So Glooscap gave it up in despair, and Wasis, sitting on the floor in the sunshine, went goo! goo! and crowed.

And to this day when you see a babe well contented, going "goo! goo!" and crowing, and no one can tell why, it is because he remembers the time when he overcame the Master who had conquered all the world. For all beings that have ever been made since the beginning, Baby is alone the invincible one.[8]

Part Four
THE BOUNTIFUL EARTH

13.

The Soil

The soil of New England—the earth itself—was in ancient times not all rich virgin loam, as many imagine. Certain early English commentators waxed enthusiastic over its excellence: "The fertility of the soil is to be admired at." Captain John Smith called it "this abounding land." Thomas Dudley, however, wrote: "Honest men who out of a desire to draw over others to them wrote somewhat hyperbolically of many things here." In overemphasizing the virtues of New England soil and overlooking or weighing lightly certain deficiencies in it, some may even have been seeking to justify their own decision to emigrate to New England.

Reliable records and cold logic indicate that in Indian times New England's basic soil was not widely different from what it is today. A small proportion could be labeled fertile loam, even by a Midwest farmer; far more was and is only fair for growing crops. Stripped of its covering of leaf mold, the greatest part, then as now, was gravelly, sandy, or rock strewn. "We found after five or six years that it grows barren beyond belief," despairs a colonist, writing perhaps from Plymouth; "the lands about the town [Concord] are very barren," writes another. Clearly the soil must have been acid also, as it is today. An early settler lamented that if he had had marl, lime, or other manure, this barrenness might in part have been cured.[1] The Indian's annual burning of wide areas had often seriously depleted the leaf cover and failed to help acidity. The native crops, however—corn, beans, Jerusalem artichokes, pumpkins, even squash—ask small favors of any gardener if provided with plenty of nitrogen.

The Indians purposely chose sandy loams and alluvial river plains, readily worked with their stone, bone, shell, and wood hand tools: such soils suited their crops perfectly. They located their planting fields intelligently—selecting, wherever possible, soils of reasonable natural fertility in spots free from unexpected frosts, near bodies of water or on hillsides with good air drainage.

King Philip and his warriors died to protect the cherished long-season, fertile, easily worked loams of their home villages at Sowams and Mt. Hope. On such lands, many reports agree, Indian women raised excellent crops. No higher mark of respect for their judgment in choosing ground for cultivation could be shown than the alacrity with which the English took over their fields. The Plymouth authorities were able to sell King Philip's fields at once; some of these fields are being tilled to this day.[2]

Heavy soils the natives could not have handled. The New World lacked animals suitable for draught purposes. New England had none at all. Black soils such as early colonists sometimes wrote home about were not for the native. Nowadays, freed of stumps by bulldozers, heavy land may be rendered tillable by ditching with mechanical diggers and by laying tile drains, once the surface has been stumped or broken up with other heavy machinery. Three centuries ago, whites and Indians alike had no means of preparing poor land.

The natives did take advantage of the natural richness of the low areas, however, and without the labor of cultivation. From swampy lands they harvested ample crops of berries, roots, and seeds for food. From the marshes also came such raw materials as rushes for mats and roof coverings and soft cattail fluff for absorbents to prevent the chafing of infants and to use as dressings for burns and scalds. Useful harvests these, without need for draining and cultivation of the land.[3] Any idea of immense untapped fertility in the original soil which prodigal farmers have since recklessly wasted is, however, as improperly descriptive of New England in the centuries before 1620 as in those since.

Neither should the soil be underrated. Southern New England especially was a fruitful land. Long since, there had been a congenial marriage of man with his environment. If the soil was no more than mediocre, the inhabitants nevertheless found its natural harvest plentiful.[4] Moreover, when intelligently cultivated, even gravel and sand could yield sufficient for their needs. That is borne out by all descriptions of early visitors, who speak with respect or admiration of the well-formed bodies, agile limbs, and excellent health of the natives they met. Frequently, though not always, these observers comment on native food supplies as being ample, even in winter. This contrasts sharply, as noted above, with the winter starvation that distressed the French Jesuit fathers to the north when they described the nonagricultural forest tribes of Eastern Canada.[5]

The near starvation of the earliest English colonists in New England should also increase respect for the "savages" whom they nearly always considered their inferiors. During their first years, the newcomers more than once, scanning the horizon with deep anxiety for the sails of food ships from England, in their absence had to call on Indians for maize. Not until the settlers adopted the native agriculture could they call themselves more than strangers and sojourners in this abounding land. The competence of the native in adapting himself to his surround-

ings and in adapting his surroundings to his personal needs will form the
heart of our study from this point on.

It has already become evident that clearings and cultivation in
aboriginal times were widespread; yet the idea of a dark, dismal stretch
of "howling wilderness" remains a popular conception. This phrase
from the Book of Jeremiah, favorite of colonial divines and early
writers, in its original context implied an unsettled or desert area; but to
moderns it is more likely to suggest a trackless forest. The evidence
offered by the earliest European visitors and colonists is otherwise.
Besides open and cultivated fields, they record considerable stretches
of woodland regularly burnt by the Indians to make hunting easier,
sometimes in both spring and fall. Verrazano commented that the
woods might all be traversed by a large army. Champlain called the
forests very thin, though abounding in oaks, beeches, ashes, and elms,
with willows in low spots. In the Penobscot Valley, he remarked, the
oaks appeared as if planted for ornament. Thoreau, a careful student of
Indian matters, believed that the woods about Concord were probably
clearer in precolonial times than in his own. He quotes William Wood's
observation that the trees, though tall, were generally not very thick
and that there was no underwood save in the swamps, where the native's
fires did not penetrate.[6] Morton also noticed that to find large trees and
good timber, it was necessary to look in low places. Other early English
observers found the trees "growinge a greatt space assonder . . . as our
parks in England" and "in the thickest part you may see a furlong or
more about."[7]

Evidence that the first generation of English settlers struggled
against overabundance of timber is missing. On the contrary, almost at
once the general courts of the colonies and town meetings began
stringent regulation of tree cutting. To them, far from an enemy to be
destroyed, woods were a resource to be conserved. In 1633 just-settled
Cambridge was ordering that "no person whatsoever shall fell any tree
near the Towne within the path which goeth from Wattertown to
Charles Towne" on pain of a fine; increasingly severe rules followed in
succeeding years. Salem, in 1636, outlawed cutting for clapboards or
pipe staves: trees were soon to be needed for ship timber. In 1638, two
years after its founding, Springfield on the Connecticut River forbade
the felling of "any tree in ye compass of grownd from ye mill river
upward . . . appoynted for house lotts."[8]

In Boston the town meeting had to give permission to cut a tree.
Inland Sudbury set up a timber warden in 1645, only seven years after
its founding. Within a quarter century, for nearly every Massachusetts
Bay and Connecticut settlement and even on the well-forested New
Hampshire coast, a principal matter of legislation was strict control of

timber cutting and prevention of its export beyond the confines of the town.[9]

Not that immense stretches of woodland were lacking. Forests blanketed all but small portions of what are now Maine, New Hampshire, and Vermont. Roger Williams attests that even in southern New England he had often been lost, "the wilderness being so vast."[10] Miles of primeval pine, hemlock, and spruce lined the upper reaches of all rivers. Yet except in rough terrain and in the highlands, in southern New England the forest was hardly as terrifying and universal as is apt to be imagined or as it may have appeared to immigrants accustomed to the close settlement and cultivation of southern England, much of which had by 1620 been deforested, some even before King William in the twelfth century surveyed his English conquest and prepared the Domesday Book. For the English countryside had gradually been molded to fit the needs of a people dependent largely on flocks and herds and broadcast-sown cereals.[11]

The witnesses so far relied on have been chiefly visitors from across the Atlantic or settlers recently arrived. They appraised the land from a European point of view, their minds envisioning the possibilities for cultivated fields smooth for wheat and barley, pasture for cattle, timber for dwellings and ships—some in the earliest days hopeful besides for precious metals or at least pelts for trade. Yet from the different standpoint of the native occupants, the New England country appeared a goodly place. The land had been considerably altered to fit its inhabitants, whose needs were different. Whether planted in corn, whether kept open and green for berries and as deer pasture to furnish meat for the tribe, whether, orchard-like, it was studded with ancient oaks, hickories, and chestnuts to yield acorns for bread and nuts for oil or whether it bore cherry trees for fruit or white birch for canoes, almost every variety of land, the growth upon it, and the animal life within it found a useful place in the indigenous economy.

14.

The Provision of Nature

By the time descriptions of New England's Indians were set down in writing, except for eastern Maine they had gone beyond the stage of full dependence on fishing, hunting, and gathering. Nevertheless, each of these resources remained so important that they took great care to husband and increase natural supplies, improve their quality, and make it easier to obtain sufficient for their needs. The Indian's wide knowledge of animals and plants enabled him to cope with a variety of problems.

Of natural food sources the most dependable day-by-day supply seems for many inhabited areas to have been fish. Almost without exception the Indian village site was beside a harbor, lake, or stream and not infrequently within reach of all three. If inland, the settlement was likely to be no more than a few days' journey from the shore, or at least near some precipitate river cascade where as earlier described spearing fish at migration seasons was the common practice. Shell heaps are now or were formerly to be met at oyster harbors and clam banks on the Connecticut shore, the largest (24 acres) at Milford, and all about Narragansett Bay. Banks of waste still remain at Apponaug (translated "Shellfish") in Warwick, Rhode Island. There were dozens at spots on Cape Cod. In Maine clam banks, scores of them, have been identified at Damariscotta, Sheepscot Bay, Medomack, York, Deer Isle, and other beaches. Many are or were three feet deep and some ten to twenty acres in extent. They are evidence of how inland villagers, including the old and infirm, would gather in great companies to obtain one mainstay of their winter diet.[1]

The purpose was to dry in the sunshine or on a frame over a smoky fire (to discourage flies) quantities of lobsters, crabs, oysters, and clams. Southern New England natives considered the quahaug or round clam an especially dainty food. John Winthrop thought it tasted like veal. His Indian friends were fond of clam broth also. Crabs they roasted. Hubbard tells what a deterrent to war it was when the fishing season began to come in, since the Indians were accustomed to dry and smoke the catch and "make provision thereof" for the greatest part of the year. Williams records the abundance of sturgeon, cod, and bass the natives acquired. Indians living on the shore could net the mackerel and

30. Making a temporary wigwam (simulation). *Town Crier* photograph.

herring that ran in schools and even on occasion in their dugout canoes hunt seal, porpoise, and whale, mammals that frequented eastern New England waters. The hunters might set up a pole in the boat, Williams says, and use their deerskin coats for sails (perhaps learned from European sailors). To harpoon a whale a group of canoes gathered. When, after sounding, the whale rose, the whalers filled its body with arrows. Mrs. Eckstorm, a Maine authority, speaks also of the collection of sea-bird eggs for food.[2]

Inland tribes gathered in spring at the great falls of the Merrimac and Connecticut, the Maine rivers, and even at lesser waterfalls, to spear salmon, bass, and sturgeon as these large fish, along with shad, pushed their way to the headwaters to spawn; they would then dry the

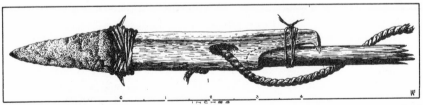

31. Early archaic harpoon holder with demountable point, showing one method of hafting. *BMAS*, 25 (1964), 61.

fish above a fire, or even on bark. The head of a bass boiled with hominy made a delicious chowder. At favorable shoal spots on minor streams, stone weirs reaching out from both banks concentrated the spring runs of herring or shad so that they could be taken by the basketful. Weirs at the outlet of Lake Winnepesaukee provided a welcome fall harvest as mature shad headed seaward. At innumerable ponds and lakes (500 on Cape Cod alone), fishing with line and hook went on all year. A Pilgrim account mentions solitary women standing waist deep to fish. William Wood was surprised that in winter the natives cut round holes in the ice, "about which they sit in their naked breeches, catching of Pikes, Pearches, Breames and other sorts of freshwater fish." In summer they caught turtles, in fall migrating eels, fat and sweet. At Fairhaven Bay on the Sudbury River, shell heaps testified to long-continued harvesting of freshwater clams in earlier centuries. New England's waters furnished its native inhabitants a valuable, readily available source of protein food the year around.[3]

Game was a second asset. Though its relative importance for food, at least in southern New England, is easy to overestimate, it was equally valuable as a source for clothing, implements, and cordage. A mature deer would dress out at a hundred pounds, a moose at perhaps eight hundred. The lip of a moose was a special delicacy; a beaver's tail was a luxury. Any notion, however, that moose, deer, and bear abounded everywhere to be taken close at hand with bow and arrow, ignores the realities. We must not forget that for the most part the New England natives were agricultural. Of the large animals just named, deer and bear raise havoc in cornfields and gardens; so do raccoons, woodchucks, and rabbits. None of these was more to be tolerated close at hand than they are by gardeners today. Nor were bears wanted in the berry pastures that the Indians maintained near their villages.

As a source of meat, therefore, every tribe had a hunting ground or deer pasture at a distance, which was kept open, and its herbage kept succulent, by seasonal fires. There the larger animals might eat their fill of browse and berries in summer and fall. The Pocumtucks of Deerfield, for example, are said to have kept the Ware River valley, twenty miles from home, so clear that from a Brookfield hill a deer could be spotted four miles distant. Squannacook swamps in Rehoboth were among King Philip's hunting grounds. The Connecticut Indians hunted in Litchfield County and kept its hills clear by fires. The Sandisfield area in the southern Berkshires and the Green Mountains were habitats for game. Speck tells how each Maine family band had its specific hunting territory up country. He emphasizes that in eastern Maine "no other regular activity occupied spirit, mind and body so incessantly as hunting." In late fall and again in late winter, hunting parties, well organized and led by experienced and skillful elders, were important events. Nearer home, traps and deadfalls, individually maintained and marked, secured the smaller animals in the months when fat, hide, and fur were at their best.[4]

The hunter took elaborate precautions to conceal his presence, for with bow and arrow he had to close in on his quarry. He learned to disguise his body, simulate bird calls and animal sounds, and use animal scents. Sometimes he lay prone for hours. Despite all this he might still return empty-handed.

Less often mentioned but another resource of spring and fall, ducks and geese broke their flight at inland fresh meadows and the salt marshes at the shores, to be hunted at night with torches. Flocks of wild pigeons in season dropped down by thousands to roost for the night on tree branches. (The manifold uses to which the Indians put the flesh, bones, skins, and feathers of the wide variety of fishes, animals, and birds have been elsewhere noted).

As pointed out in the chapter on family meals, fruits of every variety were another resource. Algonquians ate them fresh, and dried the surplus to diversify their winter stores. Among these were the berries that grow on briars. Into the edge of many a New England cultivated field, especially if it ends in a wall or headland, the native thimbleberry, raspberry, and blackberry still crowd their way today. Elderberries bordered sunny brooks, with shadberries nearby; the wild strawberry pushed into Algonquian cultivated fields once tillage was given up.

With at least two fruits, the strawberry and the grape, the likelihood of cultivation or of intelligent attention by the natives seems a distinct possibility. The strawberry was a universal fruit over much of North America. The berries of Virginia are called by Hariot "as good and as great as those in English gardens." Jesuits observed them in Canada and the Middle West; Le Jeune called the quantity almost incredible. In Indian New England the more northerly tribes called this fruit the grass-berry, and those of the southern part gave it the poetic name of heart-berry.[5]

Captain Pring, reaching the coast in 1603, described the strawberries he found as very fair and big. Brereton reported both red and white on Martha's Vineyard, and better than those of England, he said. At Plymouth the native berries got praise, and the first New World food tasted by John Winthrop's company on Massachusetts Bay soil was the "fine" Cape Ann strawberry. Wood, writing on the Bay Colony, reported strawberries in abundance, "very large ones, some being two inches about. One may gather a half bushel in a forenoon." If we suspect that his eye overestimated a trifle, Master Thomas Graves, the surveyor, at least thought the native berries of exceeding sweetness. Even usually sober Roger Williams is enthusiastic: "The berry is the wonder of all the fruits growing naturally in these parts . . . In some parts where the natives have planted, I have many times seen as many as would fill a good ship within a few miles compass." Adair, further south, corroborates Williams: "Their old fields abound with larger strawberries than I have seen in any part of the world . . . one may gather a hatfull in . . . two or three yards square."[6] In another place he tells how in strawberry time the pigeons pick over large fields "of the old grounds of the natives."

Does Williams imply that the natives planted the berries, or does he mean merely that they were growing in their cleared planting fields? Either way, to achieve such abundance, human attention would seem to have been required, if only to the extent of scattering seed on a previously cultivated cornfield. Such care becomes especially likely when the independent testimony to the size and quality of the berries is considered. It appears not accidental that Captain John Smith, in naming the "hearbes and fruits" of New England, places strawberries in a list alongside pumpkins, beans, and maize as though growing in cultivated fields, instead of with wild raspberries, gooseberries, and currants, which he also names.[7] Reinforcing the deduction is evidence from the names English settlers gave certain localities. In a countryside where brush springs up in any opening almost as soon as one's back is turned and develops within a few seasons to a thick stand of gray birch, pine, or other species propagated by the wind, the settlers on the Piscataqua in 1630 pitched their village at a harbor-side hill so thick with vines that they named it Strawbery Banke (now in Portsmouth). Sudbury pioneers, taking over Indian lands, also had their Strawberry Bank. Charlestown, Massachusetts, settled in 1628, named one of its heights Strawberry Hill; there were still others in Salem and Hull. Leicester, Massachusetts, west of Worcester, which the English bought from the Indians in 1686, was called at first Strawberry Hill. Bedford, in the Merrimac Valley in southern New Hampshire, a favorite Indian ground not settled by the English till 1755 in the second third of the eighteenth century, had a Strawberry Hill. Van der Donck, writing of New Netherland (in which the Dutch included western Connecticut), even points out differences in time of ripening among the native berries, "some of which ripen at half May, and we have them until July." This distinction could indicate human selection among differing types of berry.[8]

Indeed, it would be strange if intelligent, industrious agricultural people like the southern New England tribes should not have taken active steps, perhaps very simple ones, to ensure the success of the strawberry crop, when it filled so important a place in their diet both summer and winter. The late E. E. Edwards, a careful specialist on Indian agriculture, flatly states that the Indian had domesticated the strawberry, though certain botanists and fruit specialists disagree. In the southern continent, at any rate, the Mapuche Indians had cultivated strawberries in southern Chile before the white man arrived, and Bolivian Indians have been reported to weed patches of wild berries.[9]

Considering the lack nowadays in New England's countryside of such an abundance of wild strawberries as a dozen explorers and early colonists mention—considering also what almost universally happens today when a New England cultivated field is abandoned—it is difficult not to conclude, as already suggested, that the Indians took steps of some kind to ensure a continuing supply of a fruit they so greatly enjoyed.

A similar conclusion seems warranted with regard to the grape. Grapevines abounded in New England, the admiration of every early explorer, coming, as all white visitors did, from either wine-growing or wine-drinking countries. Brereton reported an incredible profusion of vines. Van der Donck found grapes growing to the tops of trees, which to Wood appeared natural trellises, and covering their lower branches. The clusters were of three colors: white, black and red. De Vries adds blue. "The fruit is as bigge, of some as a musket bullet, and is excellent in taste," Morton said.[10] At Plymouth John Pory counted "five serviceable sorts larger and fairer" than any he had ever seen in the South Colonies. The Plymouth colonists noted that grapevines flourished along the banks of streams. Lescarbot describes the fruit he observed in Maine as "black grapes marvellously faire, some as big as plummes growing on trunks as big as a man's fist." On an island in the Sagadahoc River in the last week of September, James Davis wondered at the "greatt store" he found there, "exceeding good and sweett of two sorts both red but the one of them a marvellous deep red." De Vries called New Netherland grapes as large as finger joints. Not all Englishmen cared for the quality of the native fruit, but Master John Endecott of Salem began to cultivate them.[11]

Testimony to the likelihood of cultivation by the natives comes from the accounts of continental visitors rather than those of English origin. Direct evidence is sparse, but its sources are reliable. First, Verrazano in the sixteenth century observed that the natives in New England had trimmed away interfering shrubbery with considerable care so that the fruit might ripen in the sun. Champlain, on Richmond Island, Maine, found near oaks and walnuts land that had been cleared (*défrichée*), plus what W. L. Grant translates "vineyards of grapes" (*force vignes*). The whole scene was so striking that he named the place "l'isle de Bacchus."[12]

To Cartier, in Canada, the loaded vines adorning the shores of rivers and lakes appeared to have been planted by the hand of man. The eye of the Jesuit Biard noted that the fruit grew in sand and gravel like that of Bordeaux, not in the best ground; but this may have been a result of natural selection.[13]

Since the natives cherished the fruit so much that they cut away competing branches, perhaps even cleared the ground where vines could flourish, it is not unreasonable to infer that they were astute enough to transplant types they liked to favorable locations near their villages. On the banks of streams or ponds open to the sun the water would furnish moisture for a dry time. In the fall, in the case of the island vines that Champlain, Lescarbot, Brereton, and Davis describe, the warmth of nearby waters would help to hold off frost until the fruit could ripen fully.

At the seashore the bayberry furnished the natives with wax. To encourage the low-bush blueberry the Indians regularly burned large areas, a practice that continues to be standard with New England's commercial blueberry growers today. The wild cranberry remains a valued community asset in the Indian town of Gay Head on Martha's Vineyard and along the Maine coast, not to mention the great industry built on today's cultivated cranberry.

So far as I have discovered, however, no calculated improvement or formal cultivation of bush and cane fruits appears to have been carried out by the natives up to the time of colonial settlement. Neither did the early English attempt to select or cultivate them when they came. Not until the nineteenth century was a beginning made with cranberry cultivation on Cape Cod and with raspberries and blackberries (the latter first in Beverly, Massachusetts). It took nearly a hundred years more before Elizabeth White, an enterprising New Jersey woman, began to select and improve blueberries.[14]

Verrazano and Captain John Smith both listed plums among fruits they saw along the New England shore, probably referring to the beach plum, earlier described, which whitens Cape Cod with its blossoms in May and bears tart fruit in the fall. The Indians of Western New York did cultivate plums, however, and plum trees were always to be found near village sites there in later times. Canadian Indians, according to Cartier, dried the fruit to make prunes. Yet in New England the Canadian plum was at best not common, though Leavitt lists it among the wild fruits of Connecticut and Western Massachusetts.[15]

As to cherries, Manasseh Cutler, an early eighteenth-century Massachusetts clergyman and botanist, mentions two native varieties of black cherries, two of red, and three shades of red chokecherries. Brereton thought that the "leaf, bark and bigness" did not differ from his in England, but the stalk "beareth the blossoms or fruit at the end . . . like a bunch of grapes." Native cherries are less commonly encountered wild today: the popularity of cherry wood among colonial cabinet makers and the ravages of caterpillars may account for their relative scarcity, though F. E. Lute avers that the tent caterpillar has been here for thousands of years and that nature arranged that the pest and its victims could get along together.[16]

Currants were referred to by explorers, but to what fruit they alluded is not always clear. Mulberries, too, were noted by Captain John Smith and by Van der Donck; exactly what they saw is also uncertain, though the red mulberry is considered by Sturtevant to be a New England native. All these fruits, as well as others ignored by the English, the natives enjoyed in season; and if the quantity sufficed, dried and stored them to flavor and fortify winter dishes.[17]

Care was surely given to the highly valued, productive acorn and nut-bearing trees of which every early traveler speaks. These include the white oak, beechnut, chestnut, butternut, hickory, and many others (thirty varieties of oak alone grow in the eastern United States). Like fruit trees, oaks and nut trees yield a larger harvest if they can spread their foliage in the open. The natives took care that less valuable trees did not interfere with the best of them; their fires cleared out competing growth.

Nowadays, because of the continuous felling of walnut trees for lumber, furniture, and gunstocks, nut trees in many places are relatively scarce. The once common beech has been made into flooring, the oak into ships and house frames. Disease has nearly wiped out the chestnut, which formerly filled entire hillsides; the shagbark hickory, highly valued as firewood, is scarce. It is difficult for moderns to measure their abundance in earlier days.

The maple tree is named by Josselyn, Wood, and in other early accounts of southern New England flora, but no mention of maple sugar and syrup appears in such writings until the end of the seventeenth century. (This subject, and a related one, the absence of a taste for sweets among the local Indians, is considered at length in the discussion above on aboriginal foods.)

One modern botanical writer is confident that in river coves and shallow waters convenient to their villages, the Indians of New England propagated the yellow water lily, important for its oily seeds and glutinous roots. It is entirely possible that some tribes arranged that this and perhaps other aquatic food plants should grow or increase in convenient locations.[18]

Wild rice was an important food source in northern New England waters. It is reported as far south as Plymouth County's North River and even in shallow Connecticut streams near head of tide. The stalks of rice were gathered in a canoe and thrashed over the side so that the grain fell into the bottom.[19] High in protein and rich in vitamin B, it was an especially nutritious food.

The natives had their spring greens too: the tender shoots of marsh marigold (or cowslip), fiddle fern, cattail, milkweed, and others held the place occupied today by spinach, asparagus, and kale. No mention is made of their cultivation in New England, though the Algonquian Delawares are said to have grown one type of milkweed. The tendrils of wild grapes, tips of tree sprouts, sliced Jerusalem artichokes, and tender young squashes all made salads.[20]

Later in the summer the native people gathered wild leeks, milkweed flowers, rose hips, and other herbs and seeds for use as flavoring for stews. Captain Levett mentions "great store of Saxifrage, Cersaparilla and Anni-seeds." Could the "parsley" that he speaks of be today's ubiquitous "pussley" or purslane, still used as a green by Indians in the West? Champlain comments on "purslane" in New England, saying that it grew in great quantities among the corn, but that the natives "made no more account of it than weeds." (For this last, modern gardeners will scarcely blame them.) Yet English colonial writers do not mention it. Purslane is a popular salad green in southern Europe; botanists consider it of Old World origin.[21]

One more possible cultivated crop. From its persistence in old-time gardens, it may well be that the valuable Indian hemp, a main source of cordage and bags, received a helping hand from aboriginal men. But of cultivation there appears no direct evidence except a veiled hint by Lescarbot, though it grew profusely near every Indian village. Champlain wrote that on Cape Cod it was so plentiful that cultivation was not needed.[22]

There remain for mention certain other resources provided by nature and helpful for human use. These include none of the valuable metals on which early European explorers had so often set their hearts, except perhaps a very little copper, some of it brought by trade from the Great Lakes region. The Indians did, however, make use of the wide variety of rocks, ledge, slate, and fieldstone which nature had lavishly provided. From each, as earlier noted, they fashioned weapons and such tools as hammers, axes, mortars, grinders, and sinkers.

Of greatest importance to man also was New England's abundant natural close-to-ground growth of woodland, marsh, and open field, its wide diversity of plant life, today often taken for granted. A variety of low trees, shrubs, and vines provided not solely valuable food, but materials for housing, tools, weapons, cordage, and medicines. All in all, in natural resources for the maintenance and development of human life, from the Indian point of view certainly, New England was a land of abundance.

15.

Preparing for Cultivation

Farming Tools

No plow had ever cut a sod on the continent of North America before the advent of the European. Even if a plow had been thought of, there was no domesticated animal large enough to pull one. Western prairie tribes used dogs to pull burdens on tote poles, but this method was unknown and would have been impractical in the wooded East. The horse that the Plains Indians so remarkably adapted to their needs had not come over until the Spaniards arrived. The natives of New England had never seen a horse before the English settled there.

The wheel, used in the Old World for at least five thousand years, was also unknown in New England, though evidence of it is said to exist in Mexico. Human beings, usually women, moved all the burdens. Only a band clasped about the head or shoulders eased the bearing of the load.

Lacking animal or mechanical helps, the natives did almost all work by hand. The sole power used, aside from that of a stream in bearing a canoe, was the resilience of the sapling as it might be made to lift a pestle for pounding grain.

There was no iron or steel—almost no metal of any kind. A little hammered or annealed copper, often brought from a long distance, is sometimes found by archaeologists in graves, but it was for adornment rather than for any practical use except arrowheads.

All the painstaking cultivation with its resulting harvests, the entire provision of food, clothing, housing, and utensils, including building the light swift canoes that so captivated European explorers, was accomplished with hand tools, and by human labor with assistance, where helpful, from fire. But it was skilled hands which held those tools, and intelligence directed the labor.

Clever methods made many manual tasks bearable. In tillage, for example, the plow was not essential. For the native types of crop, the soil needed only to be loosened in and about the hills in which seed was planted, and the spaces between them kept completely clear of weeds, all possible with hand culture alone.

For loosening the soil and preparing the hills, the New England Indian employed tools similar to the European's pickaxe, mattock, hoe, and spade. These might be of wood, stone, or bone; in southern New England a sharp or pointed stone or shell would be attached by rawhide thongs to a long wooden haft or handle. A dibble or planting stick then opened holes for the seed.

"In place of ploughs," observes Champlain of certain Maine Indians, "they use an instrument of very hard wood, shaped like a spade." Father Gabriel Sagard observed the Hurons using little wooden shovels, reminding him of an ear, with a handle at the end. Jacques Cartier estimated that a similar tool which he observed in Canada was about the size of a half-sword. What are believed to be shovel blades of sandstone are also found by New England archaeologists. In the eighteenth century Peter Kalm watched Middle Atlantic Indians turn over ground with crooked and sharpened branches. Among the Iroquois, Arthur Parker speaks of a one-piece hoe with the trunk of a sapling for a handle and its nicely angled root, the blade; or the blade might be a large flat bone. Thomas Hariot in Virginia observed wooden instruments, "almost in the form of mattocks or hoes with long handles." The scapula or shoulder blade of a deer or moose is shaped remarkably like a mattock blade. New England Indians found such bone hoes useful, and so did the related Delawares to the south and Iroquois to the west. With the working end hardened and attached to a wooden handle, the shoulder bone of either deer or moose was effective in breaking even hard ground, though more useful as a hoe for later cultivation of the crop.[1]

In these developments North American Indians behaved like people in other parts of the world. In Australia and New Zealand the aborigines dug roots for food with pointed sticks. Edward Tylor describes rough, agricultural people called Hackers, in southern Sweden, who tilled using a stick with a short projecting branch sharpened to a point which in wild places in Sweden had not even then (1873) quite gone out of use. The Basutos of Africa, according to George Gomme, use oval hoes, raising them perpendicularly overhead to descend almost of their own weight: hundreds of tribesmen assemble yearly and in a straight line raise and lower their mattocks simultaneously.[2]

Many New England fields and archaeological sites yield such stone implements, two to four inches long, some triangular and pointed, others broad with a horizontal or crescent-shaped end. At the thick or wide end a notch chipped on each side seems designed for thongs to bind the pointed stone to a haft. These are believed to be land-breaking or cultivating tools. Many examples of such stone hoes are found by archaeologists in New England.

In the constant search today by relic hunters for "arrowheads," so called, the multitude of stone tools—hoes, picks, mattocks, spades, and

32. Stone implements presumed to be hoes, with a suggested method of hafting. *BMAS*, 31 (1970), 15.

dibbles—that lie in the soil near village sites are often overlooked or ignored. Roughly chipped, ground, or shaped from gravel stones or ledge fragments of granite, sandstone, and other materials, such implements in skilled hands were capable of all loosening of earth necessary to prepare and cultivate land for the food crops on which New England natives depended. Local archaeologists conjecture that these may be adaptations to agriculture of the quarry tools of the Stone Bowl Culture that preceded pottery and agriculture in New England.

Certain long, slender stones also found near village sites may have been dibbles, used to make holes into which to drop seed. An engraving by Theodore De Bry shows a Virginian squaw standing upright, using a long-handled implement (perhaps only a single stick of wood) for this purpose. Some probable dibbles are short and shaped for use directly by the hand.[3]

Once the soil was loosened, the Indian cultivator drew it into hills. For this purpose Champlain in his coasting trip found the natives at Saco using shells; whether with a wood handle he fails to state.

When the crop had advanced so that young weeds had to be cleared from the surface, light, sharp tools would be most effective—"parers," Hariot called them, in contrast to "pickers." In Virginia, he said, the squaws rested on their knees to use either. In New England, near the shore, clamshells bound to a wooden handle were used for weeding and cultivating. The hard shells of the large sea clam were best; lacking these, the quahaug or round clam would do. "They tilled their ground with the shells of fish," wrote Samuel Sewall to his friend Nehemiah Grew.[4] In the hands of a vigorous squaw, the sharp edge of a shell hoe would be fatal to tender, growing weeds. Turtle shells were used by Indians elsewhere. (When Champlain states in a single instance that cultivation was done with the shell of the horseshoe crab, I believe him to have been misled. It is too brittle.)[5]

Considering the excellent crops that the natives obtained, their implements merit respect. Roger Williams must have considered Indian tools effective, for he records after long experience: "The Indian Narragansett women to this day, notwithstanding our hoes, do use their natural hoes of shells and wood." They may have found the heavy hand-forged English hoes hard on the back as well as less effective than the light, sharp tools to which they were accustomed.[6]

To find the most useful and reliable materials for such implements, the natives might travel miles or trade with tribes far distant. From outcroppings of flint, slate, and traprock they chipped and ground axes, hammers, picks, hoes, scrapers, mortars, pestles, gouges, and similar tools, as well as the arrowheads and knives so eagerly collected today. Among the abundant gravel stones found nearly

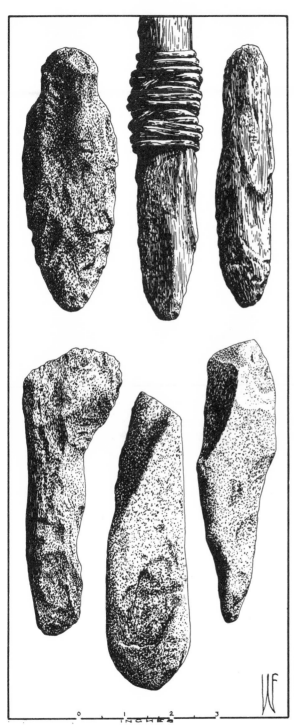

33. Stone implements presumed to be corn planters, with a suggested method of hafting. *BMAS*, 31 (1970), 17.

everywhere in glacial New England, a good eye could select a stone already roughly shaped for a needed tool or of a character easily fractured for the purpose. A round stone might serve as a grinder in a stone mortar or as a ball in some native game. A mortar shape or a long form suitable for a pestle to grind maize could be spotted by searching.

Content as they might be with their native tools, the Indian farmers promptly observed after the English began to plow that to break up land, oxen could accomplish more than men. Hence bargains between colonists and Indians for land sometimes contained a stipulation that as part payment the English should plow Indian planting land. At New Netherland, Adriaen Van der Donck noted that the natives bought metal adzes from the Dutch to work the soil. As to iron tools, Bradford at Plymouth differed from Williams: he remarked that the Wampanoags formerly had "nothing so much corn as they have since ye English have stored them with their howes, and seene their industrie in breaking up new grounds therewith." (Metal hoes are common in seventeenth century burials.)[7] The wonder is not, however, that the natives may have learned to produce more with English tools, but that for centuries they had raised sufficient crops and enjoyed food in abundance without them.

To the eye of a modern farmer, the least effective of native stone

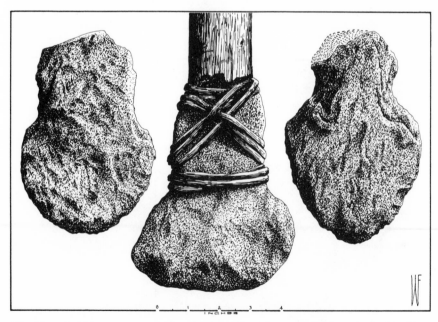

34. Stone implements presumed to be shovels, with a suggested method of hafting. *BMAS*, 31 (1970), 16.

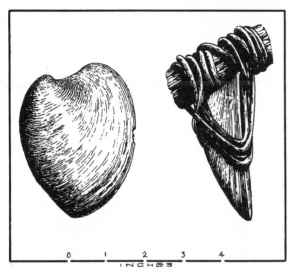

35. Quahaug shells were also used as hoes. Shown with a suggested method of hafting. *BMAS*, 31 (1970), 12.

tools was the axe. The Indian had to find a tough, seamless stone that would not split or chip and as nearly as possible of the needed shape and size, and with patient labor grind it to the proper size, then groove it for attaching the handle. The two must be bound together with thongs strong enough to stand repeated blows.

Four supple young hickory withes bent around the grooves in the axe—their boles held parallel by strips of green deerskin—formed the handle. When the deerskin thongs had dried hard, they gripped the whole tightly together. A second type of handle might be a larger sapling, cut at the desired length above the ground. The nob of roots just below the surface was trimmed, then forced apart in such a way that the axe head could be pushed through the mass of root up to its center grooves. After root and trunk dried hard, the stone axe was held firm and solid. Better still, if the axe-maker was foresighted and in no hurry, he could split a growing sapling, insert the axe head in the slit, and allow nature to tighten the grasp of wood on stone, a matter of several seasons. The abundance of axes in archaeological collections is evidence that the natives used such processes; and observers comment that the stone axe could be effective.[8] Experiments suggest that to gain the greatest effect the axe was brought down to strike at an angle to the grain of the wood.

The Fields

To clear wooded, rocky land in New England for a village site or for farming is no easy job even with today's power saws, steel axes, bulldozers, and tractors. Yet the Indians, with only hand tools, prepared for cultivation fields totaling thousands of acres, which they were using when white men first recorded them. The task was accomplished with two simple tools, the stone axe and fire. The Indian added intelligence, patience, and cooperative effort.

For one accustomed to steel tools, a stone axe, as noted, is dull, heavy, and inefficient. Yet, skillfully hafted, painstakingly sharpened, and in powerful, experienced hands, it may bring down a tree or kill an enemy.

The Indians located their planting fields on the lighter soils, where the trees were likely to be pines and soft woods, not oak and walnut. To supplement a dull stone axe, nowhere could fire work so fast and efficiently as among pines, dripping with resin and clothed with inflammable needles.

Most underbrush on the land to be farmed would long since have been cleared, either by the shade of tall and ancient trees or from regular firing of the woods. Early explorers emphasize this openness as the common state of New England forests. Thomas Morton, for example, records that the savages burnt the woods near their houses twice a year, largely destroying the underbrush so that "the trees grow here and there, as in our parks, and make the Country very beautifull and commodious."[9]

After chopping into the trunks of pine and other evergreens as far as they conveniently could, the Indians piled brush and dry branches around them and set the pile ablaze. When the hot fire had burned into the trunk a distance, they cut and burned again, assisted continually by the inflammable sap. Once the trees crashed, then dried, another fire on a brisk day would leave little on the ground but the ash and part of the trunk. Such a coating of wood ashes, rich in phosphates, lime, and potash, formed an ideal base for a healthy crop of maize or tobacco.

If the forest was mostly of hardwoods, or an easier method was preferred, the natives might strip off the bark, girdling the trees to kill them, and the next season plant in the resulting sunlight. Slow processes to our way of thinking, but effective.

(Curiously, many of the white colonists who came after, wedded at home in England to a cumbersome plow, were a long time learning how to grow crops without its aid, though in earlier centuries in Britain, Celts had done so on light soils. It was fortunate indeed for the New England colonists that there was ready to hand a "great store of plain ground without trees," and "fit for the plough.")[10]

After the land was prepared for agriculture, the natives might keep it arable for generations. Occasional resting of the land in fallow made this possible even where no sea manure was used. The common Indian practice of growing several crops simultaneously in the same field utilized both land and labor efficiently.

Once cleared, the sandy and gravelly loams that New England's Indian farmers chose were easy to work by hand. Local historians list many long-used native fields taken over by colonists from the aborigines. "Plough lands," some town records call them, or "old Indian Fields." Among Massachusetts examples are the Great Fields at Concord; Indian Field, Newbury; Indian Bottom, Hadley; and the Fairgrounds at Sturbridge. In Connecticut they include, among many, Sandy Point in Norridgewock, the Great Plain in Wethersfield, the center of Bridgeport, and Colt's Park in Hartford; in Rhode Island, Roger Williams Park at Providence.[11]

Often it was the southerly slope of a glacial hill, even the hilltop itself, that Indians chose for cultivation. This characteristic struck Captain John Smith. "Here are many rising hills, and on their tops and descents are many cornfields and delightful groves." He made this comment in the neighborhood of Ipswich, Massachusetts, where, as in many similar cases, the English bought and apportioned among themselves such areas as planting lands.[12]

At Plymouth, it will be recalled, the Pilgrims found "a high ground where there has been a great deal of land cleared and . . . planted with corn." Hillside and hilltop cultivation were common among the Nipmucks in areas near ponds and streams of northeast Connecticut and Central Massachusetts. Thus as at Fort Hill, the high land at Thompson and Mohegan in Connecticut, and at Indian Hill in Brimfield, Massachusetts may have been chosen for village sites and cultivation because it was easier to defend.[13]

On these light lands plants did well and, except in cases of extreme drought, returned sufficient crops—in favorable seasons, an abundance. Moreover, by tilling fields year after year (though sometimes with a rest between), even using the same cornhills, as was common, the cultivators saved much hard labor.

Every weed was kept down until crops were well advanced. Afterward, during the fall, grasses and weeds crowding in served to hold the soil against washing under the winter's rains and snows. In the following spring the Indians burned off the weeds and the cycle began again.

If a field was abandoned when its cultivators moved or if the land was completely played out, in the cooler parts of New England seeds of white pine or red cedar drifted in. This natural seeding may account for some of the "pine plains" so commonly mentioned in colonial records. In southern New England it might be gray birch that filtered in; on Cape Cod, aspen and pitch pine. On local soil left uncultivated it takes but a few years for forest to reclaim the land. Van der Donck was astonished when Hudson River Indians assured him that a tract already thickly grown to tall woods had been a planting field but two decades previously. About Boston Bay, between the time of the pestilence that swept away the Indians about 1616-17 and the advent of the Puritans in the 1630's, such natural afforestation had already gone far. In 1614, on his trip north, Captain John Smith had reported in Boston Harbor "many Iles all planted with corne." Bradford and Winslow, a decade later, also commented that most of the islands had been inhabited, some cleared from end to end. (Yet Wood, writing in 1634 after the Puritan settlement, has these isles abounding in woods and deer.)[14]

Indian fields were usually hard by their villages. Just as a map of English town sites of the seventeenth and early eighteenth centuries will closely proximate the locations of the villages of their native predecessors, so the cultivated fields of the colonists during their first century would largely be Indian fields and open spaces. Reams have been written about how the pioneers cleared the virgin forest. Yet until the eighteenth century there is a remarkable absence of reference to such activity in early records except as timber was cut for housing, shipbuilding, the export of lumber, and firewood.

The hard labor of clearing forested land for homesites and food production had no great lure for the English immigrants. Most of the newcomers had never swung an axe, as is clear from an examination of occupations and places of origin on the passenger lists of the first decade's incoming ships. They usually headed for lands cleared by the natives. The choicest of these the Indian chiefs were naturally slow to relinquish to the English.[15] Some cherished sites they never sold. Eventually the white newcomers increased until, fortified by firearms, they could overwhelm the native strength, reduced as it was by European diseases against which the native had no immunity. Only then could the newcomers drive the native possessors from the last of their ancestral fields and villages. King Philip had to be treacherously slain and his wife, son, and hundreds of followers sold into Spanish slavery before the Mt. Hope lands in Warren and Bristol, Rhode Island, became open to settlement. Governor John Winthrop the younger and others acquired the Indian lands in eastern Connecticut.[16]

"Old men," says Henry E. Chase in a Smithsonian report of 1883, "say that it was the habit of farmers on Cape Cod to plow up most regularly all those fields that had been already cleared by the natives, for these always gave the best crops, owing to the rich black soil that was usually found there. On the east side of Bass River, and on Indian Neck near Wellfleet Harbor the most thrifty vegetables were those growing in the dark earth and scattered shell heaps."[17]

Likewise, inland at Brookfield, Massachusetts, the hundreds of open Indian acres that stretched away later became the newcomers' planting fields. At Lancaster, Chelmsford, Newbury, Swansea, Leicester, Brimfield, Petersham, Northampton, Deerfield, Hadley, and Northfield in Massachusetts; at Warren, Middletown, Richmond, Kingstown, Providence, and elsewhere in Rhode Island; at Woodstock, Pomfret, Thompson, Mohegan, Wethersfield, Farmington, Guilford, Milford, Glastonbury, Simsbury, Bridgeport, Norwalk, and many another shore and river town in Connecticut; on the intervales of the Merrimac and the shores of Lake Winnepesaukee and Ossipee in New Hampshire; along the Oxbows of the Connecticut in both New Hampshire and Vermont; in southern Maine; in a hundred places—the twentieth-century farmer or gardener "fits" his soil on ancient Indian fields, often unaware that beyond the time of his most remote white forerunner, a shadowy line of prehistoric planters of that land stretches back into the unrecorded past.[18]

Traditional Indian cornfields have remained, however, their surface substantially undisturbed by the changes of three centuries and more. In a few such fields cornhills run parallel, row on row. In others, hills lie haphazard. Both systems are described by very early white explorers. These hills sometimes occur in permanent pasture lands,

36. Ancient Indian cornfield with original hills, according to tradition. Assonet, Massachusetts. Photograph by Howard S. Russell.

believed never to have been broken by a plow, or, sometimes, in tiers in woodlands.

If the whole expanse of pasture and forest in southern New England could be painstakingly surveyed, other so far undiscovered fields of Indian cornhills would doubtless be found. Aware of the risk of being misled by word-of-mouth tradition, we may nevertheless examine a few such reported "Indian fields."

The late E. A. Delabarre of Brown University described the appearance of a part of his own property, on the well-drained, long-season hillsides of Assonet, near Fall River, Massachusetts, sloping down to the comparatively warm waters of Mt. Hope Bay. His was one of four adjoining farms dotted with what tradition said were Indian cornhills. He calculated that once there had been 80,000 hills, covering about thirty acres. Intensively cultivated by the natives, he wrote, Assonet Neck remained in Indian possession until its ancient proprietors were driven out at the end of King Philip's War. Much of the area eventually grew up to woods, but during his lifetime Delabarre kept paths and clearings trimmed and mowed, so that the layout of regular rows of mounds showed clearly when I examined them in the 1930's.[19]

Local tradition was exact as to their origin and history, Delabarre told me. The hills had remained undisturbed because the land, before it became woods, had for generations been kept continuously in pasture instead of being broken by the plow, as so many Indian lands had been. The hills, as Delabarre described them, ran in parallel rows, N 28°E, and E 20°S, averaging about 3.75 feet apart. The soil between them was hard and vegetation comparatively meager. Once the Indians had drawn the soil into mounds, they might plant in the same cornhills season after season, adding more loam as needed. Fertilized heavily with fish for many years, these hills kept growing wild vegetation long after the time when any Indians were left to cultivate them; and the cattle and sheep that later pastured the fields never obliterated them.[20]

Dug open, the hills revealed gravel stones of all sizes. Were these stones valued for keeping the soil loose, perhaps also for retaining heat against spring frosts? From his fields Delabarre collected well-shaped slate hoes or spades and other thin stones that, hafted, might readily have served as tools. At his dwelling near Assonet River, he exhibited several carefully wrought stone mortars and pestles he had found— indispensable for grinding the harvest into meal.

Other Indian cornfields, the hills still readily observable and well backed by local tradition, have been discovered (and in some instances photographed) at West Tisbury on Martha's Vineyard; at Holbrook and Dover in Norfolk County south and west of Boston; at Northampton;

and at Mohegan, Pomfret, and Thompson, Connecticut. I have inspected them personally in all the locations mentioned except Pomfret, Connecticut. At Thompson a government radar installation appeared to have obliterated the traditional planting field located on a south-sloping hillside. At Northampton the few hills remaining after the 1938 Connecticut Valley flood were eight to twelve inches high and two feet across, aligned northeast to southeast, as Delabarre described those at Assonet. When I examined them, they were blooming with hardhack, which seemed to enjoy the higher level of the mounds and doubtless helped preserve them. Champlain describes consecutive hills at three-foot distances, apparently in regular sequence, which he saw at Saco; and one of John White's famous watercolors, carried home from Virginia in 1586, clearly depicts corn growing in rows at even distances in a village there. "De pas en pas" is the phrase Sagard uses to describe the sequence of hills in Huron fields.[21]

Regularity was by no means universal, however. At Mohegan, Connecticut, a short walk from the hilltop Indian meetinghouse and museum, plenty of corn mounds were still to be seen in a pasture in the mid 1900's. These had no symmetrical alignment; yet their appearance was not that of ordinary woodland or pasture hummocks. Unbroken tradition traced them back to the tribe of Uncas. Lafitau's Canadian drawings from the eighteenth century show similar irregular hills.[22]

As for size, plantings described by the earliest white observers appear to be of two types: extensive cornfields, and small gardens near cabins. The area of traditional fields in Delabarre's property reached thirty acres, as noted above; acreages running into the hundreds are described in several accounts by early New England travelers. These large fields may well have been cultivated in common, at least in certain aspects. The work of originally clearing and annually burning them off most likely would have been communal. J. H. Temple, in his excellent *History of North Brookfield, Massachusetts*, is one of numerous local historians who reports large fields: "The town was distinguished for its great cornfields and its defensive fort. On the northeast, west and south shores of the pond were many acres exactly suited for tillage with the native stone and shell hoes."[23]

In 1675 the colonial troops near Mt. Hope (now Bristol) and Warren, Rhode Island, passed "many fields of stately corn," a thousand acres in all, Nathaniel Saltonstall reported. As mentioned, there was no arable section of Massachusetts east of the Berkshires that did not at one time or another have cornfields. Rhode Island's Narragansett Bay area was rich in them. There were many fertile areas in Connecticut, others in New Hampshire, southwestern Maine, and the Connecticut Valley as far north as the Oxbows. The Lake Champlain area of Vermont offers credible evidence of sizable aboriginal agriculture. Allowing for the use by soldiers and travelers of round figures and excessive estimates, it is clear that even by modern standards the total area of New England Indian cornfields was substantial.[24]

Still, household plots were common, and some of them were as large as the "acre of ground" that Martin Pring mentioned. Such gardens impressed Champlain enough for him to show them on several local maps, as did Captain John Smith. They might vary in size from a half-acre to even an acre and a half. One record tells of a tribe clearing a two-acre plot for the garden of its chief.

Differences in tribal customs which may have resulted in such divergences in the size of plots and fields must remain a matter of speculation. The variety seems to indicate that both communal and individual cultivation were to be found in native New England, the practices varying from tribe to tribe, though the large fields—as Biggar suggests in relation to another area—may have been the sum of many small, individual plots.

16.

Cultivated Crops

Corn, Beans, Squashes, and Watermelons

How cultivated crops came to New England; how the natives sowed, tilled, reaped, and gathered them into barns; who did the farming, and what tools they used—all should be subjects for attention.

An Indian tradition quoted by Jacob Abbott has it that, as in the Book of Genesis, the first created men strayed from the path of righteousness. In disappointment the Great Spirit drowned them in a lake and then, starting afresh, formed one solitary man. This single human became lonely, so a sister was created to ease his solitude. In a dream one night, the brother beheld five young men come to seek marriage with his sister. (When they were created is not told!) The first four she rejected, but accepted the fifth. When the brother awakened in the morning and told of the vision, brother and sister meditated upon its meaning. They had not long to consider, for young men soon began to arrive in the flesh.

First appeared Tobacco. He was attractive, but following the pattern of the dream, the lady refused his suit, whereupon he drooped and died. Three more suitors appeared; Bean, Pumpkin, and Melon. The lady declined each in turn. But when the fifth—handsome, sturdy, upstanding Maize—appeared, she accepted him gladly. From the union of these two have come all succeeding generations of men. But that was not the end. Out of the soil where the disappointed suitors had fallen sprang up a green, leafy stalk and three differing vines. To each vine the lady gave the name of one of her disappointed suitors. All flourished under her care, and each was to prove useful to the couple and to their descendants of the remotest times.[1]

If this explanation of the origin of the chief aboriginal crops leaves the reader doubtful, others from the native Algonquians are perhaps more credible. One tale likewise credits to a lady the Indians' most valued crops.

Once upon a time, it goes, a beautiful squaw was sent by the Great Spirit to visit the tribes of New England. She brought them three gifts: in her right hand she held the seed of corn; in her left, beans and squash. After the offerings were accepted and her visit was over, from the warm earth where the bountiful visitor had been seated tobacco promptly pushed up its stalk. Roger Williams heard a different story: it was the crow who brought the welcome seeds, "an Indian graine of corne in one Eare, and an Indian or Frenche Bean in another, from the great God Kantantowit's field in the Southwest, from whence they hold come all their Corne and Beanes." Because of this belief, the New England Indians declined to kill crows, no matter how grievously they might damage the cornfields. (After the foreign newcomers arrived, however, they were not unwilling to have the less scrupulous English do it for them.)[2]

Another version had it that "a Crow brought the first Bean, and a Black-Bird the first Grain of Indian Corn into those parts," adding a second feathered pest to the sacred category. Varied stories have survived, each telling how the Indians got tobacco: one derived it from the grave of a venerated squaw, one attributes it to the sacrificing of a beautiful young princess to bring a famine to an end, and one tells of its theft from a grasshopper by the legendary tribal hero of the Maine Indians.[3]

No explanation of the great gift of maize is as charming as the legend of the Wampanoags of southern New England, as related in Weston's *History of Middleboro*.[4]

> Mon-do-min, an elderly hunter of the tribe, sat one night in his wigwam on the shore of the Nemasket River. The night was dark and stormy, for Ke-che-No-din, the Spirit of the Wind, was very angry. Mon-do-min was old and lame; his wigwam stood apart from the others; he could no longer hunt the deer or bear. He was very weak and fainting from hunger, for he had not tasted food for many days. He looked up to the Great Spirit for help. "Oh Shah-wain-ne-me-shin! Have pity upon me, and look down from your window in the southern sky, and send me help from your home in the heavens."
>
> Presently, above the wind he heard a fluttering among the long poles at the top of his wigwam. He looked up, and lo! a partridge, be-nah-nah, was caught there. Mon-do-min grasped the partridge with his hand and gave thanks: "Now has the Great Spirit had pity upon me and sent me food, that I may not die of hunger." He kindled a fire and prepared to dress the bird for his supper.
>
> But soon, amid the pauses of the storm, he heard sounds of distress. It was a woman's voice, crying bitterly. She had lost her way in the forest, and crouched for shelter beneath the corner of the Great Rock, close by his door. Out of the wigwam Mon-do-min hastened with all the strength of his old and trembling limbs. He raised the woman and brought her into his wigwam. There he laid her on his own bed of

bearskins. He chafed her limbs, for she had fallen from the rock, and tried to restore warmth to her shivering frame.

He saw that she must have food! Lifting from the fire the tiny partridge he had prepared for his own nourishment he said: "My sister, this is what the Great Spirit had given me to eat. Take it; there is not enough for thee and me. Thou wilt live, but I must die. Thus has the Great Spirit spoken. But remember me, when thou seest ones alone and perishing, and do to them as I have done to thee. Farewell."

So Mon-do-min laid himself down on the cold earth. That night the Great Spirit took him to his dwelling in the Country of Souls. In the morning the woman awoke calm and refreshed. She looked and saw Mon-do-min, dead on the floor of the wigwam. She hurried to call the chiefs of the tribe. On the bank of the river close by his wigwam they buried Mon-do-min.

When the Moon of Leaves (June) had come, behold, the ground around the grave of Mon-do-min became covered with fine green shoots, springing up like grass, but their leaves broader and more beautiful. The tribe wondered: what is this that grows around the grave of Mon-do-min? While they questioned, lo! from a bright cloud just above them, the Great Spirit spoke. "My children, listen. This that you see shall be food for you to eat when it shall be ripened into full ears of grain. It shall be called Mon-do-min, for his kindness to the poor and perishing one that stormy night, when he himself was perishing with hunger. And you shall tell it to your children, and your children's children, in all your tribes, when you see the green corne waving by the Lake of the White Stones [Assawompsett] and the river of the Nemaskets."

Believe which legend you will; suspect even that certain of them may have received a hint from the missionary's Bible; the three bountiful gifts to the red man of corn, beans, squash— "our life," "our supporters," "the three sisters"—have all been long cultivated in New England, and with them gourds, watermelons, Jerusalem artichokes, and tobacco. All, except perhaps watermelons, are native to the New World. Of these, the artichoke may have been brought into cultivation first in the eastern United States. All are well adapted to the sour soils and shifting climate of New England. Maize, originally developed from a wild grass in Central America at least 7,000 years ago, is variously estimated to have been introduced to the coastal Northeast between 1,000 and 600 years ago.[5] All must have become well established centuries before the English set foot ashore. Corn, beans, and tobacco, once newcomers, remain highly important crops to New England and to the economy of the entire continent.

In New England at the time of the earliest written records, the

northeasterly limit of corn and beans along the coast seems to have
been Maine's Kennebec and Penobscot valleys. Evidences of prehistoric agriculture have also been found near the sea in New Brunswick
village sites. Ears of the Canada Creeper, a short variety, matured in the
brief seasons of northeastern Maine, in the Canadian provinces, and
inland at Newport, Vermont.[6]

Roger Williams believed that "further north and westward of us
their corn will not grow; but to the southward better and better." The
latter half of his statement was correct. As to the first half, John
Winthrop, Jr., of Connecticut, describes maize as reaching a height of
six to eight feet near Long Island Sound. He also mentions
"Mouhawkes Corne which though planted in June will be ripe in
season."[7]

Nature is likely to bear the brunt of such climatic adaptations: T.
H. Hoskins comments that with no agricultural education beyond his
own observations, the aborigine had spread its production from the
Gulf of Mexico to the St. Lawrence and the Gaspé peninsula—an
achievement requiring both attention and skill.

The Indian has a tradition about this, says Hoskins, quoting Peol
Sesup, a Penobscot Indian. "Like all grasses . . . corn grows upward by
joints or sections. The Indians observed that the time required to
produce and perfect a joint was one phase of the moon, and as the ear
of corn starts only from a joint, there was necessarily about seven days
between the formation of ears at successive joints. Now if an ear could
be made to start at the second joint, it would mature some five weeks
in advance of that . . . formed at the seventh joint. By constantly
selecting seed from the lowest ears, he finally obtained varieties that
produced from joints lower . . . and very much earlier . . . adapted to
the short summers of the north. Slowly, but permanently, it passed into
the eight-rowed corn, producing constantly at the lower joints,
and ripening three months from the date of planting."[8] This explanation, perhaps not botanically exact, suggests Indian capacity for crop
improvement.

Height of stalk was but one aspect. The natives of America
through the centuries developed four main species of corn, and a gamut
of color and of size. One Canadian short-season corn had an ear no
larger than a caseknife handle. On the other hand, certain varieties bore
grains of very large size, or of unusual length or width. The stalks of a
tropical corn grown in the Midwest might reach a height of eighteen
feet. The New England native, so far as is known, grew only hard flint
corn.[9]

As to color, however, "Nature hath delighted itself to beautify this
Corne with a great variety of colours," wrote Winthrop. There

was white corn, reaching perfection in the gleaming flint of the Narragansetts; also black corn, cherry red corn, yellow, blue, straw-colored and greenish, speckled and striped (most of these noted by Winthrop)—all maintained true to color and variety. A mixed "squaw corn," as it was called, was still grown in southeastern Massachusetts within my own memory. Paul Dudley (1675-1761) mentions an Indian belief that maize varieties mixed through intermingling of their roots.[10]

In the whole continent there was corn eight-rowed and twelve-rowed, perhaps bearsfoot and strawberry (the last two named for outward resemblance)—according to U. P. Hedrick, a hundred or more types, and twice or thrice that number of varieties.[11]

Beans some students consider to be as important in Indian diet as maize. With these, equal skill was manifest. New England's beans were of several colors: white, red, yellow, blue, blue-spotted. "They are variegated much," commented John Josselyn, the colonial herbalist, "some being bigger a great deal than others."[12] John Winthrop, Jr., comparing them to European broad beans (of a different botanical family), thought the pods very large.

The vines that grew them varied also. Some "of the low sort" apparently were bush beans. Others were interspersed in the cornfield to climb the stalks. Speck reports that the traditional Penobscot practice was to plant the seed beside a circle of ten-foot poles slanted to meet at the top, tepee fashion, and let the vines find their way up. Paul Dudley, an observant Massachusetts Bay gentleman of the early eighteenth century, recorded that the vine climbed around its pole against the sun.[13] Some types were eaten fresh, pod and all; others were especially adapted for drying and storing. Josselyn gave to certain of them the apt title of kidney beans: botanists report that their cultivation goes back as much as 7,000 years in Mexico, where wild vines of the climbing type are still to be found in thickets in many areas. In Mexican markets as many as twenty-five varieties may be displayed.[14] Their cultivation, both climbing and bush types, spread gradually north, eventually to reach New England. In New York they have been dated as early as A.D. 1100. From the New England tribes have come the numerous sorts and colors still scrupulously perpetuated by local gardeners. Maine's present-day specialties include red kidney, yellow kidney, Jacob's cattle, and soldier beans. A Vermont bean-seed grower is reported to have on hand one hundred and thirty varieties. The native bean (*Phaseolus*), originating in the western hemisphere, is of a family altogether different from the long cultivated broad bean (*Faba faba*) of the Old World. The lima bean is a native of South America, Brazil and Peru, not of local Indian growth.

The Indian bean was to prove an important food for the New England colonists. An 1834 Boston seed catalogue lists twelve dwarf kidney and string beans and eight pole or running beans. Five years later the same firm lists twenty-one kidney and bush varieties and ten kinds of pole beans. Amelia Simmons' *American Cookery* (Hartford 1796) discusses six beans that apparently are American.

Great variations there must have been also in squash and pumpkins. "Askutasquash," the New England natives called them (to be eaten green, it means); some sorts were edible by early July. The hard winter Hubbard, Boston Marrow, and Essex Hybrid, which for years were modern New England's favorites, and the Butternut and Acorn, though American in origin, are nineteenth- and twentieth-century introductions to New England. The Hubbard probably arrived by sea from South America, the Marrow from the Western New York Indians. Direct from native America, with a cultivation record of up to 10,000 years but previously unknown in Europe, bush and crookneck summer squashes came to New England, types known elsewhere as simlins. Beginning with Champlain, all early European visitors enjoyed them.[15]

Less diversified but certainly native also are the large orange pumpkins. One of the earliest New England seed catalogues lists four varieties of pumpkin and eight of squash, at least three of the latter apparently introduced from other areas. It seems likely that all were just about the same as when the native farmers had passed them on to the English settlers, for the early colonists were far more interested in acclimating European seeds and plants than in improving the native vegetables, however important these might prove to their daily living.

Explorers and early observers all found squashes and pumpkins of great interest. "Some of them are green," Josselyn writes in 1638, "some yellow, some longish like a gourd, others round like an appel." Roger Williams called one type "vine apples" and found them "sweet" and "wholesome." Van der Donck, who explored the Connecticut shore as well as the Hudson, called the squash "a delightful fruit; as well for its variety of colors as to the mouth for its agreeable taste." The number produced on a vine in a season he pronounced incredible. The French were equally struck with this new vegetable. The New England coast natives gave Champlain some "as big as the fist," which his company ate as a salad.[16]

Carver, an early English traveler in the interior, lists "Melons or Pumpkins, by some called Squashes which serve many nations as a substitute for bread." He mentioned round, craneneck, small, flat, and large oblong squash; the small ones they ate in summer, the craneneck they hung up for winter. His large oblong appears to be what is now called a field pumpkin. Thomas Jefferson mentions a long, crooked, and warted type as having come from New Jersey, indicating an Algonquian origin. President Dwight of Yale at the end of the eighteenth century mentions both summer and winter squashes. We don't know what he saw, but a 1731 garden dictionary mentioned flat, large, white, citron-shaped, and warted squashes. Apparently the Indians had a considerable variety; and Governor Hutchinson of Massachusetts in 1764 differentiates pumpkins from squashes.[17]

Among the many varieties, Europeans promptly learned to grow at least summer crookneck and bush scallop squashes of more than one color. (U. P. Hedrick, the historian of horticulture, includes Boston Marrow and Turbans as original in New England, but Burr in 1865 says the Autumnal Marrow came from an Indian source in the Buffalo area and the Marblehead from the West Indies in 1867.)

We conclude that the New England Indians had both sugar and field pumpkins also. The pumpkin, or pompion, domesticated in Mexico between 7000 and 5000 B.C., like many another American plant had been carried to Europe within a half century after Columbus' landing. Each squash and pumpkin variety, it will be noted, had to grow separately, far enough from every other type that insects would not mix the pollen. Keeping varieties true requires a careful gardener even today.

Calabashes or gourds were selected and grown by the Indian. "It is the common water pail of the natives, and I have seen one so large that it would contain more than a [Dutch] bushel" (Van der Donck). Some botanists think that the gourd originated in Africa and floated across to the western hemisphere; others consider it native to both. At any rate, cucurbita have been associated with man in America at least 10,000 years. The gourd dates back to the earliest agriculture of Peru and Mexico, up to 7,000 years ago, perhaps more. The New England natives grew it, and found it useful for containers.[18] They used the shell, but did not eat the flesh, as was done in the Old World.

They also may have had some types of melons. Rev. Edmund Browne of seventeenth-century Sudbury describes as "naturally growing" "a muskmellon . . . soe ripened with the sunne as both in smell and taste it may compare with goodly peares." The subject is confused, however, because early writers used the terms melons, pompions, cymlings, cushaws, and, in French, *citrouilles*, without botanical precision. The early botanist De Candolle thought that the watermelon had been introduced here by Europeans, though he appears not to have been acquainted with all of the opposing testimony. Modern ethnobotanists suspect that it is from South Africa, where related plants are found wild; Hedrick believes tropical Africa. If from the eastern hemisphere, it must have spread rapidly, being found throughout the Americas.[19] Certainly the New England Indians had watermelons when the English appeared. "The watermelon . . . of a flesh color . . . is proper to this country," notes Josselyn, "a rare cooler of Feavers and excellent against the Stone." His description is precise: "Water Mellon is a large fruit, but nothing as big as a Pompion, smoother, and of a sad Grass green, rounder, or more rightly sap green with some yellowness admixt when ripe, the seeds are black, the flesh and pulpe exceedingly juicy." Thomas Graves, the land surveyor, in 1629 mentions melons as abounding, and Edmund Browne notes "a watter mellon not inferior to the best."[20]

Van der Donck in New Netherland saw a smaller variety, "the size of a man's head, somewhat oblong . . . within they are either white or red: the red have white and the white, black seeds."[21] He says that they grew rapidly and densely and were therefore useful to clear wild land. It was not grown at home in the Netherlands, he noted. Some Canadian Indians had watermelons, for Lahontan describes them accurately. Cartier in 1535 had mentioned "muskmillions" more than once, differentiating them from pompions, gourds, and cucumbers.

These vine crops as well as beans and squash, it should be noted, are invitations to the woodchuck. Here was one of the dog's few opportunities for usefulness: to dig out these "groundhogs" and bring them in to supplement the family meat supply.

Roots

Another important, cultivated crop of the New England Indians was the Jerusalem artichoke, *Helianthus tuberosus*. This plant looks like the sunflower but has a smaller blossom and an edible root. One scientist has called it and the sunflower the only crops domesticated by the Indians of the United States. Both must be today about the same as when prehistoric plant breeders left them. The Jerusalem artichoke, at least, has received little or no recent attention from North American plant breeders. Though allowed to lapse from cultivation, its native persistence has saved it.

There is no connection between it and the holy city of Jerusalem. The common English name of the plant appears to be a corruption of its name in Italian (*Girasole Articiocco*, or Sunflower Artichoke) because Rome's famed Farnese Garden early in the seventeenth century distributed it across Europe. Hedrick believes, however, that the plant originated in the American West. Candolle credits it to Indiana. Gilmore found the Nebraska Indians eating the roots raw or boiled

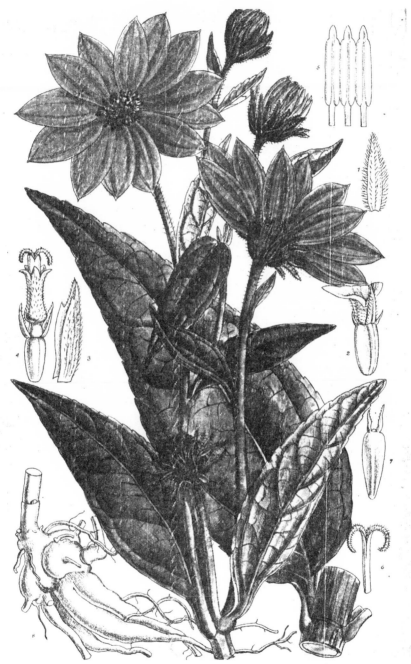

37. Jerusalem artichoke, *Helianthus tuberosus*. The Indians found its roots, both wild and cultivated, a reliable source of food. *Curtis's Botanical Magazine*, 53 (1897).

but not cultivating it. Brand thinks it native to the eastern United States. The New England Indians cultivated it and valued it for its nutritive qualities and its ability to do well in their soils. One small stream near Newburyport, named Artichoke River, is in an ancient Indian area, and the root is widely spread over the countryside elsewhere in New England.[22]

The New England coast Indians more than once treated Champlain to its tubers. He thought they tasted like real artichokes, or perhaps chard. The root had virtues besides flavor. Modern medical investigators, as noted, have considered the levulose in the roots especially beneficial for diabetics, supplying sugar to the sufferer's diet without adding excess carbohydrates.[23]

Even in poor soil artichoke plants produce tubers plentifully, and more heavily in good ground. This root has one distinct advantage over the Irish potato, a South American plant that North America received by way of Ireland: the tubers stand hard freezing in the ground.

A second potato-like root, the groundnut, *Apios tuberosa,* called "openauk" by southern New England Indians, was cultivated by several American tribes. Whether New England Indians cultivated or merely encouraged the plant there is no conclusive evidence, though Starbird asserts that the Anasaguntacooks of Maine grew many of the native wild roots; certainly they dried and stored the tubers.[24]

William Morrell, a Plymouth rhymester of 1623-24, thus describes their virtues (originally in Latin verse): "A ground-nut there runs on a grassie thread / Along the shallow earth in a bed / Yellow without, thin filmed, sweete, lilly white / Of strength to feede and cleare the appitite / From these our nature may have grand content / And good subsistence when our means is spent."[25]

As with the artichoke, their immunity to frost damage was important. In King Philip's War, after colonial soldiers had burned the stores of corn and beans of their native enemies, the uprooted Indians saved their lives as they moved from place to place in that open winter by digging these wild potatoes. Mary Rowlandson, the Lancaster pastor's wife who was captured by the Indians, tells us that "the chief and commonest food was Groundnuts: They eat also Nuts and Acorns, Hartychoaks, Lilly roots, Ground Beans, and several other weeds and roots that I know not." In Canada Le Jeune states the French called the groundnuts "rosary," because the tubers are strung like beads. Pear-shaped, rusty, or dark brown, they are rich in a starch which Edward Palmer compares to that of wheat and terms very wholesome. C. A. Potter, a student of Abenaki dialect, thought that Pennacook, the

38. Groundnut, *Apios tuberosa*. A valuable wild root widely used by the Indians as food. *The Cottage Gardener and and Country Gentleman* (April 20, 1858), p. 44.

Indian name for Concord, New Hampshire, signified "The place of groundnuts."[26]

It is sometimes asserted that sunflowers, native American and rich in oily seeds, were among New England Indian crops. If this were true, Champlain would have described such striking flowers, as he did a decade later in his account of the Hurons, and as Hariot did in Virginia. Apparently neither trade nor immigration brought them from the West, where the Senecas cultivated them. In the Northeast the plentiful supply of oil and grease to be had from bears, whales, various fishes, and nuts may have prevented it from taking hold.

This survey of native foodgrowing would be incomplete if it failed to point out that New England soils grew not just valuable food crops and plants useful for medicines and for industrial purposes, but others today regarded as undesirable weeds. In the case of some such, the native point of view may have been different, as will appear shortly.

Tobacco

Of crops cultivated by Indian gardeners there remains one—tobacco—which to the Indian was highly important. Companions of Columbus first encountered it in the West Indies in 1492. On most of the North American continent and much of South America, wherever it would grow or could be obtained by trading, the Indian used its leaf. Tobacco had been developed by the Indian from wild plants. De Candolle reports a form of it growing wild in Ecuador, in modern times. At least as far north as the Kennebec, every New England tribe cultivated tobacco.[27]

"They say they take tobacco for two causes," remarks Roger Williams, "first against rheum, which causeth the toothake, which they are impatient of; secondly, to revive and refresh them, they taking nothing but water."[28] His remark about toothache appears not to refer to chewing tobacco, though chewing was common in the Andes of South America and is said to have been practiced by some Algonquians. (Among New England's colonists, chewing tobacco seems to have been first mentioned in 1704, and then as having been introduced by sailors. The habit was not derived from the native Indians. The use of snuff, common to the south, is not reported in early New England.)[29]

Among Algonquian tribes, the chief purpose of tobacco was for smoking or "drinking," as early explorers describe the pipesmoking habit. Williams comments that "Generally all the Men throughout the

Country have a Tobacco-bag with a pipe in it." This pouch was the skin of a squirrel, otter, or other small animal, or, in Maine, was made from birch bark. Some of the stone pipes today cherished by archaeological

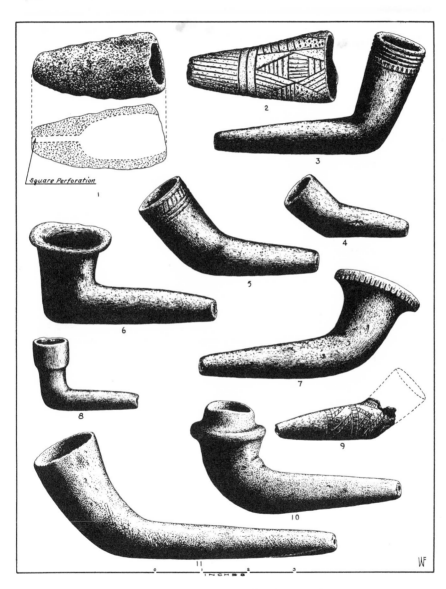

39. Clay pipes, late prehistoric. They partly replaced stone pipes. *BMAS*, 27 (1966), 65.

collectors came by native trade from distant places, the Mohawks to the west or the Cherokees to the south, although pipes made locally of clay, soapstone, or sandstone are plentiful in New England collections. The stone pipe, Wood says, might be red or black. Near the sea Captain George Waymouth saw natives using a short lobster claw. Inland a wooden pipe bowl might serve. West Indian tribes and some on the continent smoked cigars and cigarettes, but these are not reported in New England.

To prepare his smoke, the native cut or powdered dried tobacco leaf and rubbed it into bits with his fingers. He pressed the dust into the bowl of his pipe, "and laying a cole of fire upon it, at the other end sucke so long, that they fill their bodies full of smoke, till that it cometh out their mouth, and nostrils, even as out of the Tonnall of a chimney."

No tribal religious ceremony or intertribal conference began without the pipe and the smoke of tobacco. A pipe was the first courtesy offered guest or stranger.[30]

Some American tribes confined use of the pipe to their chief men. Others allowed only older men to smoke, for the young man might injure his ability to run, and it was on his stamina that the tribe must rely for safety in war. Winslow observes that the "Indians took much tobacco, but accounted it odious for their boys to do so." Women did not usually smoke, except occasionally the elderly: but in Maine, Father Ralé reported (1732) that men, women, and children were constant smokers.[31]

Tobacco served the Indian not only as a toothache remedy, but as a pain killer and antiseptic. Belief in its efficacy for these purposes has persisted into modern times. Josselyn prescribed it for open wounds. Indeed, its first use may have been as an antidote for snakebite: wild animals are said to eat one type of tobacco plant for this purpose.

Champlain saw the natives growing tobacco beside the Saco River in southern Maine and on Cape Cod. Gosnold was welcomed with it when he visited Cape Cod later. Roger Williams testifies that in Rhode Island the Indians used it frequently. As far north as it would mature between frosts, even up into the Kennebec River Valley, Indians grew tobacco. "They also plant great store of tobacco," Lescarbot wrote in 1609, "a thing most precious with them, and used universally among all those nations." Not much of it was planted in New England, Josselyn claimed, but his writing concerns chiefly the Bay coast, where Indians were few after white settlement and the colony government frowned on the tobacco habit.

The plants Captain Waymouth saw on the coast in early June

1605 were about a foot above ground. The natives made him under-
stand by signs that they would eventually grow a yard high, with leaves
as broad as both their hands.

Lescarbot's map of the coast (1609 edition) is bordered with a row
of tobacco plants, each bearing two, three, or four leaves. (The map is
likewise decorated with ears of mature corn, of large size.) Josselyn
found Massachusetts Bay Indians planting a small kind, with short,
thick, round leaves and yellow blossoms, believed to be *Nicotiana
rustica*. Pooke, they called it, a word which Trumbull interprets merely
as that which is smoked.[32]

As to quality, Captain Bartholomew Gosnold's annalist, John Brereton, thought the tobacco offered him on the New England coast
strong and pleasant, "as good as any we ever took." Rosier, with Captain
Waymouth, in Maine, called the native tobacco smoked in a lobster
claw excellent, strong, and of sweet taste. Brereton, a clergyman,
considered it much better than any he had enjoyed in England—the
latter presumably being Virginia tobacco. Josselyn said it had a bitter
taste, and was odious to white men. Several types grew in North
America; William Setchell counts fourteen species.[33]

Williams, in one place, uses a designation "Wuttammauog"—that
is, a weak tobacco. The natives often blended other sweet and fragrant
plants and barks with tobacco, as is done with certain twentieth-
century tobaccos. Among such additions and substitutes (according to
Jerome Brooks, sixteen in all), were sumac, sweet fern, leaves of the
cardinal flower, and red willow, dogwood, and other types of bark.
Certain of the additions are said to have been narcotic. The strains
used by the various tribes were of considerable variety. That of the
Neuter tribe in Ontario was so noted for superior quality that in
historic times the tribesmen traded it far and wide for furs, skins, and
porcupine quill work. So did the New York Iroquois with their
brand.[34]

Tobacco was a sacred plant; religious ceremonies attended the
planting of the seed. In some areas of America the Indians believed it a
gift from the departed. Standing in the midst of a circle marked out by
tobacco leaves, Virginia natives, with gestures and dances, offered
adoration to the sun. To honor spirit powers some tribes threw
tobacco into the fire or sacrificed it in other ways in ceremonies
connected with a wide variety of acts and events. In social intercourse
it had especial value as a proof of hospitality and as an accompaniment
for councils and similar solemn occasions. "The fondness they have
for this herbe is beyond belief. They go to sleep with their reed pipes
in their mouths; they often stop in their journeys for the same pur-

pose, and it is the first thing they do when they enter their cabins."
They "smoke when paddling a canoe. Let us say with compassion that
they pass their lives in smoke, and at their death fall into the fire."[35]

Among cultivated plants, in practically every area where the plant
was grown on this continent, tobacco was distinctly the man's crop. "It is
commonly the only plant which men labor in," was Roger Williams'
comment.[36] The art of cultivating and curing tobacco as practiced by
modern farmers in the Connecticut Valley, where for more than two
centuries it has been a staple crop, varies little in its main features from
Indian methods, except that valuable high-type cigar wrappers are
grown now under cloth tents assisted by special manures and fertilizers.
The seed of the cigar tobacco varieties now grown was brought from the
South and from Cuba, however, and not until the nineteenth century.
The original native tobacco was a considerably shorter plant than the
imported varieties.[37]

The Connecticut Valley was not where New England's English
settlers first cultivated tobacco. Even before the Puritans arrived in
Massachusetts Bay in 1630, the "old planters" at the Bay, such as Roger
Conant, had been growing the crop. Conant must have learned the art
from his Indian neighbors.

The Indians ordinarily cultivated tobacco in a separate plot, not
usually intercropping it among the corn, as they did beans, squash, and
melons. Captain Pring in one instance, however, saw "Tobacco, Pompions, Cowcumbers and such" growing together, with "Maize or Indian
wheat among them."[38]

When Virginia was settled, the natives at Jamestown planted tobacco in hills like corn, and grew it in the same spot to maturity. De
Bry's engraving shows it in serried rows. In New York, according to
Hedrick, the Indians scattered the seed (of *Nicotiana rustica*) without
pattern, then thinned the seedlings and left it to be self-sown thereafter.
Replanting, he says, might not be done for several years. McDonald
believed that this was the practice in Connecticut. (The modern imported variety *Nicotiana tabacum* is not considered self-propagating in
northern climates.) Cape Cod Indians certainly harvested seed and
preserved it for planting the following spring, for when a Pilgrim party,
landing from the anchored Mayflower, ran onto a pair of wigwams
containing food and household goods, they found also a little tobacco
seed.[39]

The modern tobacco farmer formerly set plants in the field by
hand from the seedbed with the help of a riding plant-setter. One
student of tobacco history considers this transplanting practice an
English invention, yet in early New England Josselyn saw tobacco
transplanted from the seedbed when it showed four of five leaves,

Nicotiana rustica L.

40. Indian tobacco, *Nicotiana rustica*, the cultivated variety. J. Kerner, *Figures des plantes économiques*, 6 (1786), pl. 16.

though he is not altogether clear whether he was watching Indians or English. Transplanting tobacco may well be of Indian origin.[40]

Other methods used by modern Connecticut Valley growers, said to be derived directly from the aborigines, include suckering and topping to make the leaves grow large. McDonald mentions that Indians used manure for tobacco; what type or by what tribe he does not specify. Rotted herring would have assisted tobacco, as it did maize. In Virginia, however, no account was made even of the piles of ashes from the previous year's weeds, which would have been helpful as mineral fertilizer.[41]

There is reason to believe that when the plant had made its growth, New England Indians harvested the whole stalk green, then hung it to dry in air or sun, or dried it over a fire. The next step would be stripping. On a damp day the leaves would be picked from the stalk, rolled up like tea leaves, and later, when dry again, stored.[42]

17.

The Season's Round

Planting corn and beans, both tender plants ruined by a hard frost, began only when the budding leaves of the white oak reached the size of a mouse's ear or a red squirrel's foot or when the shadbush leaf became as large as a squirrel's ear. All these aboriginal signs of the safe advance of the season are still valid. (A modern gardener, with no white oak or shadbush about, may safely plant corn when the bridal wreath spirea foams with bloom). Other considerations entered in. "In time of sowing they are governed by observing the full moon and the rising of the Pleiades," Verrazano noted.

The Indian calendar, as described by John Pynchon, one of the Connecticut Valley's earliest settlers, starts with spring corn planting time called Squannikesos, the latter part of April and the first weeks of May. In May–June the "women weed their corne." In late June and July the corn is hilled. The fourth month from planting brings the first squash and beans; next comes the time when green corn becomes fit to eat; followed by a month of ripening until it is ready to harvest. Now appears the two-month season of "white frost on ye grass & g(round)." Midwinter arrives about the second week of January. Then the sun strengthens enough so that thawing begins. By late February and early March "ye ice in ye River is all gone"; and from late March to mid-April comes the month called "Namossack Kesos, the time of catching fish," before field work once more commences.

Gladys Tantaquidgeon, a modern Mohegan, recounting the ancestral wisdom of her tribe, counsels that corn be planted in the full of the moon, and climbing vegetables when the moon is waning.[1] Whether justified or not, the notion of the moon's influence still has wide currency in the world. To the Indian the celestial powers were very real. Because they held his fate so fully in their hands, he did his best to cooperate with them, and did not fail to seek their blessing with elaborate ritual.

Besides knowing when to plant, the Indian also had means of judging and forecasting other aspects of the weather. Snapping ice in winter presaged a thaw; thunder in early spring (controlled by the four celestial thundermen or, among Western Abenaki, seven brothers) announced the winter's end, and geese flying north confirmed the omen. Three foggy mornings, a mackerel sky, bobwhites calling—any of these brought rain. High winds would follow mare's tails in the sky. Cobwebs on the grass and singing crickets meant heat. Northern lights foretold cold. When the locusts began their song, reckon six weeks to the first frost.[2]

From an agricultural point of view, the first spring job was to gather the weeds and stalks that remained in the fields from the previous season. Beating them with a hooked stick, the cultivators would wait for a still day, then burn them. The ashes provided a small amount of readily available potash and phosphoric acid for the next crop.

From some fields perhaps left fallow to regain fertility in Nature's slow renewal, no crop had been taken the previous summer. Champlain noted such fields at Nauset on Cape Cod; John Winthrop, Jr., mentions them in Rhode Island and Connecticut. He watched the Narragansetts' farming, for, he said, "The Narragansetts' land seemeth far worse than the ground of the Massachusetts."

To prepare the soil for planting, the workers, using mattocks and hoes, loosened the earth, often in the same hills as the year before. Then from the brooks where the spring run of herring or shad was on, they brought fish from their weirs in baskets and, placing two or three in each hill, covered them with a few inches of soil.

Thomas Morton explains the method. "There is a fish," he says, "called shadds, by some allizes [alewives], that at the spring of the year passe up the rivers to spawn in the ponds, and are taken in such multitudes in every river that hath a pond at the end, that the Inhabitants dung their ground with them."[3]

To do this, the natives built bush or stone weirs out into the stream from each bank, then arranged wicker cages between. When the shad or herring rushed up the stream, the weirs herded them into these narrow waters, where they were trapped. On a big job like this "all the neighbours, men and women, forty, fifty, a hundred join and come in to help freely."[4] Dipping out the fish in baskets, they bear them to waiting cornfields. The fish run ordinarily occurs about the time when spring frosts cease and corn and bean planting become safe. If time is lacking, the squaw may plant the grain first and add the fish later as what would now be called a side dressing.[5]

The Pilgrims at Plymouth found that, just as their teacher Squanto "tould them, except they gott fish and set with it in these old grounds it [the corn] would come to nothing."[6] In this feature of agriculture as well as others, the New England Algonquians were the experts and the English became their pupils.

The validity of the long-held belief that the southern New England Indians fertilized their cornhills with herring and taught the Pilgrims the practice has in recent decades been questioned by anthropological writers, notably Erhard Rostlund in the *American Journal of Geography* in 1957 and Lynn Ceci in *Science*, 1975. The doubters suggest a European rather than an American Indian origin for the method. Such a theory not only runs counter to the straightforward language of the colonial writers (as well as strong local tradition) but ignores certain agricultural and historical fundamentals.

In Plymouth manuscripts both Governor Bradford and Edward Winslow credit their learning of the practice to the teaching of Squanto, the sole survivor of the former Indian inhabitants of the Plymouth village site. Later in the century Governor Winthrop the Younger, of Connecticut, in a comprehensive description of corn culture communicated to the Royal Society of England, of which he was the first American member, states categorically that the colonists learned fish manuring from the Indians. A further bit of evidence is that the local Indian dialect has a single word (munwarwhateag) for both small fish and manure.[7]

The doubters theorize that Squanto—who taught the Pilgrims how to concentrate the wealth of fish, bear them to the fields, and lay them under the cornhills with the seed above—must have picked up the fertilizing idea in his European travels. This view pays scant attention to the reality of war-torn Europe of the seventeenth century, when fish, brought by dangerous voyages from the Grand Banks, was needed for food. As fertilizer, fish is seldom mentioned (even fish waste) by contemporary European agricultural writers. In any case, the fish-in-hill method that Squanto taught the Pilgrims had no precedent in European agriculture. For a thousand years at least, European practice, in both fertilizing and sowing grain, had been to use level, not hill, culture; Squanto could not have learned it in Spain (where he was a captive), in England later (for maize was not grown there), or in his Newfoundland stay (where waste fish was occasionally used as fertilizer for broadcast grain and vegetables but where maize does not mature). The American Indian had developed from wild plants corn (maize), potatoes, beans, squash, cocoa, and a host of other foods. In Peru and Chile he had learned to use as fertilizer not solely fish but also nitrate of soda and guano.[8] Why doubt the ability of the Plymouth Indians, in their poor soil, to learn to help their corn with herring in the hill?

Combining the arts of the skilled husbandman with observation of the weather and propitiation of the spiritual world, all signs being favorable, the Indian farmers were ready to plant. Captain John Smith, born on a farm in England, tells how planting was done. "They make a hole in the earth with a stick, and in it they put four grains of [Indian] wheate (maize) and two of beans. These holes they make four feet from one another." In New England the distance was sometimes less, as appears also from colonial records, the evidence of other explorers, and traditional cornfields still extant.[9] The squaw carried the seeds to the planting field in a neat compartmented basket made for the purpose, and dropped them into the spots opened up with the fingers or by the long planting stick.

Champlain gives a slightly different version. "Planting three or four kernels in one place, they heap about it a quantity of earth with shells of the signoc (horseshoe crab), perhaps as fertilizer, or a misunderstanding on his part. Then three feet distant they plant as much more, and thus in succession. With this corn they put in each hill three or four Brazilian (kidney) beans . . . of different colors. When they grow up they interlace with the corn, which reaches a height of five or six feet, and they keep the ground free from weeds."[10]

John Winthrop, Jr., familiar with the practices of both Connecticut and Massachusetts Indians, adds that in the vacant places and between the hills, they later planted squashes and pumpkins, letting the cornstalks serve as beanpoles and the broadleaved squash vines smother late weeds. The natives were especially likely to do this in good ground that had been well fished before, taking advantage of the cumulative effect of continued manuring.

It is enlightening to notice how astute some Indians were in agricultural practice. In the 1700's Kalm, the Swedish scientist, found the Senecas soaking seeds in hellebore, a native drug. When robber birds ate this seed, they became dizzy and drunken, like robins that have swallowed too many dogwood fruits, and their strange conduct would frighten the other bird thieves away.[11]

A first crop having been put in the ground, additional seedings such as Champlain noticed on Cape Cod could be made at intervals. Other observers and White's watercolors give evidence that this practice was not uncommon in Indian North America.

The white oak leaf having fully unfolded, and with alewives decaying under the cornhills, growth started and the fight with the crop's enemies began. "They put up little watch houses in the middle of their fields in which they, or their oldest children lodge, and early in the morning prevent the Birds," reports Roger Williams. Some of them trained hawks to guard their fields, he notes. But the children failed to "prevent" all the birds, for crows and others usually got some of the corn seed. Another enemy was the "Mouse-Squirrell," or chipmunk, "a little creature that doth much hurt in some Fields newly planted." Later, "The Great beasts, as Stagges [deer] and other beasts, as also birds do spoile it."[12]

The English colonists had to learn from the Indians how to "worm the corn," explains Wood. He may have referred to the earworm, but

Josselyn accurately describes the cutworm: dunnish colored, an inch long and he "lyes at the root all day. You may look your eyes out sooner than find any of them." He adds the despairing comment that the only means to get rid of them is the Indian method: dig up the earth about the plant, put it in a birch dish, and set it afloat in the sea![13]

Through at least a fortnight after the corn seed was planted with fish beneath, the fields had to be guarded against the dogs of the tribe, and watched by night to keep wolves from the fish "till it be rotten, which will be in fourteen days." In Maine the Indians erected enclosures around their fields to keep out four-footed marauders. A nuisance all of this; yet "agreeing together and taking turns, it is not much," philosophizes Plymouth chronicler Edward Winslow.[14]

Caring for the crop was not altogether a dull chore. "Far from being either onerous or compulsory," comments Lucian Carr, "it was carried on much in the manner of the husking and other frolics" of English farm families. Roger Williams remarks the pleasant sociable time the women had in the fields not only at planting time but all through the season, as they followed the custom now called "changing work" with neighbors.[15]

With good treatment as to fertilizer, planting, and cultivation, the corn plant and its companions could hardly fail to cooperate. At Saco, Maine, Champlain saw corn two or three feet high on July 9. This would mark satisfactory progress for well fertilized corn today: "knee-high by The Fourth of July" is a common rule of thumb in New England. When he reached Nauset, on Cape Cod, further south and with a season earlier than Saco's, Champlain noticed corn five and a half feet tall and in flower (some planted later was less advanced). He notes that beans and squashes were of various sizes, too.

When drought appeared likely to stunt the crops, the medicine man directed prayers and dances and ceremonies with which the Indians' pleas for rain to revive the wilting corn were wafted upward, and a learned eighteenth-century observer, President Ezra Stiles of Yale, comments on their remarkable success. The practice is not dead. "I have seen the rain dance in the desert four times." I overheard a white trader say in Arizona, "and believe it or not, each time there came a big rain within a day or two." Perhaps certain medicine men were especially sensitive to atmospheric pressure changes and relative humidity.[16] Records do not tell of it, but it would be surprising if in a dry time careful squaws failed to encourage wilting crops with water from the brook or spring, carried in gourds or bark containers, as those of the desert tribes did in the West.

So with rain and shine, according to contemporary testimony, Indian crops made the good progress to be expected from plants properly sown, well fertilized, carefully weeded, and systematically tended.

The corn had to be hoed at least twice, often three times, before cultivation ceased and it was "laid by"—the first time when it was a hand's length high. At a second cultivation a little earth was drawn up to the plants, and at the third, when the first ear had started, the hill was increased further. Weeds were kept strictly out of the field by the female farmers, Champlain makes clear, until the corn was high, the beans twined up the stalks, and the squash or pumpkins planted with them had covered the ground with their big leaves and sent down roots at the joints. In weeding, the Indians "exceed our English husbandmen," Wood confesses, "Keeping it so cleare with their Clammeshell-hoes as it were a garden rather than a corne field, not suffering a choaking weede to advance his audacious head above their infant corne, or an undermining worme to spoil his spurnes." Strachey, referring to the Virginia natives, says that the women and children kept the ground weedless, and when the corn had grown middle high, hilled it about as though it were a hop yard. The soil between rows was as neat as the space between the beds of a European garden.[17]

But all was not labor and worry in the fields. John Gyles, a white captive of Maine Indians, shows how the natives staggered their duties: "Then we planted corn and after planting went a fishing and to look for and dig roots, till the corn was fit to weed. After weeding we took a second tour on the same errand, then returned to hill the corn. After hilling we went some distance up the river to take salmon and other fish, where we continued till the corn was filled with milk."[18]

By August Indian families had already been enjoying for weeks the tender fruits of summer squash and the earliest beans. They eagerly watched corn silks darken, for the Feast of the Green Corn, a time of rejoicing, was at hand.

Dances—continued all night with songs of thanksgiving and feasting on the milky kernels—might fill a week. The first potful was not for human eating: it was an offering of thanks to the spirit powers. In some North American tribes, after the vessel containing the first fruits was placed on the fire, the medicine man waved cornstalks and rattled gourds in time with the singing of the tribe. No one tasted a single kernel until the offering had been made and the sacred ears had burned to black coals.

Then a completely fresh fire was laid, more corn husked, the water bubbled again, and men, women, and children fell to on the sweet ears boiled over the new fire or roasted by its embers. As the children husked the fresh-picked corn, they might scrupulously save the silks and dry them in the sun to add a delicate flavor to next winter's stews. Not even smutty kernels were wasted. Cooked with the green corn, they were counted delicious.

More days passed: the grain filled and ripened. Mature but not yet flinty, it was at its most nutritious stage. Now part of the new crop might be picked and the ears boiled or parched by a hot fire for later use. The kernels were then sliced from the cob, dried patiently in the sun to prevent spoiling, and stored, to be ground later for travel rations or to flavor and sweeten the next winter's food. The rest of the ears, unpicked, were left to mature fully in the field.

While corn ears matured and pumpkins ripened, once more the fields must be guarded. Raccoons relish green corn at least as much as humans; likewise bears. Either would by night strip the ears systematically from every hill, while any woodchucks not previously caught would gnaw at ripening squashes.

Among other uninvited harvesters, "there is a kind like starlings," De Rasieres wrote of his visit to Plymouth, "which we call maize thieves . . . They fly in large flocks, so that they flatten the corn in any place where they light, just as if cattle had lain there." Peter Kalm in the Middle Colonies also mentions maize thieves, and says their wings shine. "The Corne will be plucked out so far as they can come to it," complains John Winthrop, Jr. These writers apparently refer to grackles and redwings, commonly called blackbirds, or perhaps to true blackbirds or crows. Blackbirds the Indians had no qualms about killing, but as noted previously, they did not shoot crows, nuisance though they were: "Although they doe the corne also some hurt, yet scarce will one Native among a hundred kill them," because of the tradition that the crow had brought them the first grain of corn in one ear and a bean in the other.[19]

As September days shortened and nights lengthened, squashes and pumpkins had to be cut and piled, to be protected should a north wind presage a frost.

Beans, too, had to be pulled and dried, and the seed flailed out with a stick. In harvesting maize the reapers could take their time: frost does not harm the dry mature grain. The women would select the best-formed and best-filled ears to keep for seed, pulling back the long husks from the ears but leaving them attached to the stem end. The stripped husks of successive ears would then be braided into a single artistic rope, or "trace," which was suspended from a truss. From this each seed ear hung free and exposed to the air. If hung in the open, seed corn will keep for several years; undamaged by heat or cold, the germ remains vital and ready to sprout when planted.

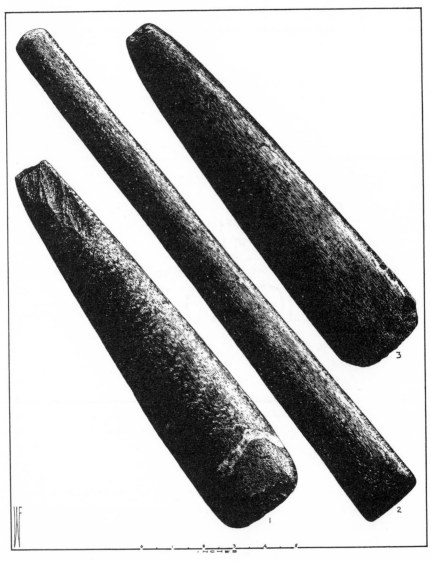

41. Tools possibly used to remove bark from trees. *BMAS*, 37 (1976), 18.

From the English pen of John Winthrop, Jr., comes a tribute to the handsome appearance of maize. It is far the most stately of all grains, he thinks (and no variety is handsomer than a long iridescent ear of New England flint). "The composure of the Eare is very beautifull . . . commonly eight rows upon the Eare and sometimes more, the number of Rowes and Grains being according to the Strength of the Ground [here Winthrop was mistaken: the number of rows is an inherited trait], the

Eare is Commonly a Span long" [nine inches]. Nine inches remains today a respectable length for an ear of flint corn, though dent corn may reach double that size.[20]

As the sun got lower and nights longer, the roots of artichokes and groundnuts had to be peeled, parboiled, dried, and stored for winter.

With crops safely harvested, the winter's stores of roots, flesh, fish, and herbs under cover, and the season's stress of labor relieved, the time had arrived for thanksgiving—tribute to the god of bounty, Cowtantowit. The tribe, or several tribes, assembled at the "place of great merrymaking" for feasting, sports, games, and dancing. Roger Williams tells what went on among the Narragansetts: "if the land be at peace . . . they set up Qun-ne-ka-muck, which signifies Long-House, sometimes a hundred, sometimes two hundred feet long near the courte, which they call Kit-Teic-Kan-ick, where many thousands, men and women, meet—where he that goes in dances in sight of all the rest, and is prepared with money, coats, small breeches, knives, or what he is able to reach to, and gives these away to the poor." While the ceremonies went forward, the crowd joined in the rhythmic "hub-hub-hub" which our forefathers borrowed as their own word for din: hubbub. At Plymouth, for the white man's first thanksgiving, the Indians joined happily in, as the Pilgrim chronicle attests.

Colored as many colonial writings were by the belief that the natives were ignorant savages, it becomes difficult to assess the true extent of the harvests, or the quality of Indian accomplishment. Good yields of corn and other crops were highly valued. The Indians sought liberal harvests. Two, three, and four ears of Indian corn to the stalk was their aim. Historical documents show that frequently they must have succeeded.

The Plymouth Pilgrims again and again bought corn raised by the Indians who lived on sandy Cape Cod: over 28 hogsheads of it in 1622. On Block Island, off the Rhode Island coast, Captain John Underhill found "great heaps of pleasant corn ready shelled." The Massachusetts Bay Puritans bought 500 bushels in one transaction. In Connecticut in 1636, Colonel John Endecott destroyed heavy crops of corn on what the white settlers later named Corn Neck. In 1637 the English and their Mohegan allies returned from a raid on the Pequots near Mystic with big booty in corn. The English loaded their barks with it. Their Indian allies filled twenty dugout canoes with corn alone. William Pynchon bargained with the Pocumtucks at Deerfield in 1638, and they ferried down 500 bushels to the Connecticut pioneers at Hartford. (This was in March, so it must have come from storage.)

Over on the Hudson River twenty years earlier, Henry Hudson had been astonished at the "great stores of corn" of the New York

Indians. De Laet estimated the corn and beans at one "house" at what is now Hudson, New York, as "sufficient to load three ships." In addition to the great quantity of the previous year's growth, more was growing in the fields.[21] The New Amsterdam Hollanders, short of food, like Pynchon bought corn from the Indians. Such records should dispel the too common notion that the Indian merely tickled the ground, lived for today, and took no thought for the future. Sheldon, the historian of Deerfield, has properly characterized the Connecticut Valley Indians as "agricultural people, industrious and provident," and they were by no means the only groups deserving such adjectives.

As to the rate of yield the natives obtained, Gookin at Wabbaquasset in Connecticut in the seventeenth century tells of forty bushels to the acre. Careful calculations indicate that such yields may not have been uncommon in favorable years. Individual Natick Indian crops ran from six to fifteen barrels, averaging eleven barrels, or close to thirty bushels per family. If the family corn grounds averaged an acre, a figure mentioned by an early explorer, this would represent a respectable yield.

Like all farmers, the Indians had occasional unproductive seasons; yet given the quantity of fish manure applied by at least some tribes and the care used in culture, yields in good seasons must have been abundant.[22]

Cultivated crops were far from the only harvests. All through the summer the children, competing with bears and deer, picked berries and fruit. Much of it they and their elders ate at once, fresh or baked in cakes. With some, perhaps, they flavored summer drinks. Great quantities, however, especially of blueberries and strawberries, they dried for winter use.

Along the shore, before frosts became severe, children harvested the bitter beach plum, and scarlet cranberries in the fresh marshes. The chiefs of the tribe perhaps set the date for gathering them, just as the selectmen of Gay Head, the Indian town on Martha's Vineyard, are said to do to this day.

As the sharp weather of October and November came on, the tribe vied with squirrels in putting away the abundant beechnuts, chestnuts, walnuts, butternuts, and acorns that plumped into the dry leaves. If the squirrels won, the family could later eat the squirrels, as well as the bears, who were also fond of nuts.

To shell flint corn the ears could be rubbed one against another, or grated against a stone. In Connecticut the natives commonly shelled corn as they gathered it, and spread it on mats in the sun to dry. To prepare it for winter storage, they covered it (perhaps the part picked before full maturity) with mats at night and opened it when the sun was hot.

Storing the Yield

During the years after World War II, in the discussion that filled the public prints about storing the immense surplus of grain accumulated by the United States government, one of the oldest and cheapest storage methods seems to have been overlooked: a hole, dug in dry or well drained earth.

In the Book of Genesis, Joseph's jealous brothers threw him into a dry pit, from which an Egyptian rescued him. Scholars think that it was an empty, underground grain-storage pit. Many peoples, both ancient and modern, in North America and in widely separated parts of the world, have stored grain and other articles of value in such pits. It was a practice not only of the Israelites and the Chaldeans in Asia Minor, but of the ancient Romans; of the ancestors of the Germans, French, and Britons in Europe; of Siberians in the Far East. In modern times, Fijians in Oceania, Kaffirs in Africa, and in North America, nineteenth-century Iroquois in Canada—all have stored supplies below ground. In

42. Aboriginal storage pits, Ware River Valley, Massachusetts. (Dividing lines superimposed). *BMAS*, 23 (1962), 48.

using the pit barn for keeping food through the winter, New England Indians were by no means unique.[23]

Governor William Bradford of Plymouth indicates one aspect of the method: "Their stores of corn are contained in great hempen bags, capable of holding five or six bushels"; but a Pilgrim party dug up carefully buried smaller baskets holding three or four bushels each.[24]

Light on the details of Indian storage is afforded by the observations of J. H. Temple. Writing in 1887 on North Brookfield, Massachusetts, on the Ware River—a town near which remains of numerous earth granaries have been found—[25] he describes the Indian barns as circular excavations from five to ten feet deep, the small ones three to five feet across and the larger ones ten to fifteen feet wide. Where the soil was tenacious and not likely to cave in, the sides converged slightly. In sandy soil it was common to line the sides with a coating of clay mortar, hardened by fire. Even in the present century this clay is sometimes found unbroken. Baked clay receptacles have been reported in southern Vermont, on Long Island, and in Woodstock, Connecticut. In Rhode Island pits have been found lined with stone, on the Massachusetts Bay South Shore with mats, in Canada with bark, in the Northwest with straw. On Iroquois village sites pits are frequent, it is said, among the Illinois. The French in 1679 noticed pits under the floor of every wigwam in a large town. Commonly in New England the pits were set into the sloping sides of a knoll or a bank so as to be dry and to shed rain. The caches were dug close together so that the contents could be protected from bears and other enemies by a picket fence. At Barre Plains in central Massachusetts, in a dry ridge, Temple notes, "the remains of fifteen Indian barns were still to be seen a century ago, for this was apparently an important Indian store town." Erosion of the adjoining river bank by the 1938 hurricane revealed what were believed to be others. The women sometimes concealed storehouses by pouring water on the soil above, or by building fires above them to remove all evidence of soil dislocation.[26]

At Chatham on Cape Cod, Champlain pictures a similar operation. They made trenches five or six feet deep in the sand on the slope of hills. Then they put their corn and other grains in large grass sacks, deposited them in the trenches, and piled sand overhead three or four feet above the surface, taking out what they needed from time to time. The food was preserved as well as it would have been in French granaries. Wood describes the stores as great holes shaped like a brass pot, dug in the ground and lined with bark. A white captive in Maine, John Gyles, himself had a hand in preparing and filling such an Indian barn.[27]

At Northfield, Massachusetts, in the Connecticut Valley, buried containers of a more lasting sort have been discovered in modern times with the contents in excellent condition. Corn, beans, pumpkin seeds, and other food had been stored in pots underground, with rawhide lashed over their tops. Across the line at South Vernon, Vermont, two ten-foot square pits have been found dug in a bank, their floors of hard pounded clay.[28]

Under some circumstances, New England Indians also stored corn above ground. In 1638, after harvest, Captain Mason marched against the new Pequot village on the Pawcatuck River. He found "the wigwams stored with abundance of corn." Four decades later another military leader, Captain Benjamin Church, commanded an expedition against a Narragansett fort. "There was a hovel inside the fort," he relates, "built after the manner of a corncrib" (the fort was in the recesses of a swamp) "and full of grain."[29]

Aboveground storage was common in other parts of North America as well. Henry Hudson came upon a bark house filled with corn and beans in 1608 when he discovered the river called by his name; sixteen years later the Dutch Van Curler described native houses on the river bank used for the same purpose. John Lamson (1714) saw houses made without windows by Virginia Indians for granaries and storages.

Some Iroquois cured corn in their cabins on long poles over smoky fires kept going day and night, drying but also darkening the kernels. Later they would shell it and put it in "great casks of bark," to be stored on high ground in tower-like granaries ventilated by numerous openings. Cartier in 1535 from Montreal recorded a similar method.[30]

The New England tribes, however, storing chiefly in the ground, kept not only corn and beans but squashes and other fruits thus protected from freezing. A modern counterpart would be the pit cellar, common on farms up to recent years for root vegetables, cabbages, and apples. None of this would have been possible if the rat, the scourge of the Old World, had been among the animals of the New. Just how the New England tribes arranged to keep uncured fruits and vegetables local records do not make clear, but evidence comes from elsewhere. Father Lafitau tells of the Iroquois to the westward piling pumpkins in bark-lined underground storages five feet deep and says that "their fruits keep perfectly sound during the winter." Le Jeune, without telling how, records that the squash sometimes lasted four or five months. On the plains of the Northwest, the Hidatsa placed squashes in the center of their underground storages, packing corn all around. Near the Great Lakes, Carver records that craneneck squash "which greatly exceed all others," are usually hung up for the winter's store and might be thus preserved for several months.

Nineteenth-century Menomini (Algonquian) cut squashes into

strips, dried them, then braided them. Peter Kalm says that these would keep for years. The Pima of the Southwest had different methods for ripe and unripe squashes. They sliced and dried the unripe fruit, later restoring succulence by soaking before cooking. Or they removed the seeds through the stem end, peeled and dried the fruit, cut the flesh into spiral strips, and dried the strips on poles, twisting them into hanks for storing.[31]

The Meskwaki, in Wisconsin, split the squash or pumpkin, sliced it in rings, strung these on poles, and dried them in the sun. Then they plaited the rings and spread the plaits on a mat on the ground, with another mat on top. A woman treaded the top mat till she flattened the whole, then dried the plaited masses further and put them away for the winter.[32]

Not only cereals, squash, roots, and other vegetable food, but dried fruits, nuts and acorns, and supplies of meat and fish went into storage—especially fish, dried or smoked on tall frames out of reach of dogs and wild animals. As for meat, no such plenitude was available (or needed) for storage in New England as Catlin saw in the West, where the Indians stored buffalo meat by the thousands of pounds. Neal does describe the drying and storage of moose meat in northern New England; and some Indians dried deer meat. Yet most New England tribes are not reported as preparing anything like the high-caloric mixture of dried ground buffalo meat and berries of the West, or the dried moose flesh, fat, and berry combination called pemmican by Hudson Bay Indians. With nourishing maize foods and plenty of fish usually available, perhaps they were not needed.[32]

Curing fish and shellfish, however, was common practice among all New England tribes. All kinds—salt-water and fresh, lobsters, clams, and oysters—were processed and stored when abundant. A favorite protein food of New England's nineteenth century, smoked salmon, now displaced by Pacific canned varieties, was only one of the most abundant of the many fish foods that the Indians habitually cured by smoking.

Fall Hunting

Fresh meat, however, was another matter. Once the harvests of the fields were safely in, the Indian males, old and young, could turn to hunting, since flesh of animals and fowl would then spoil less readily. Morning and evening were the times for ducks and geese. Following well-known flyways, these birds settled at night in river meadows and salt marshes, or rested at ease on the smooth water. The hunters would drift in quietly in canoes, light torches to cause sudden confusion among the birds, and knock them down with clubs or paddles. Then a specially trained canoe dog, sitting in the bow, would jump into the water and retrieve the game. The turkey was plentiful in the woods in Indian times (though by 1840 the colonists had exterminated the wild bird), feeding on chestnuts, acorns, and insects. Indians were able to get close by a precise imitation of the bird's call.[33]

Trails led hunters to the open inland pastures, already mentioned, where grass and browse had been encouraged so that deer might fatten on them, and bears on the blueberries they loved. In the fertile upland town of New Braintree, in central Massachusetts, where hundreds of dairy cattle have grazed each summer in verdant pastures, and in nearby Warren and Brimfield, tradition says that when the whites first came, the slopes of the gentle hills were at least as bare of trees as in the twentieth century. The Brimfield valley when settlers first saw it also had a rank growth of grass. From the top of Coy's Hill in neighboring Brookfield, at the time of the first settlement, the landscape was so open that a searcher could discover one of his beasts astray anywhere in the Ware River Valley. For no one knows how many generations or centuries the Indians had held these fields in permanent deer pasture. In the Narragansett Bay area one of King Philip's hunting grounds was at Raynham, Massachusetts, twenty-five miles inland.[34]

A bitter Indian complaint from the Canassatogoe, at a parley in Lancaster, Pennsylvania, makes it clear that this was no uncommon practice. "We are poor," the Canassatogoe chief said to the white governors of that territory, "and shall always remain so, as long as . . . the white people's cattle eat up all the grass and make deer scarce." The first settlers in Virginia's Cumberland Valley found great stretches of open grassland, and paid Indians to hunt game there for their tables.[35]

With such pastures and browse as a lure for deer and the chance of meeting an occasional moose, the hunters gathered. Under some experienced leader they arranged a concerted drive to concentrate any deer in the vicinity so as to get the greatest kill with the least effort. After the deer were brought down, the squaws were expected to carry them to a temporary camp close by. There meat, skins, and bones could be prepared for their multitudinous later uses and borne back to the winter village. Further north and in Maine, moose hunting was a late winter occupation. Even Connecticut Valley Indians pushed up the river into what is now Vermont to hunt moose in the snow.[36] In most of New England, by the time really bitter weather came, the tribes had long since left any temporary camping place and returned to snug cabins in sunny nooks. Women and children had earlier gathered wood for the fire, often from a considerable distance, and piled it at hand. The

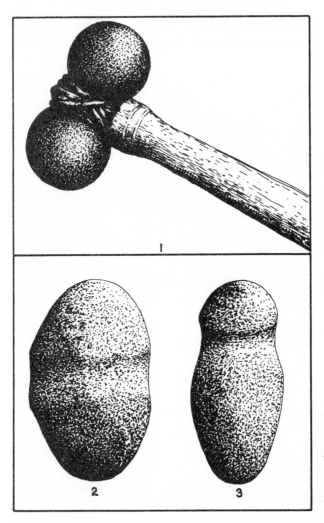

43. Ball-headed clubs. *1*, original haft, Connecticut; *2*, Greenbush, Rhode Island; *3*, Portsmouth, Rhode Island. *BMAS*, 12 (1951), 34.

storage pits were filled. Let the wind howl and snow blow, the Indian family was prepared to live and live well. "These people are not without providence," acknowledges the improvident Thomas Morton, "though they be uncivilized, but are careful to preserve food in store against winter."

Among the nonagricultural Northern Abenaki people of the north, however, hunting on snowshoes went on all winter, when depth of snow made it more difficult for moose and deer to escape.

During the winter the wife would have time to work up leather for clothing, moccasins, and snowshoes, and to plait baskets. On a proper day the brave would fish through the ice in a nearby pond or lake, or bring in over the snow a pair of squirrels. But mostly he stayed close to the good food that his wife had hung about the living quarters in the cabin and buried in underground barns to be opened from the south side on a sunny day. The skilled tool-maker entertained himself with chipping and sharpening a supply of stone tools and arrowheads; another might hollow out a canoe log or prepare fishnets to be used when spring returned. The children played with the dogs and listened carefully while their elders filled their memory with the legends of their people and the lore of woods, wind, and weather.

The winter would pass, and the season's round begin once more.

Part Five

INTERRELATIONS

18.

Trade and Conflict

There was little reason for one Indian group to trade with another. Wildlife, the soil, the waters, and their products provided every tribe with the necessities for human life. Beyond these the natives had few wants.

The desire for adornment, however, and the need to have permanent reminders of agreements and to make relations with other tribes agreeable through friendly gifts, resulted in a wide distribution of shell beads known as wampumpeague. These beads were cylindrical bits of two sorts of shell: the more desirable black, from the quahog or hardshell clam, rounded, smoothed, and pierced lengthwise; and the less favored light or white, from the mouth of the periwinkle shell. The black had twice the value of the white. Of these the Narragansetts and Block Islanders produced the best quality. They collected the shells in summer and in winter shaped, smoothed, and drilled them into beads, which they strung, and then wove the strings into belts, ornaments, and necklaces. By gift or barter these found their way as far inland as Wisconsin or even the Dakotas, and south to Virginia.

With the advent of Europeans—in the first instance the New Netherland Hollanders, but all with an insatiable appetite for beaver skins—the allure of the beads for the natives caused wampum to be widely used as currency, a medium of exchange. For a long period it had stable value: three black beads or six white to the English penny; gathered in a string as they commonly were arranged, sixty beads to the foot. Josselyn said that even the devil could not counterfeit it, but some did. As a result, in the course of (historic) time, the Narragansetts came to be termed "rich"; their wampum was eventually counterfeited. The use of wampum as money, even among the English, continued until the Revolution. It is a matter of doubt, though, whether before the arrival of Europeans and the beaver trade, wampum had value other than for personal decoration and ceremonial use. Important matters such as treaty agreements were likely to be marked by an exchange of wampum belts, with designs in the two colors, which thereafter served as visual reminders of the event itself, and to call to memory the arrangements agreed on.[1]

A second category of native exchange, though considerably less common, was copper and objects of adornment made of it. Outcrops of copper are exceedingly rare in New England. The desire for the red metal, to be made into belts and ornaments and to point spears and arrows, brought small amounts from as far away as the Great Lakes. A copper gorget has even been recovered in Vermont. For tools and arrowheads the copper was hammered out, then tempered by annealing. Yet to judge by the wealth of stone artifacts that archaeologists today discover, the use of copper was by comparison light.[2]

Among commodities that entered into trade, another was tobacco pipes. Some were blue, some white, some of steatite (soapstone), a mineral not difficult to work and possessing the advantage of being unaffected by fire. The Indians also made pipes of clay. The stem might be of reed and as much as two feet long, so that the bowl would rest on the knee or the ground (Williams). The bowl might be plain—or its surface might be ornamented with figures of beasts, birds, or men—and either sculptured or etched by a sharp-edged tool.[3]

Since pipes and smoking were part of ordinary hospitality as well as of intertribal gatherings, there was wide distribution of attractive specimens by gift or barter, and New England archaeological collections often display not only local pipes but examples from the South and West. Domestic pottery was another type of possession which, if not actually acquired from other regions, showed their influence, especially that of the Iroquois, in art and design.

Aside from pipes and pottery, the influence of the powerful Iroquois confederacy, concentrated around the lakes of Western New York, reached into and across New England. By the beginning of English settlement Iroquois power had become so great that some of the local Indians considered the coming of the English fortunate and their protection welcome. The Iroquois were of different blood and culture from the Algonquians and spoke a different language. They had advanced in the art of government to the point where in the fifteenth century fifty years before Columbus five contiguous tribes (later six) had joined to form a league that ensured internal peace and overawed its neighbors. Whether their power over an extensive territory of neighbors came chiefly because of their combined strength or, as some historians suggest, because of their purchase of firearms from the Hollanders before their Indian neighbors had acquired them from the French and English, is not clear.[4] It is certain, however, that by the time the English arrived, the fertile and attractive Champlain area of Vermont had become uninhabited except for villages at Swanton (Missisquoi). The pleasant upper Connecticut Valley, except for a Squakheag or Sokoki village at Vernon just above the present Massachusetts line and a Cowassuck settlement at Newbury, was lightly inhabited. In the seventeenth century many of Vermont's valleys were deserted and served tribes from the South as a beaver hunting ground and for moose tracking. At Vernon in Vermont and Northfield in Massachusetts, the Squakheags had villages. At Deerfield the populous Pocumtucks continued to live and farm under a treaty with the Mohawks or Maquas, nearest of the Iroquois tribes. Eventually, well into historic time, as a result of French influence from Canada, disagreement arose and the Pocumtucks refused tribute. After Mohawk ambassadors were somehow slain, the latter tribe struck and destroyed the villages and their people.[5]

The Indian population of the lower Connecticut Valley as far south as Wethersfield, with ten Algonquian subtribes, had earlier come to be so much in fear of the Mohawks that a Connecticut chief traveled to Plymouth and Boston to invite the English with their firearms to settle there, and both Plymouth and Massachusetts Bay governments accepted the invitation. Yet the power of the Mohawks by no means ended at the Connecticut River. Their emissaries collected tribute among the scattered Nipmuck villages of central Massachusetts, among the Pennacooks of New Hampshire, and among the Indians of Maine.

In hilly western Connecticut and Massachusetts the valleys had been once inhabited, then deserted. After the advent of the English made them safer, Mahicans repeopled some of them. The Mohawks were not the sole oppressors, however. After the pestilence of 1616-17 weakened the Massachusetts and their neighbors, the Tarrantines, Abenaki from the Canadian provinces, were likely to invade by sea and, as far west as Massachusetts Bay, rob the Massachusetts of their crops. When Roger Conant and his small company arrived at Cape Ann and Salem about 1626, the local Indians welcomed the newcomers as protectors, and shared their cornfields.

It is not easy to determine with certainty the extent of war among New England's natives before the advent of Europeans. Some students of their life and habits conclude that they were not by nature warlike and that most tribes avoided fighting. Yet jealousy or enmity between populous powerful tribes appear from time to time to have brought on conflict. Where Connecticut and Rhode Island meet, there the Pequots squeezed and divided the Niantics and Nipmucks. When in 1637 the English made war on the Pequots, destroyed their principal village and fort, and confiscated their corn, a company of jealous subtribe Mohegans acted as guides and scouts and rejoiced at the breakup of the Pequots as a tribe. A band of the surviving Pequots, forced out of New England, found a home eventually beside Lake Winnebago in Wisconsin, where George Catlin found 400 of them living, "having brought with them from their former country (New England) a knowledge of agriculture which they had effectually learned and practiced."[6]

This is not the sole recorded conflict. All was peace about Massachusetts Bay when the English arrived, but the Massachusetts had formerly been at war with both tribes south of them, the Wampanoags and the Narragansetts, and the latter two had warred with each other, Williams tells of naval warfare, with forty or fifty dugouts filled with warriors on each side. The Gookin narrative, by contrast, remarks on the good feeling between the Massachusetts and their northern neighbors, the Pawtuckets or Pennacooks, of the Merrimac and Androscoggin valleys. It is clear, therefore, that the various tribes had from time to time battled or displaced one another even though speaking dialects of a common language.

Indians in war employed three chief tactics: surprise, ambush, and stratagem. An Algonquian village might suppose the Mohawks to be 200 miles distant, yet an onslaught at dawn could bring disaster. Or, beating off an enemy and in hot pursuit, the defenders might run into an ambush in a ravine or swamp where escape was almost out of the question. Judging from the vividly recorded experience of the English, the only limit to the variety of stratagems used to beguile and trap a foe was the imagination and resolution of the enemy. However, given the often equal wile and skill of their opponents, losses would seldom be as heavy proportionately as those of a European battlefield, with its close formations of artillery, cavalry, and foot soldiers.

To avoid the possibility of undetected attack, an Indian village was likely to be located on a hill, with open land about it, and perhaps also protected by a stockade. Two such are reported overlooking planting fields at Agawam opposite Springfield and there were three Pennacook forts above the Merrimac near Franklin, New Hampshire. Another was that of Sassacus, chief of the Pequots, set on an eminence between the Mystic and Thames estuaries on the Connecticut shore. A clear description of this one has come down to us because of the surprise attack on the stronghold and its unsuspecting occupants by Captain John Mason on July 16, 1637, and the destruction that resulted. On the open hilltop the Pequots had built a village of seventy wigwams. Knowing the enmity borne them by their subject Mohegans, they surrounded the two-acre area with a palisade of tree trunks ten feet high and sunk three feet deep into the ground, pierced by loopholes for marksmen and having only two openings. It was so heavily supplied with food and necessaries stored from the previous season that the victors bore away a large stock.[7]

The record of King Philip's war tells that on December 18, 1675,

Captain Benjamin Church and a company of English assisted by friendly Indians took unawares a much larger fort of the Narragansetts at South Kingstown, Rhode Island. On a five-acre island in the midst of a great swamp, a formidable tree-trunk stockade enclosed a village of 500 cabins, reached only by a single bridge. Here again, by a surprise attack, this time in a December snowstorm, the English gained entrance and set the mat-and-rush-covered wigwams afire. A holocaust resulted.[8]

Both these examples of fort building occurred in historic times; the defenses may therefore bear the mark of European as well as native influence. Indeed a renegade colonist, Joshua Tift, was accused of supervising the Kingstown work and was executed by the English. However, forts in other parts of eastern North America are known to date from prehistoric times.

By contrast, although Champlain in his account of the New England Indians mentions a stockade at Saco, neither his maps nor written descriptions record defensive works at Gloucester or Plymouth, or on Cape Cod. If Gloucester was a village of the numerous and powerful Pawtuckets, this would account for its openness. Plymouth was under the jurisdiction of the Wampanoags, and Chatham under the related Nausets. War by the allied Massachusetts and Wampanoags against the Narragansetts had been known in the past, but at the time of Champlain's visit all appear to have been at peace. The Saco tribe had predatory Down-East neighbors, however, and the Mohawks were perhaps demanding tribute from them, as they did later.

Certain local earthworks and ditches remaining from former times have been traditionally considered Indian forts. Yet it appears more likely that most if not all such earthworks are of colonial origin, sometimes intended to enclose or restrict cattle. It is to be kept in mind that the amount of ditching involved would have been a considerable feat to accomplish with Indian stone or wood picks and shovels. All in all, in Indian warfare surprise was the most effective offense, watchfulness the best defense.

"Their weapons heretofore were bows and arrows, clubs, and tomahawks, made of wood like a pole axe [indicating a long handle] with a sharpened stone fastened therein," Gookin says. Wood describes a tomahawk that was slightly different but equally lethal: the handle or pole was about two and one-half feet long, and its deadly work was done by "a knob at one end as round and bigge as a football [of that period] . . . one blow or thrust will not neede a second to hasten death." Among the Penobscots whom Speck studied two centuries later the knob Wood speaks of might be natural, formed by trimming the enlargement at ground level of the roots of a birch and left attached to the lower end of the trunk, or perhaps with a stone imbedded. In the hands of a strong man this could crack a skull, whether of man or beast.[9]

It is clear that the original tomahawk was a very different instrument from the iron or steel axe that today is known as a tomahawk and is so pictured. The latter was European, not native, and did not appear until historic time, when traders furnished axes to the Indians in exchange for furs.

As for bows and arrows, tradition is more nearly correct. A bow might be from three to as much as six feet tall (one colonial observer estimated seven) and notched at each end. The shorter type was for hunting, the longer for war. Several light, strong woods are recorded:

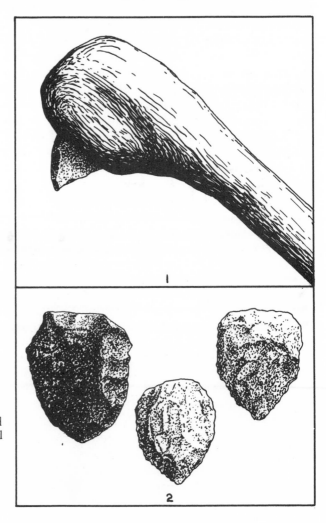

44. *1,* Stone-pronged wooden clubs, original haft, Connecticut; *2,* Points for clubs, Greenbush, Rhode Island. *BMAS,* 12 (1951), 34.

hickory, beech, white ash, rock maple, witch hazel—all tough, yet limber enough to give the arrow its spring. The cord that bound the notches together at each end was of sinew. The bow-maker doubled a strip of sinew, perhaps chewing it first to make it pliable, and rolled it tightly against his thigh to make a long twist. Then he looped it at the proper distance into the notches or holes prepared at the two ends of the bow. He carried it in his left hand. James Rosier tells that once when an Indian let him try his bow, he found that the spring of the bow would carry his arrow "five or six score yards strongly."[10]

For the arrow the maker would pick a straight, slender, dried alder sprout two or three feet long, or split out the heart of a section of white ash or white cedar, both of which split straight. He might bring one end to a point, leaving the other end thicker. More likely he would notch one end and drive in a thin, sharp bit of a chippable stone—flint or quartz (Verrazano said emery, jasper, or hard marble)—or an eagle claw or a slender bit of bone from a deer's shank. Brereton saw copper arrowheads also. The arrow-maker would decorate the back end with from two to five half-feathers split lengthwise, from a crow or a hawk, the shaft between. When he shot, he would draw the arrow back against the bowstring with his thumb and forefinger.[11] To make sure there would be no dispute as to who brought down the goose or the deer, as a final touch he engraved his mark somewhere, and hoped to retrieve the arrow for a second use.

The brave carried his stock of arrows, as many as forty or fifty perhaps, in a leather or rush quiver at his shoulder, either front or back, where he could promptly reach up the opposite hand and grasp one. If his tribe was at war, he would very likely wear over his heart a shield of two or three thicknesses of untanned dry rawhide which the sharpest arrow could not pierce.[12]

Partly to make his appearance ferocious, partly perhaps to make himself less visible among the foliage and shadows of the forest, for war the brave painted his skin, just as the modern soldier adopts camouflage. Mention should also be made of the dog, which was useful in certain types of hunting.

Cruelty in war and the torture of captives cannot be gainsaid. The gruesome accounts of the torture of captured colonists tend to create a picture of deliberately vicious treatment of enemies by New England Indians. The widespread use of torture by the Iroquois Five Nations to the west about this period is well documented; therefore, once the Iroquois had entered New England and harassed the natives, retaliation against them by eastern Indians might be expected. Cases of torture of individual captives such as are recorded in accounts of colonial wars may well have occurred before the arrival of Europeans.

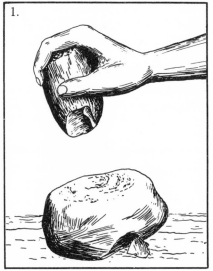

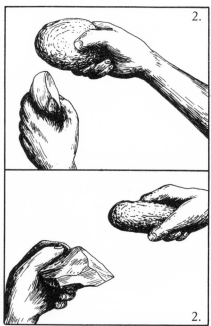

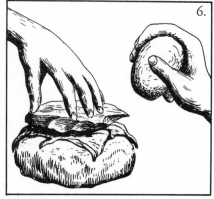

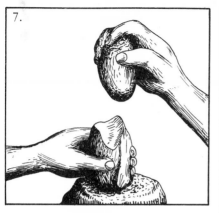

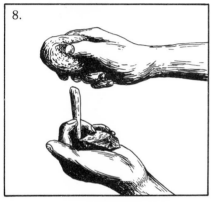

45. Methods of chipping stone to make tools and weapons. *1*, direct percussion on "anvil"; *2*, direct percussion using hammerstone; *3*, direct percussion using hafted stone hammer; *4*, direct percussion using hafted antler; *5*, direct percussion using billet; *6*, direct percussion flatwise on anvil; *7*, direct percussion edgewise on anvil; *8*, indirect percussion, one man; *9*, indirect percussion, two men. *BMAS*, 24 (1963), 61-63.

On the other hand, Nathaniel Knowles, who has made an exhaustive study of documents on the subject for the entire eastern United States and Canada, concludes that evidence is lacking to show that the eastern Algonquian tribes practiced systematic torture as distinct from brutality (on which there is no dispute) before they were harassed by the Iroquois. Another student of Algonquian culture, Regina Flannery, earlier voiced a similar conclusion.[13]

Torture did not ordinarily extend to women and children. The victors were likely to add these to their own tribe to increase its numbers and food potential.

The taking of scalps as war trophies is not mentioned by the earliest writers on New England. The practice appears to have developed, or at least increased, as a proof of death in order that the scalper might collect rewards offered by French and English. The first printed reference, according to the Oxford English Dictionary, is in 1670.

19.
Travel and Communication

The Indian's crowning achievement in handicraft was the canoe. Having no wheeled vehicle or beast of burden, but dwelling in a country indented by numerous safe harbors and interspersed with a multitude of lakes and streams, New England's natives carried travel by water to a high degree of perfection. European observers gave their artistically shaped, lightweight birch bark canoes unstinted admiration.

The shell of the canoe ideally was one long, wide strip of bark from the trunk of a single white birch. Making a vertical slit in the tree's bark of the intended length of the canoe, perhaps twenty feet, was the first step. Gradual separation of the bark from the trunk followed, with care not to split or gouge the sheet. Bearing the strip to the spot where the canoe was to be fashioned, the builders first flattened the bark gently, then, between two rows of stakes, gave it a canoe's rough shape. With ingenious tools and methods, the gunwales, thwarts, ribs, and lining of white cedar were installed, and the lines of the sides and the ends determined. Wooden pegs and root fibers fastened the two pointed ends together. Any openings were sewn together with thread of tamarack root. All was finally sealed with pitch, one hand of the worker holding a hot coal inserted in a cleft stick, the thumb of the other hand pressing in gum to stop any opening in the bark. The result was a handsome craft, its nose made rising, as Lescarbot describes it; of a size to hold three or four persons. It was highly maneuverable, yet light enough (perhaps as little as 60 pounds, at most 100) to be borne across a portage on the shoulders of a single person. If intended for poling against a swift current, width would be reduced. A paddle of maple or spruce about two yards long in the hands of the boatman furnished both motive power and steering. Catlin, on his northwestern tour in a later century, admiring the craft of the Chippewas, rated the birch bark canoe "the most beautiful light model of all the water craft that ever were invented." Who would differ, at least as to a craft for fresh water? And Wood tells of their dexterous use among sea waves also.[1] They would "endure an incredibly great sea," as Josselyn put it, "mounting upon the working billows like a piece of cork." Where birch was not available or haste was needed, a canoe of elm or spruce bark or moose hide would serve as a substitute. For sea employment the length would be twenty

46. Penobscot Indian birch bark canoe, historic period previous to 1830. Courtesy of Peabody Museum of Salem, Massachusetts. The canoe was presented to the Museum in 1835. How much earlier Indian builders may have constructed it is unknown. This date was only three quarters of a century after the first colonial settler arrived at Bangor—a place where Indians congregated—hence it appears reasonable to conclude that the materials, lines, and structure follow original native patterns. However, its builders appear to have shaped and smoothed ribs and sheathing with metal rather than original native tools.

feet or more, the width perhaps as much as four feet, the bottom flat, and fitted with a stone anchor and a fiber rope.

Champlain reports birch bark canoes in Maine, and as far south as Thacher's Island off Cape Ann. Beyond that point, however, the canoe became a dugout, more suitable for salt water waves and used even for whaling. Roger Williams in Rhode Island offers indirect evidence of the division, a result at least partly of a scarcity of white birch south of the Merrimac. His lexicon of Indian words includes separate terms for pine, oak, and chestnut canoes, but none for one of birch bark. At New Amsterdam De Vries reported bark canoes for four or five persons, presumably up the Hudson where the white birch would be found; but he also records boats hollowed out of tree trunks. "I have frequently seen eighteen or twenty seated in a hollow log," he wrote. In fact he himself had fashioned one large enough to carry 225 bushels of maize. Another writer gives the dimensions of a certain pine canoe as 20 feet long and 2½ feet wide; but John Winthrop records a Long Island dugout that held eighty men. Williams lists several sizes between.[2]

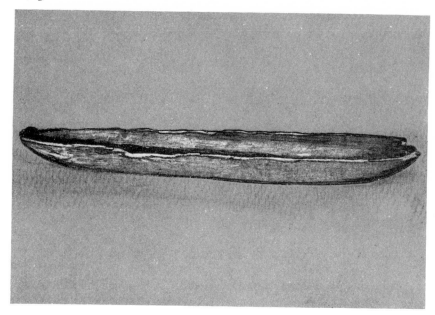

47. Indian dugout canoe, discovered in Weymouth Great Pond, South Weymouth, Massachusetts, in 1965. It was made around A.D. 1400 from a single white pine, by means of stone and shell tools and fire. *Length*: 10 feet, 11 inches overall. *Beam*: 2 feet, 3 inches. *Inside depth*: 10¼ x 11¾ inches. *Weight*: approximately 290 pounds. Courtesy of Chester B. Kevitt and Weymouth Historical Commission. A similar dugout in the possession of the New Hampshire Antiquarian Society, Hopkinton, N. H. is 14½ feet long; width 22 inches, tapering to 20.

Even using steel tools, to complete such a wooden vessel would have been a formidable task. Champlain explains the way the natives went at it: "After cutting down at the cost of much labor the largest and tallest tree they can find, by means of stone hatchets . . . they remove the bark and round off the tree except on one side, where they apply fire gradually along its entire length and sometimes put red-hot pebble-stones on top." Then with stone chisels and scrapers they remove the charred wood and begin afresh, using what in the previous century Verrazano had termed "admirable skill." To finish, Wood states, they smooth the whole with clam and oyster shells. Williams tells how an Indian would go off into the woods with his tools, a bag of corn, and flints for fire; he would fell a chestnut, make a boat from its trunk, and in ten or twelve days get his friends to help bring out the finished craft. The paddle might be of birch where that grew, otherwise of ash or maple.[3]

Verrazano and Champlain speak of dugout-building in the summer, but Phineas Pratt, a later colonial, called it a job "done amidst the snow." A birch bark canoe, on the other hand, was best fashioned in warm weather, when the bark was less stiff, and under a shady tree.

For winter travel snowshoes of white ash with hide mesh permitted a five-mile-an-hour steady gait. Among the Abenaki of the north an ash

48. Hollowing a dugout canoe. Simulated diorama. *Town Crier* photo.

or birch toboggan drawn by a strap from the hunter's chest brought back the deer.

The forest primeval before New England history was written down was far from trackless. Between the numerous Indian villages with their cultivated fields and from one harbor, pond, fishing place, clam bed, or hunting ground to another, well-trodden "little brown paths went winding." Often they had been worn deep by the passage of countless thousands of feet over centuries. A fleet messenger might press a hundred miles over them in a single day. Along them also the plodding squaw with her little ones could slowly bear essential family chattels from the winter village to and from the salmon falls, the clam bed, and the oyster harbor. By their means in the fall she brought home to the village the deer and bear her husband and sons had taken in the tribal hunt.

Except in Maine, Vermont, and northern New England in general, travel by water was limited. In tidal waters, on lakes, ponds, and the largest rivers, the birch canoe or pine dugout offered easy transportation in summer. For portage from one lake or stream to another the shortest or least laborious route would be well known. But New England's surface is hilly and broken; all but the largest watercourses are likely to have steep or stony beds. The water, for most of the summer, is often shallow, and falls are frequent. During the four months or more of winter, ice makes rivers useless for canoe travel, though suitable at times for snowshoes. As a result, paths were likely to follow alongside the principal water courses.[4]

Paths led also across country from one river valley to another, between or over mountains, where usable streams were absent. For safety the path might skirt the side of a hill or wind along the crest of a range rather than follow a stream. Footpaths thus crisscrossed the New England country in all directions, from the Atlantic to the Hudson and from Long Island Sound to the St. Lawrence Valley. No signboard or tree blaze marked them: for an Indian, markers were not needed.

By means of these widespread paths, King Philip's warriors in 1676 could appear as if by magic to burn one frontier town after another, then as suddenly melt away. The New York Iroquois could cross the Berkshires or the Green Mountains to bring terror to the Indians of inland Massachusetts, New Hampshire, and Maine. In the French and Indian Wars, over well-known ancient paths and waterways, the Indians from northern Vermont and the St. Lawrence Valley, of Abenaki blood and allied with the French, again and again attacked New England villages, then transported their white captives swiftly to Montreal. Trade went on from tribe to tribe; wampum from Atlantic

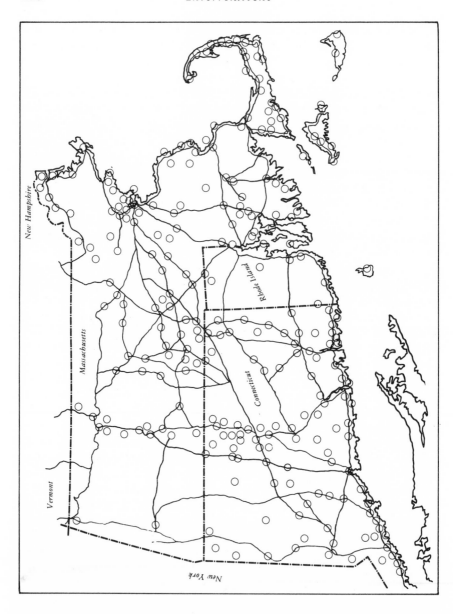

49. A compilation (incomplete) of recorded Indian trails and villages in southern New England as the seventeenth century began.

Coast Indians might serve as currency in the Dakotas, as noted, while Minnesota copper found its way east to turn up in Algonquian graves.

It was by use of these immemorial ways, not, as some historians have imagined, by trail blazing, that English colonists from Massachusetts Bay reached and founded Hartford, Springfield, Providence, Lancaster, Concord, and Wolfeboro in New Hampshire, and many another promising spot for settlement. As one result, Indian village sites and cornfields frequently became the seats of their colonial successors. The landmarks of the aborigine turned into roadmarks for the succeeding English. Hulbert has called these paths "the greatest asset bequeathed by the red man to the first Europeans." Beside them at intervals would be some boulder with a hollowed-out depression where the traveling squaw could grind corn or nuts. There might even be a fallen tree trunk with a hollow burned in it, in which with the aid of red hot stones she could boil a soup or chowder.[5]

Unmapped, unmarked except in the atlas of memory, these prehistoric ways of communication for centuries formed a familiar and essential feature of the landscape all through the eastern United States. The modern engineer has evened their surfaces but, until the advent of earth-moving machinery, has seldom found better routes. The natives picked the most practical, the easiest, and the fastest routes, the shallowest and safest fordways, or the stream crossings that a single felled tree would bridge. If mountains loomed ahead, the path climbed to the lowest notch. The routes took note of springs and dry, safe camping places but avoided swamps and excessive grades.

The trails were narrow, seldom broader than a cart's rut, Wood says, and usually not over a foot broad, Johnson declares in his "Wonder-Working Providence." Pilgrim leaders Bradford and Winslow estimate two feet. Yet they were entirely suitable for persons walking Indian file on tough bare feet or on snowshoes and setting one foot before the other, while clear enough to speed the fleetest messenger. Some heavily used paths were broader. One of them still discernible from central Connecticut to Providence is two feet deep in places. Well into the twentieth century a highway remained traceable on Martha's Vineyard, still known as "The Savage Path" and, in certain areas, clearly evident except for ingrown trees. Crossing the originally well-peopled island from one shore to the other, it measured three feet or more in width and was deeply worn from centuries of travel by unnumbered Indian feet.[6]

The first Indian way to be extensively used by the English was the ancient route between Massachusetts Bay and the Connecticut River near Hartford. Still known today as The Old Connecticut Path, it winds

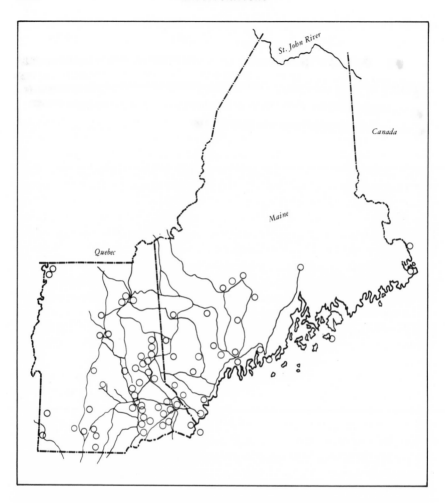

50. A compilation of certain recorded northern New England Indian trails and villages of the seventeenth and eighteenth centuries. Note that no attempt is made to trace trails in eastern Maine and Vermont. In eastern and northern Maine the chief means of travel was the vast network of rivers and lakes connected by brief portages. Vermont, at the time of European discovery, had trails, but only a handful of villages at its borders, which were served by water transport.

southwestward around ledges, avoiding swales, just as when Thomas Hooker's Cambridge congregation in 1636 set out over it with their cattle and goods to become the settlers of central Connecticut. This path was the road of the interior Nipmuck Indians to the Bay, and for Bay Indians a thoroughfare to the west. A branch that led westerly to what is now Springfield and thence to today's Albany is still known in western Massachusetts as the Bay Path. Over it Springfield's earliest settler and merchant, William Pynchon, dispatched his messages to the Massachusetts General Court and drove his cattle to the Boston market. A second branch turned northerly at Wayland, sixteen miles from Boston, and went west by way of Lancaster, making logical the early settlement of each of these river-meadow villages.[7]

Still another east–west path is the so-called Mohawk Trail, rising up the valley of the Deerfield River from that of the Connecticut and winding around Hoosac Mountain to reach the Hudson Valley. Easterly from the Connecticut Valley with its great falls, now called Turner's and Bellow's, it connected via Miller's River Valley with the falls of the Nashua at Fitchburg, and from there continued to the coast.[8]

Cascades like those on the Connecticut and the Merrimac were meccas for the natives, and were neutral zones. Indians gathered there by the hundreds and thousands when the salmon were running—not only to fish but for days of frolic and competition. Wide-ranging paths brought tribes that might normally be enemies, satisfied to meet as neighbors and sports competitors, all thought of fighting banished at least for the duration of the fish run. Families feasted, youngsters competed in games, and all helped to accumulate stores of smoked and dried food for the future.[9]

Further to the south, the Pequot Path skirted the shore along Narragansett Bay and Long Island Sound from what is now Providence to New London, New Haven, and beyond. Travelers now know it as The Old Boston Post Road; eventually it reaches New York.[10]

Other narrow highways led north and south. A path from Long Island Sound followed the Connecticut River north to the great falls at Holyoke, then to Turner's Falls, then to Bellows Falls, clear to the Upper Coos in New Hampshire and Vermont, and thence to Quebec. From the Nipmuck country in central Massachusetts, paths led down the Quinebaug to New London, and down the Blackstone to Providence. Woodstock, in northeast Connecticut, was a hub for trails in all directions. In western Connecticut, paths followed the Farmington, Naugatuck, and Housatonic rivers. Quinnipiac, today's New Haven, was the center of a nest of trails leading to what are now New York, Danbury, Middletown, Hartford, and even into Canada.[11]

In southeastern Massachusetts the Taunton River and its

tributaries, their courses heavily populated, were all paralleled by footways. Paths crisscrossed Cape Cod. The Bay Path connected Boston and Taunton, and a second path near the shore reached Plymouth from Boston Bay. Another way, now Route 44, led from Plymouth west to the head of Narragansett Bay.[12]

The North Shore of Massachusetts Bay; the Merrimac River country, populous clear to Lake Winnepesaukee; the Saco, Androscoggin, and other western Maine rivers—all had their pathways. The Ossipee Trail connected the southern Maine coast with New Hampshire lakes and mountains; several routes led from Maine and New Hampshire into Canada. Vermont's stream valleys were laced with paths. In northern and eastern Maine the seacoast is indented by tidal estuaries and watered by broad, often deep rivers reaching far inland to drain hundreds of lakes; here canoe travel was the logical method. The upland portions of the path might each be but a few miles long to bypass a fall or connect a stream with a lake. Yet the whole would form a practical pattern and pathway.[13]

Besides such through routes, local trails were innumerable. Such were the Metacomb Path to King Philip's Mt. Hope, and the Narragansett Trail, which crossed from Massachusetts Bay to Buzzard's Bay. An "Indian Trail," as it is named, runs today down to the shore at North Scituate (Massachusetts). The Mill Path crosses the island of Martha's Vineyard; on Cape Cod the Wading Place Path leads from Chatham to Orleans; the Salem Path goes from the Mystic River east to Massachusetts Bay. Many a modern Main Street, Central Avenue, or River Road is the English-language designation for a way used by aboriginal feet a thousand years ago, to connect a village to the planting field, the fishing place, or the hunting grounds, or just to the local spring, always an important objective.[14]

Comments Roger Williams: "It is admirable to see what paths their naked hardened feet have worn through the wilderness, even in the most stony places. Guides and porters are found for hire to conduct to remote hunting houses for lodging in the vast forests at night." To unaccustomed English eyes these pathways might be hidden. "A man may travel many days and never find one." The Indian, however, "sees it instantly . . . and will mark his courses as he runs more readily than most Travellers who steer by the Compass. The Ranges of the Mountains, the Courses of the Rivers, the Bearings of the Peaks, the Knobs and Gaps . . . are all landmarks, and Picture the Face of the Country on his Mind."[15] Indian boys learned all this so early that a father would not hesitate to send a son of only ten or twelve years to guide an English colonist lost and bewildered in the woods, perhaps a dozen miles to his destination.

To remind themselves or their later generations of historic events, the Indians erected no monuments or stone markers. Instead of records and chronicles, "where any remarkable act is done, in memory of it, either in the place, or by some pathway near adjoining, they make a round hole in the ground about a foot deep and as much over." The occasion for it once made known, "they are careful to acquaint all men, as occasion serveth, therewith." Such a hole they carefully renew as needed, "by which many things of antiquity are held fresh in memory," and a journey made less tedious for the traveler (including the colonist) by the relation of historical occurrences.[16]

Over the selfsame paths, around the same physical obstacles, often to the identical destinations, modern route numbers guide automobiles today. Cities spread out from sites that harbored wigwams, and the salmon falls are the power sources for the milltowns of New England.

Afterword: A Promising Society

The foregoing chapters have offered a picture of a settled, intelligent people, supplying themselves with the necessities of life, and with considerable to spare. They were a society contentedly functioning—on a communal basis in some respects, individualistic in others. Everything its members needed the land and sea afforded, through cultivation, hunting, fishing, gathering, or manufacture.

These Indians cared for their old and infirm. They knew how to adapt to circumstances and to make the most of possibilities. Of laying up treasure in enduring form there was very little, and equally little cause for it. The few needs that could not be met locally, barter could supply. The Mathers and other Puritans called the natives savages, infidels, pagans. The Indians had not yet learned to live together peaceably, any more than have many peoples today; yet, appraising them now, examining their skills and attainments, in particular their esteem for nature and its provision, we may agree that it is scarcely possible to view them with other than respect.

For an appreciation of New England's native peoples and their characteristics, one important factor is an understanding of their point of view. This was, in essence, the conception that nature, however its innumerable aspects and manifestations might differ or even appear in conflict, was an organic whole. Every part of it—man, beast, fruit, flower, soil, sun, or shower—had its role and special value as an intrinsic part of creation. Each deserved regard and, if made use of, man's appreciation. Hence the wealth of nature's resources was to be used—but used judiciously, not squandered.

Another aspect of the natives caught the notice of Edward Ward. The Indians, he commented, valued their liberty above all else (the English were never able to make good servants of them). Beyond that, he observed, "they neither covet Riches or dread Poverty; But all are Content with their own conditions, which are in a manner Equal."

From the Indian, colonial New England derived directly what was for three centuries to be its most important field crop, corn, and the methods of growing and fertilizing it. Corn was not only its leading bread grain but, of almost equal importance, feed for the domestic animals and fowl which the newcomers brought with them. Along with corn the Indians added two other valuable foods, beans and squashes. Not that the local tribes had originated them, but they had adapted them to the sour soils and shifty climate of New England and developed methods of combining their cultivation so as to require a minimum of soil area and labor. In order to survive in the new strange land and climate, the English found it expedient to use the Indians' seeds and learn the Indian method of hill cultivation, unknown in Europe, and their fish fertilization. In doing so the newcomers also adopted, or adapted, Indian recipes for palatable food preparation that have provided pleasure and nutrition to all succeeding generations.

There is much else for which modern New England is indebted to the Indians. Travel in any direction, except for modern bulldozed speedways and turnpikes, and you will follow the winding ways and easy grades originally worn deep by moccasined feet. The very names of a number of the principal highways—"Bay Path," "Ossipee Trail," "Mohawk Trail," "Old Connecticut Path"—bespeak their origin. The hills, rivers, ponds, and mountains that these roads skirt have the musical titles the original inhabitants gave them: Winnepesaukee, Quinsigamond, Quinnipiac, Narragansett, Monadnock, Connecticut, Kennebec, Katahdin, Merrimac, Wachusett. Flourishing cities and charming towns are seated on the spots that in the distant past vanished tribes selected as the most suitable for habitation.

Today but a few thousand New England Indians remain. Others of a different race have preempted their lands, their town sites, their cultivated fields, their crops, even their special dishes. This book has sought to offer a faithful description of those earlier inhabitants as persons, of the food they ate, the way they lived, and the land they lived in. It has emphasized the profound debt we owe them. It has also tried to present a just assessment of their character and of the promise for a future which, up to the present has remained unfulfilled.

Yet hope remains. A healthy new interest in New England's Indians has recently arisen—in their way of life, the way their lands were acquired by newcomers from across the sea, the way their concerns were subordinated to those of the newcomers. More striking still, after being quiescent and ignored for generations, the New Englanders of Indian blood begin to feel new pride in their heritage and culture as they seek to revivify the values of their ancestors.

If the reader's knowledge has been increased, his respect for the attainments of the native race and culture heightened, his understanding of certain aspects of New England's past deepened, this book will have attained its object.

Appendix

Uses of Trees, Shrubs, and Herbaceous Plants

The following listing lays no claim to completeness in either number or usage. Items are included only if a contemporary document or other reliable source attributes their use to some New England tribe or area at or about the time when European settlement is first recorded. Many plants known to have been used by later Indians, but of foreign origin, are therefore omitted. Not all usages listed, especially those designated as medicinal, were known to all tribes or all native practitioners. Readers are warned not to eat, drink, or use unaccustomed edible or medicinal items listed except upon the advice of persons of experience. With these reservations, I hope that the compilation will be informative.

Plant names are listed as found in *Gray's Manual of Botany*, Eighth Edition.

Common Name	Botanical Designation	Use
Alder	Alnus rugosa (DuRoi) Spreng.	Arrows, medicine
Apple (see Crabapple)		
Arrow Arum	Peltandra virginica (L.) Schott & Endl.	Root, medicine
Arrowhead	Sagittaria latifolia Willd.	Root for food
Artichoke (see Jerusalem Artichoke)		
Ash, Black	Fraxinus nigra Marsh.	Basketry, bows, arrows, medicine
Ash, White	Fraxinus americana L.	
Balm of Gilead	Populus gileadensis Rouleau	Medicine
Balsam Fir	Abies balsamea (L.) Mill	Gum for sealing, medicine
Baneberry (see Bunchberry)		
Basswood (Spoonwood)	Tilia americana L.	Fibers for mats, fish nets; bark for splints; roofing, siding for cabins; wood for bowls, spoons
Bayberry	Myrica pennsylvanica Loisel.	Food, wax

209

Common Name	Botanical Designation	Use
Beach Pea	Lathyrus japonicus Willd.	Food
Beach Plum	Prunus maritima Marsh.	Food
Bean, Bush	Phaseolus vulgaris, variety humulis Alef.	Food
Bean, Pole or Climbing	Phaseolus vulgaris L.	Food
Beech	Fagus grandifolia Ehrh.	Nuts for food, flavoring; wood for bows, snowshoes
Berries (see individual varieties)		
Birch, Gray	Betula lutea Michx.	Punk for ignition; medicine
Birch, White	Betula papyrifera Marsh.	Bark for dishes, boxes, canoes, medicine
Blackberry	Rubus allegheniensis Porter	Food; medicine
Bloodroot	Sanguinaria canadensis L.	Dye, medicine
Blueberry, Canada	Vaccinium myrtilloides Michx.	Food
Blueberry, Dryland	Vaccinium pallidum Ait.	Food
Blueberry, High-bush or Swamp	Vaccinium corymbosum L.	Food
Blueberry, Lowbush	Vaccinium vacillans Torr.	Food
Boneset	Eupatorium perfoliatum L.	Medicine
Box Elder	Acer Negundo L.	Sap for food
Bunchberry, White	Actaea pachypoda Ell.	Medicine
Butternut (White Walnut)	Juglans cinerea L.	Food, dye, oil, medicine
Cardinal Flower	Lobelia cardinalis L.	Tobacco blend
Cattail	Typha latifolia L.	Thatching, weaving, roots for food
Cedar, Red	Juniperus virginiana L.	Dishes, roots for thread, medicine
Cedar, White	Chamaecyparis thyoides (L.) BSP.	Arrows, canoes, roots for thread
Cherry, Appalachian	Prunus susquehanae Wild.	Food
Cherry, Black	Prunus serotina Ehrh.	Food, medicine

Common Name	Botanical Designation	Use
Cherry, Red or Pin	Prunus pennsylvanica L.	Food
Cherry, Sand or Dwarf	Prunus pumila L.	Food
Chestnut	Castanea dentata (Marsh.) Borkh.	Food, dugout canoes
Chokeberry, Black	Pyrus melanocarpa (Michx.) Wild.	Food, medicine
Chokeberry, Purple	Pyrus floribunda Lindl.	Food
Chokecherry	Prunus virginiana L.	Food
Clematis (see Virgin's Bower)		
Columbine	Aquilegia canadensis L.	Medicine
Corn (see Maize)		
Cowslip	Caltha palustris L.	Food
Crabapple	Pyrus coronaria L.	Food
Cranberry	Vaccinium macrocarpon Ait.	Food, medicine
Currant, Wild Red	Ribes triste Pall.	Food
Dogwood	Cornus florida L.	Bark for medicine, tobacco blend
Elderberry	Sambucus canadensis L.	Food, medicine
Elm, Slippery	Ulmus rubra Muhl.	Medicine
Elm, White	Ulmus americana L.	Dugout canoes, dishes, wigwam cover; inner bark for fishnets, textiles, medicine
Fern, Fiddle or Bracken Fern	Pteridium aquilinum Var. pubescens Underw.	Food Food
Fern, Sweet	Comptonia peregrina (L.) Coult.	Tobacco blend
Fir (see Balsam Fir)		
Flag (see Sweet Flag)		
Ginseng	Panax quinquefolius L.	Medicine
Gooseberry	Ribes oxyacanthoides L.	Food
Goosegrass	Galium Aparine L.	Medicine
Gourd*	Cucurbita Pepo L.	Dishes, pails, storage

Common Name	Botanical Designation	Use
Grape, Downy	Vitis cinerea Engelm.	Food
Grape, Frost, Chicken, Possum, or Fox	Vitis vulpina L.	Food
Grape, Pigeon	Vitis aestivalis Michx.	Food
Grape, Riverside, Sweet Scented, Winter, or Frost	Vitis riparia Michx.	Food
Grape, Sand, Sugar, or Mountain	Vitis rupestris Scheele	Food
Grape, Summer or Silverleaf	Vitis aestivalis var. argentifolia (Munson) Fern.	Food
Grape, White or Fox	Vitis Labrusca L.	Food
Great Solomon's Seal	Polygonatum biflorum (Walt.) Ell.	Medicine
Groundnut	Apios americana Medic.	Food
Hackmatack (see Tamarack)		
Hardhack	Spiraea tomentosa L.	Medicine
Hellebore	Veratrum viride Ait.	Medicine
Hemlock	Tsuga canadensis (L.) Carr.	Medicine
Hemp (see Indian Hemp)		
Hickory	Carya ovata (Mill) K. Koch	Food, baby food, bows, roofing, tool handles
Hop	Humulus Lupulus L.	Medicine
Hop Hornbeam	Ostrya virginiana (Mill) K. Koch	Bowls, mortar, food
Indian Hemp	Apocynum cannabinum L.	Cordage, baskets, fisheries, medicine
Jack-in-the-Pulpit (Indian Turnip)	Arisaema triphyllum (L.) Schott	Medicine
Jerusalem Artichoke	Helianthus tuberosus L.	Food
Juniper, Ground or Prostrate	Juniperus communis, Var. depressa Pursh.	Fruits, medicine
Lady's Slipper (Nerve-root) (see also Yellow Lady's Slipper)	Cypripedium reginae Walt.	Medicine
Larch, American	Larix laricina (DuRoi) K. Koch	Decoration, medicine

Common Name	Botanical Designation	Use
Laurel, Mountain (see Mountain)		
Leek, Wild	Allium tricoccum Ait.	Food
Lichens (many species)		Emergency food
Lily, Turkscap	Lilium superbum L.	Roots for food
Linden (see Basswood)		
Lobelia (Indian Tobacco)	Lobelia inflata L.	Medicine
Maize (Corn)	Zea mays L.	Food, stalks for roofing, husks for mats, baskets
Maple, Black	Acer nigrum Michx.	Sap for food
Maple, Silver	Acer saccharinum L.	Sap for food
Maple, Rock or Sugar	Acer saccharum Marsh.	Food, bows, paddles, dishes
Marsh Marigold (see Cowslip)		
Milkweed, Common	Asclepias syriaca L.	Food, medicine
Mountain Laurel	Kalmia latifolia L.	Roots for spoons
Oak, Red	Quercus rubra L.	Food, bark for roofing, touchwood, ashes for lye, medicine
Oak, White	Quercus alba L.	Food, canoes, dishes, bark for roofing, medicine
Onion, Wild	Allium cernuum Roth	Food
Partridge Berry	Mitchella repens L.	Medicine
Pea (see Beach Pea)		
Pennyroyal	Hedeoma pulegioides (L.) Pers.	Medicine
Pigweed	Amaranthus retroflexus L.	Food
Pine, Pitch	Pinus rigida Mill.	Torches, medicine
Pine, White	Pinus Strobus L.	Dugout canoes, bark for medicine
Pipsissewa (see Prince's Pine)		
Plum	Prunus nigra Ait.	Food
Plum (see Beach Plum)		
Pokeberry	Phytolacca americana L.	Medicine

Common Name	Botanical Designation	Use
Prince's Pine (Pipsissewa)	Chimaphila umbellata var. cisatlantica Blake	Medicine
Pumpkin*	Cucurbita Pepo L. and Cucurbita moschata Duchesne	Food
Pyrola (Shinleaf)	Pyrola elliptica Nutt.	Medicine
Ragweed	Ambrosia artemisiifolia var. elatior (L.) Descourtils	Bruised leaves for nausea
Raspberry, Black	Rubus occidentalis L.	Food
Raspberry, Red	Rubus idaeus L.	Food, medicine
Rattlesnake Root, or Seneca Snakeroot	Polygala Senega L.	Medicine (snake-bite)
Rice, Wild	Zizania aquatica L.	Food
Rose, Wild	Rosa blanda Ait., Rosa carolina L., Rosa virginiana Mill. or Rosa nitida Willd.	Hips for food, medicine
Sarsaparilla	Aralia nudicaulis L.	Medicine
Sassafras	Sassafras albidum var. molle (Raf.) Fern.	Roots for tea, oil, medicine
Shadbush	Amelanchier canadensis (L.) Medic.	Food, medicine
Shagbark (see Hickory)		
Shinleaf (see Pyrola)		
Skunk Cabbage	Symplocarpus foetidus (L.) Nutt.	Medicine
Slippery Elm (see Elm)		
Smartweed	Polygonum pennsylvanicum L.	Medicine
Snakeroot, Virginia	Aristolochia Serpentaria L.	Medicine
Solomon's-seal	Polygonatum canaliculatum (Muhl.) Pursh	Medicine
Spatter-dock (see Lily)		
Sphagnum Moss	Sphagnum obtusifolium Ehrh.	Baby care
Spoonwood (see Basswood)		
Spruce	Picea glauca (Moench) Voss	Medicine
Squash*	Cucurbita Pepo L. (or) C. moschata Duchesne	Food
Strawberry (Red)	Fragaria virginiana Duchesne Fragaria vesca L.	Food

Common Name	Botanical Designation	Use
Sumac, Smooth	Rhus glabra L.	Berries for food, tobacco blend, medicine
Sweet Flag	Acorus Calamus L.	Roofing, gum for caulking, roots for food, medicine
Sweet Grass	Hierochloe odorata (L.) Beauv.	Scented baskets, deodorant
Tamarack (Hackmatack)	Larix laricina (DuRoi) K. Koch	Roots for thread, medicine
Thimbleberry	Rubus odoratus L.	Food
	Rubus argutus Link.	Food
Tobacco	Nicotiana rustica L.	Smoking, antiseptic, pain relief, medicine
Turk's-Cap Lily	Lilium superbum L.	Roots for food
Turnip, Indian (see Jack-in-the-Pulpit)		
Virgin's Bower (Clematis)	Clematis virginiana L.	Medicine
Wake Robin (see Jack-in-the-Pulpit)		
Walnut, White (see Butternut)		
Walnut, Black	Juglans nigra L.	Food, mortars, dye
Water-lily, White	Nymphaea odorata Ait.	Roots for food
Water-lily, Yellow (Yellow Pond-lily)	Nuphar advena Ait.	Roots for food
Water-lily, Yellow	Nelumbo lutea (Willd.) Pers.	Roots for food
Watermelon*	Citrullus vulgaris Schrad.	Food
White Bunchberry (Baneberry)	Actaea pachypoda Ell.	Decoction of root, medicine
Whitewood (see Basswood)		
Willow, Pussy	Salix discolor Muhl.	Hoops and handles
Wintergreen (see Pyrola)		
Witch Hazel	Hamamelis virginiana L.	Bows, medicine
Yellow Lady's Slipper	Cypripedium Calceolus var. pubescens (Willd.) Correll	Roots for medicine

*Not native, according to *Gray's Manual of Botany,* but naturalized prehistorically in America.

Notes

1. The Region and Its Resources

1. Jesse D. Jennings, *Prehistory of North America* (New York McGraw-Hill, 1968), 40-44.

2. James B. Griffin, "The Northeast Woodlands Area," in Jesse D. Jennings and Edward Norbeck, eds., *Prehistoric Man in the New World* (Chicago, University of Chicago Press, 1964, reprint 1965), 128. Douglas S. Byers, "Radiocarbon Dates from Bull Brook," Mass. Arch. Soc., *Bulletin*, 20, no. 3 (1959), 33.

3. Gordon R. Willey, *An Introduction to American Archaeologoy, I: North and Middle America* (Englewood Cliffs, N.J., Prentice-Hall, 1966), 50-51. Jennings, *Prehistory*, 112, 125.

4. Mark Nathan Cohen, *The Food Crisis in Prehistory: Overpopulation and the Origins of Agriculture* (New Haven, Yale University Press, 1977), 189, 192. John Collier, *The Indians of the Americas* (New York, Norton, 1947), 172. Griffin, "Northeast" 237, 256.

5. Margaret A. Towle, *The Ethnobotany of Pre-Columbian Peru*, Viking Fund Publications in Anthropology, 30 (New York, Wenner-Gren Foundation for Anthropological Research, 1961), 21, 55, 91, 93. Walton C. Galinat, "The Evolutionary Emergence of Maize," Torrey Botanical Club, *Bulletin*, 102, no. 6 (1975), 315-324. Lawrence Kaplan, "Archeology and Domestication in American Phaseolus (Beans)," *Economic Botany*, 19 (1965), 358-368. Howard Scott Gentry, "Origin of the Common Bean, *Phaseolus vulgaris*," ibid., 23 (1969), 55-69. C. Earl Smith, Jr., "The Archeological Record of Cultivated Crops of New World Origins," ibid., 19 (1965), 323-324.

6. Donald D. Brand, "The Origin and Early Distribution of New World Cultivated Plants," *Agricultural History*, 13 (April 1939), 109-117. Berthold Laufer, "The American Plant Migration," *Scientific Monthly*, 28 (1929), 239-251. Herbert J. Spinden, "Thank the American Indian," *Scientific American*, 138 (1928), 330-332. E. Lewis Sturtevant, "Kitchen Garden Esculents of American Origin," *American Naturalist*, 19 (1885), 444.

7. Everett E. Edwards, *American Indian Contributions to Civilization*, U.S. Dept. Ag., Bureau of Agricultural Economics, pamphlet, 1934.

8. Walton C. Galinat, "The Origin of Corn," in *Corn and Corn Improvement*, ed. G. F. Sprague, *Agronomy*, 18 (Madison, Wis., Am. Soc. of Agronomy, 1977), 1-47. Alvin M. Josephy, Jr., *The Indian Heritage of America* (New York, Knopf, 1968), 28, 32.

9. William Brandon, *The Last Americans* (New York, McGraw-Hill, 1973), 41, 74.

10. Walton C. Galinat, "The Origin of Corn," 13, 17. Paul C. Mangelsdorf, *Corn: Its Origin and Improvement* (Cambridge, Harvard University Press, 1974), 163.

2. The First Europeans

1. "The Voyage of John de Verazzano along the Coast of North America," tr. Joseph G. Cogswell, New York Hist. Soc., *Collections*, 2nd series, 1 (1841), 48.

2. George Parker Winship, ed., *Sailors Narratives of Voyages along the New England*

Coast, 1524-1624 (Boston, Houghton Mifflin, 1905), 89. James Rosier, "A True Relation of the Most Prosperous Voyage of Captain George Waymouth," Mass. Hist. Soc., *Collections*, 3rd series, 8 (1843), 125-157.

3. Sieur Samuel de Champlain, *Voyages*, tr. Charles Pomeroy Otis, (Boston Prince Society, 1878), 65, 72, 75.

4. *Mourt's Relation*, probably by William Bradford and Edward Winslow, ed., Henry Martyn Dexter (Boston, 1865), 64.

5. John Smith, "A Description of New England," Mass. Hist. Soc., *Collections*, 3rd series, 6 (1837), 103-140.

6. The depopulating disease was formerly thought to have been yellow fever (surviving Indians said the bodies turned yellow). Recent studies rule this out and suggest smallpox, chicken pox, or influenza, caught from sailors carrying germs to which their own systems were immune. A recent article concludes: "The best definition is probably that of Bradford—an infectious fever": see Billee Hoornbeck, "An Investigation into the Cause or Causes of the Epidemic . . . 1616-1619," *New Hampshire Archaeologist*, 19 (1976-77), 35-46. Edward L. Bynner, "Topography and Landmarks of the Colonial Period," in Justin Winsor, ed., *The Memorial History of Boston*, 4 vols. (Boston, 1880-81), 1:521. Roger Clap, *Memoirs, 1630* (Boston, 1731), reprinted in Dorchester Antiquarian and Historical Soc., *Collections*, 1 (1844), 41.

7. Francis Higginson, "New-England's Plantation," in Alexander Young, *Chronicles of . . . Massachusetts Bay* (Boston, 1846), 244.

8. Thomas Graves, "Letter from New England," in Young, *Chronicles of . . . Mass. Bay,* 11.

9. Thomas Morton, *The New English Canaan*, intro. Charles Francis Adams, Jr. (Boston, 1883), 11. William Wood, "New England's Prospect," in Young, *Chronicles of . . . Mass. Bay,* 395. A. K. Teele, *Noted Men and Historical Narrations of Ancient Milton* (Boston, 1900).

10. *Mourt's Relation*, 64.

11. Winship, *Sailors Narratives*, 41.

12. *Mourt's Relation*, 103, 104.

13. James D. Knowles, *Memoir of Roger Williams* (Boston, 1834), 19. John Winthrop, *The History of New England from 1630 to 1649*, ed. James Savage (Boston, 1825), 1:47.

14. John W. De Forest, *History of the Indians of Connecticut . . . to 1850* (Hartford, 1851), 69, 92. Winthrop, *History*, 1:194.

15. De Forest, 99.

16. George H. Ford, Comp., *Historical Sketches of Milford* (New Haven, 1914), 12, 14, 18 (and numerous other local histories). Federal Writers' Project, American Guide Series, *Connecticut* (Boston, 1938), local references to the areas named.

17. For Connecticut Valley areas mentioned in Connecticut and Massachusetts, see local histories. For New Hampshire, see Edwin D. Sanborn, *History of New Hampshire* (Manchester, 1875); Everett S. Stackpole, *History of New Hampshire* (New York, Am. Hist. Soc., 1916); Grant Powers, *Historical Sketches of . . . Coos Country 1754-1785* (Haverhill, N.H., 1880), 30. For Vermont, see Gordon M. Day, "The Indian Occupation of Vermont," *Vermont History*, 33, no. 3 (1965), 367, 373; Mary R. Cabot, ed. *Annals of Brattleboro, 1681-1895* (Brattleboro, 1921), 3, 4; Federal Writers' Project, *Vermont* (Boston, 1937), 175, 209; Frederic P. Wells, *History of Newbury, Vermont* (St. Johnsbury, Vt., 1902), 30; and other local histories. Walter Hill Crockett, *Vermont, the Green Mountain State* (New York, 1921), 1:59.

18. Sherman W. Adams and H. R. Stiles, *The History of Ancient Wethersfield* (New York, 1904), 31. Sylvester Judd, *History of Hadley* (Springfield, Mass., 1905), 97.

19. George Sheldon, *A History of Deerfield*, 2 vols. (Deerfield, 1895-96), 1:52.

20. Grace Greylock Niles, *The Hoosac Valley: Its Legends and Its History* (New York, 1912), 29. Samuel Orcutt, *The Indians of the Housatonic and Naugatuck Valleys* (Hartford, 1882), 15, 17, 102.

21. Mathias Spiess, *The Indians of Connecticut* (New Haven, Yale University Press, 1933), 23, 27. Charles F. Sedgwick, *General History . . . of Sharon . . . Connecticut*, 3rd ed. (Amenia, N.Y., 1898), and local histories of other places named in the pages just preceding. Also Clarence Winthrop Bowen, *Woodstock: An Historical Sketch* (New York, 1886), 73.

22. John J. Currier, *History of Newbury, Mass., 1635-1902* (Boston, 1902), 183-184. Sanborn, *New Hampshire*, 91, 125; and numerous local histories.

23. Anonymous, "A Relation of a Voyage to Sagadahoc, 1607-1608," in Henry S. Burrage, *Early English and French Voyages* (New York, 1906), 414. Ferdinando Gorges the Younger, *America Painted to the Life* (London, 1659), 43. Clarence A. Day, *A History of Maine Agriculture, 1604-1860* (Orono, 1954), 19, 20. Charles M. Starbird, *The Indians of the Androscoggin Valley* (Lewiston, Lewiston Journal Printshop, 1928), 30. Winship, *Sailors Narratives*, 262.

3. The Tribes and Their Distribution

1. Roger Williams, "An Helpe to the Native Language of that part of America Called New England (commonly called Williams' *Key*)," in *Writings*, 6 vols., ed. J. Hammond Trumbull, Narragansett Club Publications (Providence, 1866-74), 1:1-219, 103. De Forest, *Connecticut Indians*, 31ff. Maurice Robbins, "Indians of the Old Colony," Mass. Arch. Soc., *Bulletin*, 17, no. 4 (1956), 59-74. David I. Bushnell, Jr., *Native Villages and Village Sites East of the Mississippi*, Bureau of American Ethnology, *Bulletin* 69 (Washington, 1919), 199. "Hutchinson Papers," Mass. Hist. Soc., *Collections*, 3rd series, 1 (1825), 24, 211.

2. De Forest, 41ff. Francis Jennings, *The Invasion of America: Indians, Colonialism and the Cant of Conquest* (Chapel Hill, University of North Carolina Press, 1975), 111-115. "A Brief Narrative of . . . Nanhiganset Country," Mass. Hist. Soc., *Collections*, 3rd series, 1 (1825), 211. Charles C. Willoughby, "The Wilderness and the Indian," in A. B. Hart, *Commonwealth History of Massachusetts* (New York, 1927-30), 1:127-159.

3. *North American Indians in Historical Perspective* Eleanore Burke Leacock and Nancy Oestreich Lurie, eds., (New York, Random House, 1971), 22. Brinley, 210, 212. *Connecticut Register and Memorial* (Hartford, 1842), 384. Simon G. Griffin, *A History of. . . Keene from 1732 . . . to 1874,* (Keene, 1904), 33, 141.

4. Daniel Neal, *The History of New-England . . . to 1700*, 2 vols. (London, 1720, 1747), 1:39, 43, 44.

5. Fannie H. Eckstorm, "The Indians of Maine," in Louis C. Hatch, ed., *Maine: A History*, 5 vols. (New York, Amer. Hist. Soc., 1919), 1:59. Lewis H. Morgan. *Houses and House-Life of the American Aborigines*, Contributions to North American Ethnology, 4 (Washington, 1881) 7, 11.

6. D'Arcy McNickle, "Americans Called Indians," in Leacock and Lurie (above) p. 39. James Hammond Trumbull, "The Indian Tongue and Its Literature," in Justin Winsor, ed., *Memorial History of Boston, 1630-1880*, 4 vols. (Boston, 1880), 1:468.

7. Williams, *Key*, 120. Mrs. Anne Grant, *Memoirs of an American Lady*, 2 vols. (New York, 1901), 1:157.

8. Marc Lescarbot, *Nova Francia*, tr. P. Erondelle (London, 1609), 282. Edward Winslow, "Good News From New England," Massachusetts Historical Society, *Collec-*

tions, 2nd series, 9 (1832), 95. Regina Flannery, *An Analysis of Coastal Algonquian Culture* (Washington, 1939), 77. James Sullivan, "The History of the Penobscot Indians," Massachusetts Historical Society, *Collections*, 9 (1804), 213.

9. Williams, *Key*, 120. Frank G. Speck, *Penobscot Man* (Philadelphia, University of Pennsylvania Press, 1940), 104.

10. John R. Swanton, *The Indian Tribes of North America*, U.S. Bureau Am. Ethnology, *Bulletin*, 145 (Washington, 1953, reprinted 1968), 28, 30, 31. Federal Writers' Project, *Rhode Island: A Guide to the Smallest State* (Boston, 1937), 26.

11. Swanton, 24, 27. Henry E. Chase, "Notes on the Wampanoag Indians," Smithsonian Institution, *Annual Reports*, (1883), 878-907. Marion Vuilleumier, *Indians on Olde Cape Cod* (Taunton, Mass., Sullwold, 1970), 17.

12. Swanton, 23. Chandler E. Potter, *The History of Manchester, . . . N.H.* (Manchester, 1856), 25. William Hubbard, "A General History of New England," 2nd ed., Massachusetts Historical Society, *Collections*, 2nd series, 5 (1848), 34.

13. Swanton, 13. Eckstorm, in Hatch, ed., *Maine*, 1:43-48. Speck, 3. Starbird, *Androscoggin Valley*, 10.

14. Edwin M. Bacon, *The Connecticut River and the Valley of the Connecticut* (New York, Putnam, 1906), 82. Sheldon, *Deerfield*, 52. Niles, *Hoosac Valley*, 5, 20.

15. Charles C. Willoughby, *Antiquities of the New England Indians* (Cambridge, Harvard University, Peabody Museum of American Archaeology and Ethnology, 1935), 278. Starbird, 14. Thomas Williams Bicknell, *The History of the State of Rhode Island and Providence Plantations*, 5 vols. (New York, Amer. Hist. Soc., 1920), 1:6-9.

16. Chase, 890. Vuilleumier, 27. Henry F. Howe, *Salt Rivers of the Massachusetts Shore* (New York, Rinehart, 1951), 23.

17. Jennings, *Invasion*, 6, 26, 27. Daniel Gookin, *Historical Collections of the Indians in New England*, annotated by Jeffrey H. Fiske (1792; reprinted Towtaid, [n.p.], 1974), 102, 104.

18. De Forest, *Connecticut Indians*, 62. Sherburne F. Cook, "Interracial Warfare and Population Decline among the New England Indians," *Ethnohistory*, 20, no. 1 (1973), 9, 11. T. J. C. Brasser, "The Coastal Algonkians" (in Leacock and Lurie, above), 65. Brandon, *Last Americans*, 199. Sheldon, *Deerfield*, 1:52. Federal Writers, *Rhode Island*, 28.

19. Edward Johnson, *Wonder-Working Providence of Sions Saviour in New England* (London, 1654; reprinted Andover, Mass., 1867), 23. Adams Tolman, *Indian Relics in Concord* (Concord, Mass., Concord Antiquarian Society, 1902), 15.

20. Sanborn, *New Hampshire*, 21. James Duane Squires, *The Granite State of the United States*, 4 vols. (New York, Amer. Hist. Co., 1956), 1:14.

21. Sheldon, *Deerfield*, 52.

22. J. Wingate Thornton, "Ancient Pemaquid," Maine Hist. Soc., *Collections*, 5 (1857), 156. Rufus King Sewall, *Ancient Dominions of Maine* (Bath, 1859), 51.

23. Edmund B. Delabarre and Harris H. Wilder, "Indian Corn Hills in Massachusetts," *Am. Anthropologist*, 22 (1920), 203-225 (and personal communication).

4. Personal Characteristics

1. Wood, in Young, ed., *Chronicles . . . of Massachusetts Bay*, 70. Smith, "A Description of New-England", in Mass. Hist. Soc., *Collections*, 3rd series, 6 (1837), 108. Winship, *Sailors Narratives*, 15, 113. Bartholomew Gosnold, "Letter to His Father, Touching His First Voyage to Virginia", Massachusetts Historical Society, *Collections*, 3rd series, 8 (1843), 69-72. Emma Schemel, ed. and tr., "A Swiss Surgeon Visits

Rhode Island, 1661-1662," *New England Quarterly*, 10 (1937), 539. George W. Pierce, "History of Winchester," in *History of Cheshire and Sullivan Counties* (Philadelphia, 1886), 557. Capt. John Underhill, "History of the Pequot War," in *Nevves from America* (London, 1638), reprinted Mass. Hist. Soc., *Collections*, 3rd series, 6 (1837), 5, speaks of his opponents as "men straight as arrows, very tall, and of active bodies." Brereton calls the Indians of the same area taller than the English. In Maine Governor James Sullivan rates the Penobscot Indians as tall as Europeans but much better proportioned. Capt. Gilbert, in the Androscoggin Valley in 1607 met "near 50 able men, very straight and tall such as their like we had not seen." (Quoted by Starbird, *Androscoggin Valley*, 50.) Warner F. Gookin and Philip L. Barbour, *Bartholomew Gosnold, Discoverer and Planter* (Hamden, Conn., 1963), 54.

2. Verazzano, "Voyage," N.Y. Hist. Soc., *Collections*, 2nd series, 1 (1841), 46. Daniel Ricketson, *The History of New Bedford, . . . Massachusetts* (New Bedford, 1858), 36. Nicolaes Van Wassenaer, "Historisch Verhael," in J. Franklin Jameson, ed., *Narratives of New Netherland* (New York, Scribners, 1909), 72. Adriaen van der Donck, "Description of the New Netherlands," New-York Hist. Soc., *Collections*, 2nd series, 1 (1841), 190. John Josselyn, *An Account of Two Voyages*, London, 1674, (reprinted Boston, 1865), 124. Winship, *Sailors Narratives*, 15.

3. Wood, 69, 70. *Letters of Samuel Lee and Samuel Sewall Relating to New England and the Indians*, George Lyman Kittredge, ed. Colonial Soc. of Mass., *Publications*, 14 (1912), 147. Willoughby, *Antiquities*, 282.

4. Verazzano, "Voyage," 1:47. Isaack de Rasieres, "Letter to Samuel Blommaert," in *Narratives*, ed. Jameson, 106. Donck, 1:191.

5. Josselyn, 124. "John Dunton's Journal," Mass. Hist. Soc., *Collections*, 2nd series, 2 (1814), 97-124. Winship, 47.

6. Samuel Orcutt, *The History of the Old Town of Derby, Connecticut* (Springfield, 1880), 1-i.

7. Edward Ward, "A Trip to New England," in *Boston in 1682 and 1699*, ed. George P. Winship (Providence, 1905), 69. Morton, *Canaan*, 145, 147. See also Louis Hennepin, *A New Discovery of a Vast Country in America*, ed. Reuben Gold Thwaites, 2 vols. (Chicago, McClurg, 1903), 2:490. But Fr. Du Peron speaks of insane people among the Hurons: Reuben Gold Thwaites, *The Jesuit Relations and Allied Documents*, 22 vols. (Cleveland, 1896-1901), 4:155, and Cartier at Montreal in 1535 was asked to heal blind and crippled Indians: Samuel Eliot Morison, *The European Discovery of America: The Northern Voyages, A.D. 500-1600* (New York, Oxford University Press, 1971), 414.

8. John Heckewelder, "History, Manners and Customs of the Indian Nations . . . [of] Pennsylvania . . .," Am. Philos. Soc., *Transactions*, 1 (1819), 154.

9. Verazzano, "Voyage," 46. Champlain, *Voyages*, ed. Grant, 61. Thomas Lechford, *Plain Dealing: or, News from New England*, ed. J. Hammond Trumbull (reprinted Boston, 1867), 115.

10. Williams, *Key*, 77. Wood (above, note 3).

11. Paul Le Jeune, "Relation," in *Jesuit Relations*, Thwaites, ed., 6:157, 17:199. Pierre Biard, writings in ibid., 2:11.

12. Johnson, *Wonder-Working Providence*, 117, 227. Also in Winsor, ed., *Boston*, 1:256.

13. William Apes (of the Pequod Tribe) *A Son of the Forest* (New York, 1829), 131. See also John G. Whittier introduction to Stanley Pumphrey, *Indian Civilization* (Philadelphia, 1877), and Jennings, *Invasion*, 160.

14. Benjamin Church, *The History of King Philip's War*, ed. Henry M. Dexter (Boston, 1865), 1:127, and editor's notes, 128. Samuel E. Morison, *The Story of the "Old*

Colony" of New Plymouth (New York, Knopf, 1956), 274, 276, 283. Douglas E. Leach, *Flintlock and Tomahawk: New England in King Philip's War* (New York, Macmillan, 1958). William J. Miller, *Notes Concerning the Wampanoag Tribe of Indians* (Providence, 1880), 116.

15. Underhill, in Mass. Hist. Soc., *Collections*, 3rd series, 6 (1837), 8-24. John Stetson Barry, *The History of Massachusetts*, 3 vols. (Boston, 1855), 1:428. Morgan, *Houses*, 4:12. Federal Writers, *Connecticut*, 230.

5. Health and Illness

1. Alfred Goldsworthy Bailey, *The Conflict of European and Eastern Algonkian Cultures, 1504-1700*, Monograph Series, 2 (Sackville, N.B., New Brunswick Museum, 1937), 75. Calvin S. Martin, "The European Impact on the Culture of a Northeastern Algonquian Tribe: An Ecological Interpretation," *William and Mary Quarterly*, 3rd series, 31 (1974), 17. Nicolas Denys, *The Description and Natural History of the Coasts of North America (Acadia)* (Toronto, Champlain Society, 1908), 399. Baron de Lahontan, in *New Voyages to North-America*, ed. Reuben Gold Thwaites (Chicago, McClurg, 1905), 2:415, 418. Neal, *New-England*, 1:29. Eric Stone, *Medicine among the American Indians* (New York, Hoeber, 1932), 49, 56, 61, 78. Emily C. Davis, *Ancient Americans* (New York, 1931), 37. John Bakeless, *The Eyes of Discovery* (Philadelphia, Lippincott, 1950), 129.

2. Leaman F. Hallett, "Medicine and Pharmacy of the New England Indians," Mass. Arch. Soc., *Bulletin*, 17, no. 3 (1956), 47. Heber H. Youngken, "The Drugs of the North American Indians," *American Journal of Pharmacy*, 97, no. 3 (1925), 158-185, 257-271. Virgil J. Vogel, *American Indian Medicine* (Norman, Okla., University of Oklahoma Press, 1970), 6.

3. Rather than attempt individual references for the data recorded in the succeeding paragraphs, I offer this assurance. Items are included only if my research has developed reasonable evidence of their use specifically by New England Indians at or about the time the English and French met them and recorded their practices. Thus certain remedies attributed to Indians by tradition or by their presence in lists of folk medicine may be missing here. Ruled out also are plant remedies of European origin, often adopted by later Indians, such as dandelion, mullein, shepherd's purse, tansy, plantain, and others—as well as Indian medicines of Western, or Central and South American derivation. For the reader interested in specific or more extended information than is here presented, I suggest in particular the Youngken study. Also, Gladys Tantaquidgeon, *Folk Medicine of the Delaware and Related Algonkian Indians* (Harrisburg, Penn., Pennsylvania Historical and Museum Commission, 1972); Nicholas N. Smith, "Indian Medicine, Fact or Fiction?" Mass. Arch. Soc., *Bulletin*, 26, no. 1 (1964), 13-17; Virginia Scully, *A Treasury of American Indian Herbs* (New York, Crown, 1970); C. A. Weslager, *Magic Medicines of the Indians* (Somerset, N. J., 1943); Virgil J. Vogel, *American Indian Medicine* (Norman, Okla., 1970); M. R. Harrington, *The Indians of New Jersey: Dickon among the Lenapes* (New Brunswick, Rutgers University Press, 1963); Michael A. Weiner, *Earth Medicine—Earth Foods (New York, 1972)*; and Stone, *Medicine* (above, note 1). Nor should the valuable observations of the French missionaries to Canada in Thwaites, ed., *Jesuit Relations* and similar accounts, or the data afforded by early New England naturalists, be overlooked.

4. Gladys Tantaquidgeon, "Mohegan Medicinal Practices, Weather-lore, and Superstitions," U.S. Bureau of American Ethnology, *Annual Report*, 43 (1928), 264-275.

Williams, *Key*, 212, 221. Dunton, "Journal," 119. James M. Thompson (quoting James Corse, "Journal"), *History of Greenfield, Mass., 1692-1900* (Greenfield, 1904), 38. *Lee and Sewall Letters*, Kittredge, ed., 29.

5. Denys, *Natural History*, 403. Jonathan Carver, *Travels through the Interior Parts of North America . . . 1766-1768* (London, 1778), 235. George Catlin, *Letters and Notes on the Manners, Customs, and Condition of the North American Indians*, 2 vols. (New York, 1844, reprinted Philadelphia, 1913), 2:258. Williams, *Key*, 212. Dunton, "Journal," 119.

6. Speck, *Penobscot Man*, 252. Melvin R. Gilmore, "Uses of Plants by the Indians of the Missouri River Region," U.S. Bureau of American Ethnology, *Annual Report*, 33 (1911-12), 64.

7. Speck, 76. Ward, *New England*, 69.

8. Ralph May, *Early Portsmouth History* (Boston, Goodspeed, 1926), 70.

9. Morton, *Canaan*, 145. Ward, 65. Denys, 403. Wassenaer, "Historisch Verhael," 72.

10. Lahontan, *New Voyages*, 2:418. Denys, 399. Claude C. Coffin, "Connecticut Indian Burials," Arch. Soc. of Conn., *Bulletin*, 32 (1963), 63.

11. Neal, *New-England*, 29. Le Jeune, in *Jesuit Relations*, Thwaites, ed., 6:189. J. H. Temple, *History of Framingham, Massachusetts* (Framingham, 1887), 43. Eva L. Butler, "Sweat Houses in the Southern New England Area," Mass. Arch. Soc., *Bulletin*, 7, no. 1 (1945), 11-15.

12. H. E. Pulling, "Farmers before Columbus," unpublished lecture before New England Section, Am. Chemical Soc., September 18, 1936.

13. William H. Clark, *History of Winthrop, Massachusetts* (Winthrop, 1952), 32.

14. Daniel J. Boorstin, *The Americans: The Colonial Experience* (New York, Random House, 1958), 201. John Duffy, *The Healers: The Rise of the Medical Establishment* (New York, McGraw-Hill, 1976), 34.

15. Gookin, *Historical Collections*, 21. Frank Hamilton Cushing, "Remarks on Shamanism," Am. Philos. Soc., *Proceedings*, 36 (1897), 184-187.

16. Denys, 415. Vogel, *Medicine*, 15, 22.

17. John Lee Maddox, *The Medicine Man* (New York, Macmillan, 1923), 190.

6. Religion and Philosophy

1. Gookin, *Historical Collections*, 21.

2. Daniel Strock, Jr., *Pictorial History of King Philip's War* (Hartford, Conn., 1851), 19. Johnson, *Wonder-Working Providence*, 117, 227. George H. Ellis, "The Indians of Eastern Massachusetts," in Winsor, *Boston*, 256, 264.

3. Samuel Greene Arnold, *History of the State of Rhode Island and Providence Plantations* (New York, 1859-60), 75. Lahontan, *New Voyages*, 2:413. Thomas Hutchinson, *The History of the Colony and Province of Massachusetts Bay*, ed. Lawrence S. Mayo, 3 vols. (Cambridge, Harvard University Press, 1936), 1:394.

4. Clark Wissler, *Indians of the United States* (Garden City, N.Y., Doubleday, 1940, ed., 1966), 278.

5. Ellis, 260. Bicknell, *Rhode Island*, 79, 80.

6. Lechford, *Plain Dealing*, 120.

7. Frederick Webb Hodge, ed., *Handbook of American Indians North of Mexico*, 2 vols. Smithsonian Institution, (Bureau of American Ethnology, *Bulletin*, 30, 1907-10), 2:768. Natalie Curtis, *The Indian's Book* (New York, 1907), xxiii, 4. *Jesuit Relations*, ed. Thwaites, 13:259.

8. Coffin, in Arch. Soc. of Conn., *Bulletin*, 32 (1963), 6-11. Denys, *Natural History*, 438. William S. Fowler, "Two Indian Burials," Mass. Arch. Soc., *Bulletin*, 35, nos. 3 and 4 (1974), 15.

7. A Place to Live

1. James Sullivan, "The History of the Penobscott Indians," Mass. Hist. Soc., *Collections* 9 (1804), 213. Thomas Weston, *History of the Town of Middleboro, Massachusetts* (Boston, 1906), 2.
2. Quinebaug Historical Leaflets, Quinebaug Hist. Soc., Sturbridge, Mass., 1 (R.I. . . .), 73-78. Stebbins, *Hinsdale*, 357. G. M. Fessenden, *The History of Warren*, (Providence, 1845), Supplement, 23. Bushnell, *Native Villages*, 18. De Forest, *Connecticut Indians*, 207. *Jesuit Relations*, Thwaites, ed., 3:77. Henry F. Howe, "Archaeology of the Lower North River Valley," Mass. Arch. Soc., *Bulletin*, 10, no. 2 (1949), 41.
3. Josselyn, *Two Voyages*, 138. Morton, *Canaan*, 3. Donck, "New Netherlands," 128.
4. Verazzano, "Voyage," 1:48. Mary A. Proctor, *The Indians of the Winnipesaukee and Pemigewasset Valleys* (Franklin, N. H., 1931), 19. Morton, 87, 92. Nathaniel Saltonstall, "State of New England," in Lincoln, ed., *Narratives of the Indian Wars*, 55.
5. Williams, "Key," Mass. Hist. Soc., *Collections*, 3 (1794), 215. Neal, *New-England*, 3:26.
6. Morton, 134. Josselyn, 126. Champlain, *Voyages*, ed. Grant, 71. *Mourt's Relation*, 35. Speck, *Penobscot Man*, 27-31.
7. Dunton, John, "Journal," Mass. Hist. Soc., *Collections*, 2nd series, 2 (1814), 97-124. Ezra Stiles, *Extracts from the Itineraries . . ., 1755-1794*, ed. Franklin Bowditch Dexter (New Haven, Yale University Press, 1916), 131. Morton, above.
8. Ward, *New-England*, 68. Champlain, 63. Frederic H. Douglas, *New England Indian Houses, Forts, and Villages*, Leaflet 39, Denver Art Museum (1932). Morton, above. Philip Vincent, "A True Relation of the Late Battell . . . Pequot War," Mass. Hist. Soc., *Collections*, 3rd series, 6 (1837), 39. Williams, *Key*, 60. Higginson, in Young's *Chronicles of . . . Massachusetts Bay*, 256.
9. Champlain, 76, 124. Speck, 32. Stiles, above, Lechford, *Plain Dealing*, 118.
10. *Mourt's Relation*, 35. Bushnell, *Native Villages*, 19-22.
11. Williams, *Key*, 60. Champlain, 90. Morton, 134. Benjamin Tompson, *New-England's Crisis* (Boston, 1894), 18.
12. Williams, 213. Chase, "Wampanoag Indians," 906.
13. Bushnell, 54. Higginson, 256. Alexander F. Chamberlain, "Algonkian Words in American English," *Journal of American Folklore*, 15 (1902), 266.
14. *Mourt's Relation*, 33, 159. Higginson, 257. Henry W. Haynes, "Notes on Indian Hemp," Mass. Hist. Soc., *Proceedings*, 2nd series, 6 (1890), 35. Speck, 118. Ruth M. Underhill, *Red Man's America* (Chicago, University of Chicago Press, 1953 and 1971), 61.
15. Lucien Carr, "The Food of Certain American Indians and Their Methods of Preparing It," Am. Antiquarian Soc., *Proceedings*, new series 10, (1896), 175. Josselyn, *Two Voyages*, 111.
16. George Catlin, *North American Indians* (Philadelphia, Leary, Stuart, 1913), I:259. Eva L. Butler and Wendell S. Hadlock, "Dogs of the Northeastern Woodland Indians," Mass. Arch. Soc., *Bulletin*, 10, no. 2 (1949), 17-35. Denys, *Natural History*, 429-431. Glover M. Allen, "Dogs of the American Aborigines," Museum of Comparative Zoology, Harvard University, *Bulletin*, 63, no. 9 (1920), 429-517.

8. Household and Personal Equipment

1. Willoughby, *Antiquities*, photo on 109. I have examined such boulder mortars at numberous places, including (in Massachusetts) Sudbury, Sandwich, and Martha's Vineyard; and have notations of others in all New England states except Vermont. An interested reader, if near an ancient thoroughfare, will do well to inquire in his neighborhood.

2. Mortars of this type are on exhibit in numerous museums. The Massachusetts Archaeological Society, at its Bronson Museum, Attleboro, has excellent examples; likewise Harvard's Peabody Museum, Amherst College, and many others.

3. The Mohegan Museum, at Montville, Connecticut, has a well turned wood mortar handed down in the Tantaquidgeon family.

4. Joseph Lafitau, *Moeurs des Sauvages Ameriquains*, Books I and II (Paris, 1724), 181.

5. Virginia Baker, *Massasoit's Town, Sowams in Pokonoket* (Warren, R.I., 1904), 37.

6. Underhill, *Red Man's America*, 67.

7. Gookin, *Historical Collections*, Fiske edition, 16. *Mourt's Relation,* 35. Josselyn, *Two Voyages*, 111. John Underhill, "History of the Pequot War," Mass. Hist. Soc., *Collections*, 3rd series, 6 (1837), 7. Fulmer Mood, "John Winthrop, Jr., on Indian Corn," *New England Quarterly*, 10 (1937), p. 129.

8. Gookin, above. Philip Vincent, Mass. Hist. Soc., *Collections*, 3rd series, 6 (1837), 39. "John Smith's Description of New-England," 120. Champlain, *Voyages*, Grant ed., 68.

9. Josselyn, above. See also Otis Tufton Mason, "Aboriginal American Basketry: Studies in a Textile Art without Machinery," U.S. National Museum, *Annual Report* (1902), (Washington, 1904), pp. 211, 216, 228. Eva L. Butler and Wendell S. Hadlock, "Some Uses of Birch Bark in Northern New England," Mass. Arch. Soc., *Bulletin*, 18, no. 4 (1957), 72-75. Speck, *Penobscot Man*, 109.

10. Willoughby, *Antiquities*, 157-161. William S. Fowler, "Stone Bowl Making at the Westfield Quarry," Mass. Arch. Soc., *Bulletin*, 30 (1968), 6-16. "The Diagnostic Stone Bowl Industry," ibid., 36, nos. 3 and 4 (1975), 1-10.

11. Champlain, *Voyages*, 86. William J. Howes, "Aboriginal New England Pottery," Mass. Arch. Soc., *Bulletin*, 15, no. 4 (1954), 82-86. Gookin, *Historical Collections*, 16. Lescarbot, *Nova Francia*, 232. Newton D. Mereness, *Travels in the American Colonies, 1690-1783* (New York, 1916), 220. Morton, *Canaan*, 159.

12. Willoughby, 190-200. Claude C. Coffin, "Seaside Indian Village Site: Fort Trumbull Beach," Arch. Soc. of Conn., *Bulletin*, 32 (1963), 15. Charles F. Sherman, "Pottery Traits of the Plymouth District," Mass. Arch. Soc., *Bulletin*, 8, no. 2 (1947), 27-29. Thomas Morton, *Manners and Customs of the Indians*, Old South Leaflet, vol. 4, no. 87 (Boston, 1897), 7. Lescarbot, 232.

13. *Mourt's Relation*, 33-35. Willoughby, 258-264. Hennepin, *New Discovery*, 2:527. Thomas E. Daniels, *Vermont Indians* (Orwell, Vermont, privately printed, 1963), 41. Wood, *New England's Prospect* (Prince Society edition, 1865), 20.

14. Wood, 77. William S. Fowler, "Eating Practices in Aboriginal New England," Mass. Arch. Soc., *Bulletin*, 36, nos. 3 and 4 (1975), 21-27. Cutler, ". . . *Vegetable Productions . . .*", Am. Acad. of Arts and Sciences, *Memoirs* (1785), 1:442. Hodge, *Handbook*, 164.

15. Jennings, *Prehistory*, 18. Wissler, *Indians*, 247. McNickle, "Indians," 34. Roland Allison, "Shell Heaps around Deer Isle," Arch. Soc. of Maine, *Bulletin*, 2 (1964), 3-5; 12 (1975), 1-3.

16. Ward, "New-England," 68. Willoughby, *Antiquities*, 279. Denys, *Natural History*, 411, 413. Charles Knowles Bolton, quoting Rev. William Morrell, in *The Real Founders of New England* (Boston, Faxon, 1929), 3. Lechford, *Plain Dealing*, 116, 411.

17. Verazzano, "Voyage," 1:47. Roger Williams, *Complete Writings* (New York, Russell and Russell, 1963), 1:145.

18. Daniels, *Vermont Indians*, 49. Morton, *Canaan*, Prince Society edition, 142. Denys, 411, 412. Williams, above. Brereton, in Winship, *Sailors Narratives*, 46.

19. Denys, 214. Wissler, *Indians*, 83. Sewall, *Ancient Dominions*, 38.

20. Denys, above.

21. Lechford, 116; Verrazano, quoted by Bicknell, *Rhode Island*, 66.

22. Bowen, *Woodstock*, 540. Harrington, *Indians of New Jersey*, 220. Speck, *Penobscot Man*, 99. *Jesuit Relations*, Thwaites, ed., 6:217.

9. The Family Meals

1. I am not aware of any previous systematic attempt to discuss in detail the character and scope of the diet of the New England Indians, despite traditions relating to the Indian origin of numerous local New England food specialties and practices. The data here presented are assembled from a wide variety of sources.

2. Donck, "New Netherlands," 1:187. Willey, *Introduction to American Archaeology*, 22.

3. Joseph Nicolar, *The Life and Traditions of the Red Man* (Old Town, Maine, 1893), 144. Diamond Jenness, *The Indians of Canada*, National Museum of Canada, *Bulletin*, 65, 3rd ed. (1953), 31. Speck, *Penobscot Man*, 101.

4. Denys, *Natural History*, 402. Daniels, *Vermont Indians*, 42. William A. Ritchie, *The Archaeology of Martha's Vineyard*, American Museum of Natural History (Garden City, New York, Natural History Press, 1969), 23, 52.

5. Rosier, "True Relation," Mass. Hist. Soc., *Collections*, 3rd series, 8 (1848), 143. Morton, *Canaan*, 137. Bowen, *Woodstock*, 540.

6. Coffin in Arch. Soc. of Conn., *Bulletin*, 32 (1963), 12-25. Dena F. Dincauze, *The Neville Site: 8000 Years at Amoskeag*, Peabody Museum, *Monographs*, 4 (Cambridge, Harvard University, 1976), 8. Neal, *New-England*, 1:27. Sebastian Ralé, "Letter to His Brother," in John F. Sprague, *Sebastian Ralé, A Maine Tragedy of the Eighteenth Century* (Boston, 1906), 109. *Letters of Lee and Sewall,* ed. Kittredge, 150. Mary Rowlandson, *The Narrative of the Captivity and Restoration of Mrs. Mary Rowlandson* (Lancaster, Mass., 1903), 60. George Faber Clark, *A History of . . . Norton . . . Massachusetts* (Boston, 1859), 55.

7. Daniel Williams Harmon, *A Journal of Voyages and Travels in the Interior of North America* (New York, 1903), 279. Oliver La Farge, *A Pictorial History of the American Indian* (New York, Crown, 1956), 113.

8. Speck, *Penobscot Man*, 65, 97. Ritchie, 52, 55. The observant Roger Williams, the original Rhode Islander, fails to mention the clambake in his description of Indian life, but Speck in Maine terms it "a native procedure."

9. Arthur C. Parker, *Iroquois Uses of Maize and Other Food Plants*, New York State Museum, *Bulletin*, 144 (Albany, 1910), 65.

10. Wood, *New England's Prospect*, 75.

11. Williams, *Key*, 40. Carr, "Food," 178.

12. Timothy Alden, "Memorabilia of Yarmouth," Mass. Hist. Soc., *Collections*, 1st series, 5 (1798), 55.

13. Rasieres, in *Narratives*, ed. Jameson, 107.

14. Mood, "Winthrop, Jr.," 129, 131. Carr, 184. Morgan, *Houses*, 119. Heckewelder, "History . . . of Indian Nations," 185. *Letters of Lee and Sewell*, Kittredge, ed., 150.

15. James Grant Wilson, "Arent Van Curler and His Journals," Am. Hist. Assn., *Annual Report* (1895), 87, 91. Johnson, *Wonder-Working Providence*, 109. Edward

Palmer, "Food Products of the North American Indians," U.S. Department of Agriculture, *Report*, 15 (1870), 415. Jenness, *Indians of Canada*, 43.

16. Gookin, *Historical Collections*, 15. Parker, *Uses of Maize*, 72. Alanson Skinner, "Some Wyandot Corn Foods," Milwaukee Public Museum, *Yearbook* (n.d.), 3:109. Johnson, 109. Mood, "Winthrop, Jr.," 129. Nicola Tenesles, *The Indian of New England*, ed. Joseph Barratt (Middletown, Conn., 1851), 19.

17. Heckewelder, 185. Lechford, *Plain Dealing*, 112. Hennepin, *New Discovery*, 1:149. William Strachey, *The Historie of Travaile into Virginia*, ed. R. H. Major (London, 1849), 73.

18. Schemel, in *N.E. Quarterly*, 10 (1937), 540. Nicolar, *Red Man*, 118.

19. Mood. "Winthrop, Jr.," 131. Samuel G. Drake, *Indian Captivities, or, Life in the Wigwam* (New York, 1855), 83.

20. Mood, 129.

21. Wood, *New England's Prospect*, 129. John Bartram, *Observations on . . . Soils, Rivers* (London, 1751, reprinted Rochester, 1895), 71. Lahontan, in Thwaites, *New Voyages*, 1:155.

22. U.S. Dept. of Agriculture, *Yearbook* (1925), 412.

23. Ulysses Prentiss Hedrick, *A History of Horticulture in America to 1860* (New York, Oxford University Press, 1950), 13. Which of the numerous varieties of beans the New England Indians grew and cooked is not clear. That they included the Boston-baked pea bean there is no proof.

24. Carver, *Travels*, 263. Hubbard, "History of New England," 214. Wilkes Allen, "A Memoir of the Pawtuckett Indians" in *The History of Chelmsford* (Haverhill, 1820), 150. John Josselyn, *New-England's Rarities Discovered*, ed. Edward Tuckerman (Boston, 1865), 103. Donck, "New Netherlands," 192. Speck, *Penobscot Man*, 94.

25. Francis Daniel Pastorius, *Description of Pennsylvania (1700)*, Old South Leaflets, vol. 4, no. 95 (Boston, 1898), 11.

26. Champlain, *Voyages*, 67. Williams, *Key*, 125. Josselyn, 109.

27. Merrit Lyndon Fernald and Albert Charles Kinsey, *Edible Wild Plants of Eastern North America* (Cornwall-on-Hudson, Idlewild Press, 1943), 357-359. Liberty H. Bailey, ed., *Cyclopedia of American Agriculture* (New York, Macmillan, 1917), 5th ed., 2:542.

28. Henry David Thoreau, *Writings*, 20 vols., ed. Bradford Torrey (Boston, Houghton Mifflin, 1906), 3:384. Henry F. Howe, *Prologue to New England* (New York, Farrar and Rinehart, 1943), 60. Huron H. Smith, *Ethnobotany of the Menomini Indians*, Milwaukee Public Museum, *Bulletin*, 4, no. 1 (1923), 65. Colonel James Smith, "An Account of the Remarkable Occurrences . . . during His Captivity with the Indians in the Years 1755-59," (Lexington, 1799, reprinted, Cincinnati, 1870), 26. Rowlandson, *Captivity*, 60. William Morrell, "Poem on New England," Mass. Hist. Soc., *Collections*, 1 (1792), 128.

29. Johnson, *Wonder-Working Providence*, 109. James Adair, *History of the American Indians*, ed. Samuel C. Williams (Johnson City, Tenn., 1930), 439.

30. Emma L. Coleman, *New England Captives Carried to Canada*, 2 vols. (Portland, 1925), 2:162. Elizabeth Hanson, *An Account of the Captivity of Elizabeth Hanson* (London, 1760), 16. F. W. Waugh, *Iroquois Foods and Food Preparation*, Geological Survey of Canada, Anthropological Series, 12 *Memoir*, 86, (Ottawa, 1916), 123.

31. Fernald and Kinsey, 159. C. Hart Merriam, "The Acorn: A Possibly Neglected Source of Food," *National Geographic*, 34 (1918), 129. John Long, *Voyages and Travels . . . 1768-1788*, ed. Milo Milton Quaife (Chicago, 1922), 80.

32. Taylor A. Steeves, "Wild Rice—Indian Food and a Modern Delicacy," *Economic Botany*, 6 (1952), 108-116. Josselyn, *Rarities*, ed. Tuckerman, 86. Edward Palmer,

"Food Products of North American Indians," U.S.D.A., *Report*, 15 (1870), 407. Ethel Hinckley Hausman, *The Illustrated Encyclopedia of American Wild Flowers* (Garden City, N.Y., 1947), xiv. Fernald and Kinsey, 84. Jannette May Lucas, *Indian Harvest: Wild Food Plants of America* (Philadelphia, Lippincott, 1945), 34, 46, 49, 51. A. B. Stout, "Vegetable Foods of the American Indian," New York Botanical Garden, *Bulletin*, 15 (1914), 54.

33. Parker, *Uses of Maize*, 96. Josselyn, *Two Voyages*, 20. Melvin R. Gilmore, "Indian Lore and Indian Gardens," *Field and Camp Notebook* (Ithaca, Slingerland-Comstock Company), 24.

34. Lescarbot, *Nova Francia*, 281. Thoreau, *Writings*, 14:308.

35. Mrs. Wilfrid O. White, "The Beach Plum," Garden Club of America, *Bulletin*, n.p., 1940. Oliver P. Medsger, *Edible Wild Plants* (New York, Macmillan, 1939), 41, 44, 48, 50. Hedrick, *Horticulture*, 41. Cutler, "Indigenous Plants," 149.

36. Anonymous, *Voyage to Sagadahoc*, 414. Donck, "New Netherlands," 192. Speck, *Penobscot Man*, 94. David Pieterszen de Vries, "My Second Voyage to the Coast of America," N.Y. Hist. Soc., *Collections*, 3 (1857), 90.

37. H.E. Pulling, "Farmers before Columbus," unpublished lecture. Gilmore, "Uses of Plants," 65. Smith, *Ethnobotany of the Menomini*, 62. Frances Densmore, *Chippewa Customs*, Smithsonian Institution, Bur. Am. Ethnology, *Bulletin*, 86 (Washington, 1929), 39. Valery Havard, "Drink Plants of the North American Indians," Torrey Botanical Club, *Bulletin*, 23 (1896), 33-46.

38. Lechford, *Plain Dealing*, 119.

39. Knowles, *Memoir of Roger Williams*, 131. Henry C. Dorr, "The Narragansetts," R.I. Hist. Soc., *Collections*, 7 (1885), 160.

40. Josiah Cotton, "Vocabulary of the Massachusetts (or Natick) Indian Language," Mass. Hist. Soc., *Collections*, 3rd series, 2 (1830), 145.

41. H. A. Schuette and A. J. Ihde, "Maple Sugar: A Bibliography of Early Records, Part II", Wisconsin Acad. of Sciences, Arts, and Letters, *Transactions*, 38 (1946), 89-184.

42. Paul Dudley, "An Account of the Method of Making Sugar," quoted by A. E. Chamberlain in "Maple Sugar and the Indians," *American Anthropologist*, 4 (1891), 382. H. A. and Sybil C. Schuette, "Maple Sugar: A Bibliography of Early Records," Wisconsin Academy of Sciences, Arts, and Letters, *Transactions*, 29 (1935), 216.

43. Samuel Hopkins, *Historical Memoirs Relating to the Housatonnuck Indians* (Boston, 1753), 27.

44. Lafitau, *Moeurs*, 2:155. Speck, *Penobscot Man*, 104. Cabot, *Brattleboro*, 4. Bailey, *Conflict of Cultures*, maintains that sugar making was not practiced by the Algonquians (p. 58). M. K. Bennett, "The Food Economy of the New England Indians," *Journal of Political Economy*, 63 (1955), 384, reaches a similar conclusion. Regina Flannery in her *Analysis of Coastal Algonquian Culture* earlier cited, calls the practice doubtful.

45. Charles A. Eastman, *Indian Boyhood* (Boston, Little, Brown, 1924), 29-36.

46. Smith, *Remarkable Occurrences during Captivity*, 36, 69. J. W. Powell, U.S. Bureau of Ethnology, *Reports*, 14 (1892), 287-290.

47. Peter Kalm, "Description of Sugar Making," *Agricultural History*, 13 (1939), 151-156. Thomas L. McKenney, *Sketches of a Tour to the Lakes, of the Character and Customs of the Chippeway Indians* (Baltimore, 1827), 193. Parker, *Uses of Maize*, 102 ff.

48. J. F. Wojta, "A Visit to the Indian Sugar Bush Ceremonials," *Wisconsin Archaeologist*, 11, no. 4 (1932), 172-175.

49. Sieur de Dièreville, *Relation of the Voyage to Port Royal in Acadia or New France* (Toronto, Champlain Society, 1933), 117.

50. Kalm, 156.

51. McKenney, above.

52. Church, *King Philip's War*, 30. Wood, *New England's Prospect*, 75. Hutchinson, *Massachusetts Bay*, 392. Nicolar, *Red Man*, 144. Elijah Kellogg, "Passamaquoddy Vocabulary," Mass. Hist. Soc., *Collections*, 3rd series, 3 (1833), 181-182, gives the Quoddy word as "Solowai." In other parts of the continent, however, the use of salt is well authenticated; see C. A. Browne, "The Chemical Industries of the American Aborigines," *Isis*, 23 (1935), 406-424; Driver, *Indians of North America*, 72-74; Edith V. Murphey, *Indian Uses of Native Plants* (Palm Desert, Cal., Desert Princes, 1959), 29.

53. Morton, *Canaan*, 161. Nehemiah How, "A Narrative of the Captivity of . . .," in Samuel G. Drake, *Tragedies of the Wilderness* (Boston, 1748), entry for October 7, 1745.

54. Le Jeune, in *Jesuit Relations*, Thwaites, ed., 5:97. Stephen Laurent, "The Diet That Made the Red Man," *New Hampshire Archaeologist*, 9 (1959), 7.

55. Winthrop, *History*, 2:331.

56. Benjamin Church, *History of King Philip's War*, I:50

57. John Asch, *The Story of Plants* (New York, Putnam, 1948), 116.

58. Pulling, "Farmers before Columbus," 3.

59. Palmer, "Food Products," 428. Smith, *Ethnobotany of the Menomini*, 59.

60. Rowlandson, *Captivity*, 60. Hanson, *Captivity*, 16. Heckewelder, quoted by Parker, *Uses of Maize*, 62. Williams, *Complete Writings*, 1:40. Carr, "Food," 188.

10. The Roles of the Sexes

1. Winslow, "Good News," 96. Williams, *Complete Writings*, 1:123.

2. Lechford, "Plain Dealing," 115. Levett, in Winship, *Sailors Narratives*, 285.

3. Joseph Jouvency, in *Jesuit Relations*, Thwaites, ed., 1:257. Biard, ibid., 3:101, 103. Winthrop, *History*, 1:122.

4. Benjamin B. Thatcher, *Indian Biography*, 2 vols. (New York, 1832), 1:305, 2:10. Ralph D. Smith, *The History of Guilford, Connecticut* (Albany, 1877), 9. George H. Tilton, *A History of Rehoboth, Massachusetts*, 1643-1918 (Boston, 1918), 62. William L. Stone, *Life and Times of Sir William Johnson, Bart.* (Albany, 1865), 2:181. *North American Indians in Historical Perspective*, Leacock and Lurie, eds., 22.

5. Lahontan, in Thwaites, *New Voyages*, 2:453. Arnold, *Rhode Island*, 75ff. Driver, *Indians of North America*, 443.

6. Gookin, *Historical Collections*, ed. Fiske, 13. Winslow, 97. Neal, *New-England*, 1:41.

7. Jenkins, *Connecticut Agriculture*, 2:295. Lahontan, in Thwaites, ed., *New Voyages*, 461.

8. Williams, *Key*, 212, 221. Morton, *Canaan*, 145. Dunton, "Journal," 110. Catlin, *North American Indians*, 2:258.

9. Hallett, Mass. Arch. Soc., *Bulletin*, 16, no. 2 (1955), 28. Adair, *History of the American Indians*, 437. See also George F. Will and George E. Hyde, *Corn among the Indians of the Upper Missouri* (Lincoln, University of Nebraska Press, 1976), 75, 93.

10. Heckewelder, "History of Indian Nations," 142.

11. Robert R. Walcott, "Husbandry in Colonial New England," *New England Quarterly*, 9 (1936), 251. Mildred Campbell, *The English Yeoman under Elizabeth and the Early Stuarts* (New Haven, Yale University Press, 1942), 230, 251. Waugh, *Iroquois Foods*, 9.

12. John M. Cooper, "The Culture of the Northeastern Indian Hunters," in Frederick Johnson, ed., *Man in Northeastern North America* (Andover, Peabody Foundation, 1946), 300. Heckewelder, "History of Indian Nations," 146. Parker, *Uses of Maize*, 23. Nicola Tenesles, in Barratt, ed., *Indians of New England*, 1:4. Williams, *Key*, 221.

13. Williams, *Complete Writings*, 1:75, 123, 141, 189. Hopkins, *Housatonnuck Indians*, 251. Driver, *Indians of North America*, 178-181.

12. Beyond the Round

1. For details on native games beyond the brief descriptions provided here, an excellent source is Allan Forbes's *Other Indian Events of New England*, published in 1941 by the State Street Trust Company of Boston (of which Mr. Forbes was the head), pp. 31-36. Willoughby's *Antiquities* has discussions on pp. 110, 226, and 260. In the *Bulletin* of the Massachusetts Archaeological Society, 16, no. 2 (1955), 25-28, Leaman F. Hallett describes Indian games of numerous types. All draw from colonial records.

2. "Captivity of Colonel James Smith," in Drake, *Indian Captivities*, 219. McKenney, *Tour to the Lakes*, 180. Church, *King Philip's War*, 1:29.

3. Forbes, *Other Indian Events*, 23.

4. Harrington, *Indians of New Jersey*, 51.

5. Willoughby, 110. Hallett, 26.

6. Willoughby, 226.

7. Harrington, 57. Hallett, 25.

8. Charles G. Leland, *The Algonquin Legends of New England* (Boston, Houghton Mifflin, 1884). "Told by Maria Saksis, a very intelligent Penobscot woman."

13. The Soil

1. Quoted by John C. Gray, "Remarks on New England Agriculture," in *Essays: Agricultural and Literary* (Boston, 1856), 2, 3. Alfred S. Hudson, *The History of Concord, Massachusetts* (Concord, 1904), 318. Hutchinson, *Massachusetts Bay*, ed., Mayo, 1:404.

2. Chase, "Wampanoag Indians," 878. Church, *King Philip's War*, 1:127 (and note), 148-152.

3. Josselyn, *Rarities*, ed. Tuckerman, 6. Stout, "Vegetable Foods," 50-60. Palmer, "Food Products," 405, 409, 415.

4. Hubbard, "History of New England," 23. Johnson, *Wonder-Working Providence*, 175. Champlain, *Voyages*, tr. Otis, 121. Speck, *Penobscot Man*, 94-98.

5. *Jesuit Relations*, Thwaites, ed., 3:84, 5:171, 6:277.

6. Verazzano, "Voyages," 1:57-67. Sieur Samuel de Champlain, *Voyages*, ed. Grant (New York, Scribners, 1907), 63. Thoreau, *Writings*, 7:133.

7. Morton, *Manners and Customs*, 17. Sagadahoc, 412. Johnson, *Wonder-Working Providence*, 56. John Brereton, "A Brief and True Relation ..." (London, 1602), reprinted Mass. Hist. Soc., *Collections*, 3rd series, 8 (1843), 89.

8. Walcott, *N.E. Quarterly*, 9 (1936), 220-224. *Town and Selectmen's Records, 1630-1702* (Cambridge, 1901), 6. James D. Phillips, *Salem in the Seventeenth Century* (Boston, Houghton Mifflin, 1933), 97. Mason A. Green, *Springfield, 1634-1886: History of Town and City* (Springfield, 1888), 47.

9. Alfred S. Hudson, *The History of Sudbury, Massachusetts* (Boston, 1889), 3.

10. Roger Williams, "An Helpe to the Native Language of America," in *Writings*, ed. J. Hammond Trumbull. Narragansett Club, 6 vols. (Providence, 1864), 1:96, 97.

11. Mabel E. Seebohm, *The Evolution of the English Farm* (London, 1927), 36, 152.

14. The Provision of Nature

1. Chase, "Wampanoag Indians," 897. Fannie H. Eckstorm, "Review of Willoughby's

'Antiquities,' "*N.E. Quarterly*, 9 (1936), 347. Federal Writers, *Connecticut, 476*. Federal Writers, *Rhode Island*, 30. Nicolar, *Red Man*, 118.

2. John Winthrop, *Selections from an Ancient Catalogue of Objects of Natural History* (1734, reprinted New Haven, 1844), 5. William Hubbard, *A Narrative of the Indian Wars in New England . . . 1607-1677* (Worcester, 1801), 214. *The Letters of Roger Williams*, ed. John R. Bartlett (Providence, Narragansett Club, 1874), 197. Speck, *Penobscot Man*, 36.

3. Hutchinson, *Mass. Bay*, 1:390. Clifford K. Shipton, *Roger Conant, A Founder of Massachusetts* (Cambridge, Harvard University Press, 1944), 47. Wood, *New England's Prospect*, 101.

4. Frank G. Speck, "Territorial Subdivisions and Boundaries of the Wampanoag, Massachusett, and Nauset Indians," *Indian Notes and Monographs* 44 (New York, Heye Foundation, 1928), 57. Orcutt, *Housatonic Valley*, 4. Powers, *Coos Country*, 236.

5. Thomas Hariot, *A Briefe and True Report of the New Found Land of Virginia*, facsimile of 1588 ed. (New York, Dodd, Mead, 1903), D. For the derivation of modern strawberries, see E. Lewis Sturtevant's "Notes on Edible Plants," ed. U. P. Hedrick, New York Agricultural Experiment Station, *Report, 2*, pt. 2 (Albany, 1919), 276-282. Le Jeune, *Jesuit Relations*, Thwaites, ed., 1:103.

6. Winship, *Sailors Narratives*, 59. Winthrop, *History*, 1:27. Wood, *New England's Prospect*, 15. Williams, *Key*, 121. Adair, *American Indians*, 434.

7. John Smith, in Winship, *Sailors Narratives*, 244.

8. Donck, "New Netherlands," 152.

9. Everett E. Edwards, "The Agriculture of the American Indians prior to the European Conquest," U.S. Dept. Ag., *Bulletin*, 23, 2nd ed. (Washington, 1934), 2. My conclusions about the strawberry are based not only on numerous seventeenth-century writings, but on considerable correspondence and discussion with botanists and a lifetime of local observation.

10. Brereton, "Brief Relation," 87. Donck, above. Morton, *Canaan*, 186.

11. John Pory, *Lost Description of the Plymouth Colony*, ed. Champlin Burrage (Boston, Houghton Mifflin, 1918). Lescarbot, *Nova Francia*, 93. "Voyage to Sagadahoc," in Burrage, *Early Voyages*, 414. Vries, "Second Voyage," 90.

12. Verazzano, "Voyage," 54. Champlain, *Voyages*, 1:194.

13. Jacques Cartier, "On the St. Lawrence 1534-5," in *American History Told by Contemporaries*, 112. *Jesuit Relations*, Thwaites, ed., 3:67.

14. Hedrick, *Horticulture*, 444, 448. S. B. Phinney, "Cranberry Culture," U.S. Dept. of Agriculture, *Report* (1863), 131.

15. Verazzano, 48. Winship, 244. Champlain, ed. Grant, 61, 62, 65, 88. *Mourt's Relation*, 136. Wood, *New England's Prospect*, 15. Edmund Browne, "Report on Massachusetts," Col. Soc. of Mass., *Transactions*, 7 (1900), 77. Medsger, *Edible Wild Plants*, states that wild plums range from Connecticut west (41).

16. Cutler, "Vegetable Productions," 449. Brereton, "Brief Relation," 75-79. Donck, "New Netherlands," 1:152.

17. Sturtevant, "Notes on Edible Plants," 44, 149.

18. Lucas, *Indian Harvest*, 63. Stout, "Vegetable Foods," 43, 54, 57.

19. Steeves, "Wild Rice," 108-116. Eastman, *Indian Boyhood*, 234ff. Jenkins, *Connecticut Agriculture*, 293.

20. Lucas, 34-51. Gilmore, "Indian Lore," 20. *Mourt's Relation*, 62, 131.

21. Christopher Levett, "A Voyage into New England," Mass. Hist. Soc., *Collections*, 3rd series, 8 (1843), 167, 168. Hedrick doubts that what Champlain and Levett saw was *Portulaca oleracea* (*Horticulture*, 67); but if it was not, what was it that filled Indian rows so abundantly?

22. Josiah G. Holland, *History of Western Massachusetts*, 2 vols. (Springfield, 1855), 1:21.

15. Preparing for Cultivation

1. Champlain, *Voyages*, ed. Grant, 62. F. Gabriel Sagard, "Le Grand Voyage Fait au Pays des Hurons," in *Trois Voyages* by Bertrand Guégan, (Paris, Edition du Carrefour, 1929), 119. Lafitau, *Moeurs*, 2:76. Jacques Cartier, "Second Voyage," in *Trois Voyages*, 42. Waugh, *Iroquois Foods*, 24. Parker, *Uses of Maize*, 24. Hariot, *Virginia*, c-2. See also William S. Fowler, "Agricultural Tools and Techniques of the Northeast," Mass. Arch. Soc., *Bulletin*, 15, no. 3 (1954), 41-51.
2. Edward B. Tylor, "Primitive Society Part II," *Contemporary Review*, 22 (1873), 63. George L. Gomme, *The Village Community* (New York, 1890), 281.
3. Williams S. Fowler, "Classification of Stone Implements of the Northeast," Mass. Arch. Soc., *Bulletin*, 25, no. 1 (1963), 25, and "Comparative Study of Hoe and Spade Blades," ibid., 35, nos. 1 and 2 (1973-74), 1.
4. Hariot, above. Williams, *Key*, 124. *Letters of Samuel Lee and Sewall*, ed. Kittredge, 153.
5. Waugh, 11. Frederick S. Dellenbaugh, *The North-Americans of Yesterday* (New York, Putnam, 1901), 270.
6. Williams, above. Wood, *New England's Prospect*, 106. Rasieres, in Jameson, ed., *Narratives*, 109. Champlain, 62.
7. William Bradford, *"Of Plimouth Plantation," from the Original Manuscript* (Boston, 1898), 123.
8. Willoughby, *Antiquities*, 130-141.
9. Brereton, "Brief Relation," 89. Morton, *Canaan*, 172.
10. Electa F. Jones, quoting Capt. Henry Aupanmurt (an Indian), in *Stockbridge, Past and Present: or, Records of an Old Mission Station* (Springfield, 1854), 15. Adair, *American Indians*, 232, 434. Champlain, *Voyages*, 115. William Wood, "Description of Massachusetts," in Young, *Chronicles of . . . Mass. Bay*, 395, 408.
11. Chase, "Wampanoag Indians," 878. Mood, "Winthrop, Jr.," 128.
12. Smith, "New-England," 118. John White, "The Planter's Plea," *The Founding of Massachusetts* (Boston, Massachusetts Historical Society, 1930), 161. See such local histories as Hudson, *Concord, Massachusetts*; Judd, *Hadley;* Adams, *Wethersfield, Connecticut*; John W. Hanson, *History of . . . Norridgewock and Canaan* (Boston, 1849); and Holland, *Western Massachusetts*.
13. Winship, *Sailors Narratives*, 240. Alexander Young, ed., *Chronicles of the Pilgrim Fathers* (Boston, 1844), 229. Wood, in Young, *Chronicles of . . . Mass. Bay*, 405.
14. Systematic examination of local histories of the 50 to 60 towns settled during the first half century of settlement makes the point amply clear.
15. "Early Attempts at Rhode Island History," ed. William E. Foster, R.I. Hist. Soc., *Collections*, 7 (1885), 5-109. Benjamin Bourne, *An Account of the Settlement of the Town of Bristol in the State of Rhode-Island* (Providence, 1785).
16. Chase, "Wampanoag Indians," 878.
17. Though many such fields have in recent decades been covered by developments as housing has displaced farms, a comprehensive study of local history and tradition makes this evident.
18. Delabarre and Wilder, "Indian Corn-hills," 203-205.
19. The last time I visited the Delabarre property, a considerable period after his death, the growth of the woodland and natural vegetation had made identification of cornhills difficult. The present condition of this and other localities mentioned I do not know.

20. F. Gabriel Sagard, "Le Grand Voyage Fait au Pays des Hurons," in *Trois Voyages*, (above), 119. John White drawing reprinted in American Heritage, *Book of Indians* (New York, 1961), 167.

21. Lafitau, *Moeurs*, 2:155. *Pageant of America*, Ralph H. Gabriel, ed. (New Haven, 1925-29), 3:31.

22. J. H. Temple, *History of North Brookfield, Massachusetts* (North Brookfield, Mass., 1887), 30.

23. Samuel G. Drake, *The Aboriginal Races of North America*, 15th ed. rev. (New York, 1880), 209; see Sanborn, *New Hampshire*, 91. Stackpole, *New Hampshire, 176.* Day, *Maine Agriculture*, 20. Orcutt, *Housatonic Valley*, 102. Currier, *Newbury*, 183, 184. Also numerous other local references to extensive cultivation.

24. Winship, *Sailors Narratives*, 59. Smith, Mass. Hist. Soc., *Collections,* 3rd series, 4 (1834), 108, 117, 118, 120.

16. Cultivated Crops

1. Jacob Abbott, *American History*, 8 vols. (New York, 1860-65), 1:83.

2. Williams, "Key," 114.

3. Nicolar, *Red Man*, 57.

4. Thomas Weston, *History of the Town of Middleboro, Massachusetts* (Boston, 1906), 3.

5. Galinat, in Sprague, ed., *Corn and Corn Improvement*, 13.

6. M. K. Bennett, "The Food Economy of the New England Indians," *Journal of Political Economy*, 63 (1955), 370, 371.

7. Mood, "Winthrop, Jr.," 127.

8. T. H. Hoskins, with Peol Susup, "An Indian on Indian Corn," *Garden and Forest*, 8 (1895), 23.

9. Driver, *Indians of North America*, 41.

10. Winthrop, *History, 125.* J. Howard Biggar, "The Old and the New in Corn Culture," U.S. Dept. Ag., *Report* (1918), 125. J. H. Kempton, "Maize: Our Heritage from the Indian," Smithsonian Institution, *Annual Report*, 1937 (Washington, 1938), 386.

11. Hedrick, *History of Agriculture*, 23.

12. Josselyn, *Two Voyages*, 23.

13. Speck, *Penobscot Man*, 91. Paul Dudley, "Observations on Some of the Plants in New England," Mass. Hist. Soc., *Collections*, 1st series, 9 (1804), 200.

14. Gentry, *Economic Botany*, 23 (1969), 64-66.

15. John L. Stoutenburgh, *Dictionary of the American Indian* (New York, 1960). Victor R. Boswell, of the U. S. Dept. of Agriculture, "Fossils or Plants?" in *American Vegetable Grower*, (December 1965), 37, states: "Common varieties that we call squash include three species: Cucurbita pepo, C. moschata, and C. maxima. The same is true of pumpkins. Mere custom rather than use or botanical relations determined which varieties are called squash and which pumpkins."

16. Josselyn, *Rarities*, ed. Tuckerman, 109. Williams, *Key*, 125. Donck, "New Netherlands," 186.

17. Carver, *Travels*, 525.

18. Donck, 186-188. Charles B. Heiser, Jr., "Cultivated Plants and Cultural Diffusion in Nuclear America," *Am. Anthropologist*, 67, no. 4 (1965), 937. Thomas W. Whitaker, "Gourds and People," *Am. Hort. Mag.* (October 1964), 209. Towle, *Ethnobotany of Peru*, 93. Willey, *Introduction to Archaeology*, 22.

19. Jasper Danckaerts and Peter Sluyter, "Journal of a Voyage to New York . . . in

1679-80," L.I. Hist. Soc., *Memoirs*, 1 (1867), 128. Lyda A. Taylor, *Plants Used as Curatives by Certain Southeastern Tribes*, (Cambridge, Harvard University Botanical Museum, 1940). Hedrick, *Horticulture*, 15. Alphonse de Candolle, *Origin of Cultivated Plants* (New York, 1887), 264.

20. Josselyn, above. Browne, "Report on Massachusetts," 77.

21. Donck, 186, 187.

22. Hedrick, 17. Candolle, 445. Gilmore, "Uses of Plants," 131. Brand, *Ag. History*, 13 (1939), 109.

23. Champlain, 81, 86. Lescarbot, *Nova Francia*, 279.

24. Starbird, *Androscoggin Valley*, 31. Thoreau, *Writings*, 3:384, 4:490.

25. Morrell, Mass. Hist. Soc., *Collections*, 1 (1792), 128.

26. Rowlandson, *Captivity*, 60. C. E. Potter, "Appendix to 'Abnaquies'," Maine Hist. Soc., *Collections*, 4 (1850), 193.

27. George A. West, *Tobacco, Pipes and Smoking Customs of the American Indians*, Milwaukee Public Museum, *Bulletin*, 17 (1934), 30, 54, 59, 117. Driver, *Indians of North America*, 90. Candolle, *Origin of Cultivated Plants*, 141.

28. Williams, *Key*, 43.

29. Gregory Mason, "Native American Food," *Natural History*, 37 (1936), 313. Lucia S. Chamberlain, "Plants Used by the Indians of Eastern North America," *American Naturalist*, 35 (1901), 2. Elizabeth Ramsey, *History of Tobacco Production in the Connecticut Valley*, Smith College Studies in History, 15 (Northampton, 1930), 113. Adrian F. McDonald, *History of Tobacco Production in Connecticut* (New Haven, Yale University Press, 1936), 3.

30. Catlin, *North American Indians*, 1:165. Williams, 72.

31. Winslow, "Good News," 97. Ralé, in *Sebastian Ralé*, ed. Sprague, 110.

32. Lescarbot, *Nova Francia*. See map decoration in 1609 London edition, opp. 136; also 277. Josselyn, *Rarities*, ed. Tuckerman, 103. Josselyn, *Two Voyages*, 76.

33. Brereton, "Brief Relation," 88. Winship, *Sailors Narratives*, 123. William A. Setchell, "Aboriginal Tobaccos," *Am. Anthropologist*, new series, 23, no. 4 (1921), 398, 403.

34. Jerome E. Brooks, *The Mighty Leaf: Tobacco through the Centuries* (Boston, Little, Brown, 1952), 23. Nicholas N. Smith, "Smoking Habits of the Wabanaki," Mass. Arch. Soc., *Bulletin*, 18, no. 4 (1957), 76. Catlin, 1:263. Parker, *Uses of Maize*, 32.

35. Le Jeune, in *Jesuit Relations*, Thwaites, ed. 7:137.

36. Williams, 43. George K. Holmes, "Some Features of Tobacco History," Am. Hist. Assn., *Annual Report*, 1 (1919), 387.

37. Holmes, 393

38. Williams, 43. Howe, *Prologue to New England*, 72. Champlain, ed. Grant, 62.

39. Holmes, 387, 393. Hedrick, *History of Agriculture*, 30. McDonald, 1. *Mourt's Relation*, 36.

40. Josselyn, *Two Voyages*, 61.

41. Hariot, *Virginia*, C-2.

42. Holmes, 151.

17. The Season's Round

1. Gladys Tantaquidgeon, "Mohegan Medicinal Practices," U.S. Bureau of American Ethnology, *Annual Report*, 43 (1928), 270, 271. Young, *Pilgrim Fathers*, 370. Waugh, *Iroquois Foods*, 24.

2. Tantaquidgeon, 270.

3. Thomas Morton, *Canaan*, 224.

4. Williams, *Key*, 123.

5. Mood, "Winthrop, Jr.," 127.

6. Bradford, "Of Plimouth Plantation," 121.

7. Winthrop, 182, *Mourt's Relation*, D. W. Prowse, *History of Newfoundland*, New York, Macmillan, (1895), 106, 128, 129. Chamberlain, *Journal of American Folklore*, 15 (1902), 248.

8. G. Browne Goode, "The Use of Agricultural Fertilizers by the American Indians and the Early English Colonists," *Am. Naturalist*, 14 (1880), 476, quoting Garcilasco de la Vega, *The Royal Commentaries of Peru*, tr. Sir Paul Rycaut (London, 1688). Alexander Grobman, et al., *Races of Maize in Peru*, Nat. Academy of Sciences– National Research Council, *Publications*, 915 (Washington, 1961), 25. Browne, *Isis*, 23 (1935), 407. Marc Lescarbot, in his *Nova Francia*, P. Erondelle translation (London 1609, p. 232), stated that the Massachusetts Bay Indians "do fatten [their soil] with the shells of fish." An 1844 report states that formerly, Cape Cod Bayside farmers split up the horse-foot or king crab for fertilizing cornhills. Did they learn this from the Indians?

9. Sebastian Ralé, *Sebastian Ralé*, Sprague, ed., 110. Delabarre and Wilder, "Indian Corn-hills," 203ff.

10. Champlain, *Voyages*, ed. Grant, 64.

11. Parker, *Uses of Maize*, 26. The Yumans of the Southwest had learned that sprinkling plants with water in which fish had been cooked would deter rabbits. Edward F. Castetter and Willis H. Bell, *Yuman Indian Agriculture* (Albuquerque, University of New Mexico Press, 1951), 155.

12. Williams, *Key*, 114. Winthrop, 127.

13. Josselyn, *Two Voyages*, 115.

14. Day, *Maine Agriculture*, 22. Young, *Chronicles of the Pilgrim Fathers*, 370.

15. Carr, "Food," 162. Williams, 123.

16. Stiles, *Itineraries*, 142. Driver, *Indians of North America*, 399.

17. Champlain, 62. Wood, *New England's Prospect*, Prince ed., 106. Strachey, *Travaile*, ed. Major, 117.

18. Drake, *Indian Captivities*, 83.

19. Rasieres, in Jameson, *Narratives*, 114. Peter Kalm, "Travels," in *Pinkerton's Travels* (London, 1812), 470. Mood, "Winthrop, Jr.," 126.

20. Winthrop, 125, 127.

21. John de Laet, "Extracts from 'The New World,'" N.Y. Hist. Soc., *Collections*, 2nd series, 1 (1841), 300.

22. Temple, *Framingham*, 36.

23. Madeleine S. and J. Lane Miller, *Harper's Bible Dictionary* (New York, 1955), 350. Peter H. Blair, *Roman Britain and Early England* (N.Y., Norton, 1966), 117. Lescarbot, *Nova Francia*, 275.

24. Bradford, *Of Plimouth Plantation*, 123.

25. Temple, *North Brookfield*, 27.

26. I have discussed this subject more fully in "How Aboriginal Planters Stored Food," Mass. Arch. Soc., *Bulletin*, 23, nos. 3 and 4 (1962), 47-49.

27. Champlain, *Voyages*, ed. Grant, 95. Wood, *New England's Prospect*, Prince ed., 106. Drake, *Indian Captivities*, 83.

28. A. Hyatt Verrill, *The Heart of Old New England* (New York, 1936), 14. Walter Needham and Barrows Mussey, *A Book of Country Things* (Brattleboro, 1965), 148.

29. De Forest, *Connecticut Indians*, 169. Elisha R. Potter, Jr., "Early History of Narragansett," R. I. Hist. Soc., *Collections*, 3 (1835), 88. Nathaniel Bouton, "History of the Ancient Pennacooks," in *History of Concord . . . 1725-1853* (Concord, N. H., 1856), 19.

30. Wilson, American Hist. Assn., *Annual Report* (1895), 87, 90. Parker, *Uses of Maize*, 34. Le Jeune, in *Jesuit Relations*, Thwaites, ed., 1:103. Carver, *Travels*, 525.

31. Smith, Milwaukee Public Museum, *Bulletin*, 4, no. 1 (1923), 33, and plate 26, p. 155. Hennepin, *New Discovery*, 2:652. Adair, *American Indians*, 439.

32. Huron H. Smith, *Ethnobotany of the Meskwaki Indians*, Milwaukee Public Museum, *Bulletin*, 4, no. 2 (1928), 257. Catlin, *North American Indians*, 1:140. Neal, *New-England*, 1:28. See also Edward N. Wentworth, "Dried Meat—Early Man's Travel Ration," *Ag. History*, 30 (1956), 2ff.

33. Denys, *Natural History*, 435. *The Animal Kingdom*, Frederick Drimmer, ed., 3 vols. (Garden City, N.Y., 1954), 4:991. Coffin, Arch. Soc. of Conn., *Bulletin*, 32 (1963), 33.

34. Holland, *Western Massachusetts*, 2:5, 16, 202. John W. Barber, *Historical Collections of Massachusetts* (Worcester, 1844), 214. Speck, "Territorial Subdivisions," 57, and "The Family Hunting Band as the Basis of Algonkian Social Organization," *Am. Anthropologist*, 17 (1915), 294, 297.

35. Harriette S. Arnow, *Seedtime on the Cumberland* (New York, 1960), 56. William L. Stone, *The Life and Times of Sir William Johnson, Bart.*, 2 vols. (Albany, 1865), 2:108.

36. De Forest, *Connecticut Indians*, 207. Bushnell, *Native Villages*, 32.

18. Trade and Conflict

1. Arnold, *Rhode Island*, 81. Baker, *Massasoit's Town*, 3ff Hutchinson, *Massachusetts Bay*, 1:386. Jennings, *Invasion*, 92. Williams, *Complete Writings*, 1:173-177.

2. Willoughby, *Antiquities*, 112-118.

3. Ibid., 186-188.

4. Collier, *Indians of the Americas*, 199. McNickle, in *North American Indians*, ed. Leacock and Lurie, 166.

5. Sheldon, *Deerfield*, 152. Spiess, *Indians of Connecticut*, 18.

6. Eckstorm, "Indians of Maine," 47. Joseph B. Felt, *Annals of Salem*, 2 vols. (Salem, 1845), 1:21.

7. Alden T. Vaughan, *New England Frontier: Puritans and Indians* (Boston, Little, Brown, 1965), 145. Porter E. Sargent, *A Handbook of New England* (Boston, 1916), 169.

8. Gookin, *Historical Collections*, 18.

9. Brandon, *Last Americans*, 183. Gookin, above.

10. Speck, *Penobscot Man*, 11, 115. Harrington, *Indians of New Jersey*, 96. Daniels, *Vermont Indians*, 19.

11. Sewall, *Ancient Dominions*, 96. Denys, *Natural History*, 419. Bicknell, *Rhode Island*, 1:68.

12. Speck, 115. Electa F. Jones, quoting Indian source in *Stockbridge*, 16. Clark Wissler disagrees.

13. Nathaniel Knowles, "The Torture of Captives by the Indians of Eastern North America," Am. Philos. Soc., *Proceedings*, 82 (1940), 190.

19. Travel and Communication

1. Le Jeune, in *Jesuit Relations*, Thwaites, ed., 5:133. McKenney, *Tour to the Lakes*, 199, 200, 338. Catlin, *North American Indians*, 2:157. Denys, 420.

2. Champlain, *Voyages*, ed. Grant, 66. Verrazano, in Winship, *Sailors Narratives*, 18. Williams, *Key*, 107. Winthrop, *History*, 112. Vries, "Second Voyage," 95.

3. Chester B. Kevitt, "Aboriginal Dugout Discovered at Weymouth," Mass. Arch. Soc., *Bulletin*, 30, no. 1 (1968), 1-5.

4. A number of historians have been misled on this. Not, however, Archer B. Hulbert, *Historic Highways of America*, 16 vols. (Cleveland, 1902-1905), 2:14, 19.

5. Hodge, *Handbook*, 2:799. Wood, *New England's Prospect*, 79. Archer B. Hulbert, *Soil: Its Influence on the History of the United States* (New Haven, Yale University Press, 1930), 50, 51. Gookin, *Historical Collections* Fiske, ed., 32-37. Mrs. Harriet S. Caswell, *Our Life among the Iroquois Indians* (Boston, 1892), 276.

6. Williams, *Key*, 216. Wood, *New England's Prospect*, 79. *Mourt's Relation*, 32.

7. George F. Marlowe, *The Old Bay Paths* (New York, 1942), 96. Leaman F. Hallett, "Indian Trails and Their Importance to the Early Colonists," Mass. Arch. Soc., *Bulletin*, 17, no. 3 (1956), 42. Levi B. Chase, *The Bay Path and Along the Way* (Norwood, Mass., privately printed, 1919).

8. William B. Browne, *The Mohawk Trail* (Pittsfield, Mass., 1920), 5ff.

9. Hubbard, "History of New England," 5:30.

10. Sidney S. Rider, *The Lands of Rhode Island* (Providence, 1904), 235.

11. Stackpole, *New Hampshire*, 2:41. Spiess, *Indians of Connecticut*, 10, 26. Harral Ayres, *The Great Trail of New England* (Boston, 1940), 96, 153, 163, 186, 189. Wells, *Newbury, Vermont*, 31, and other local histories.

12. Howe, *Salt Rivers*, 24.

13. Starbird, *Androscoggin Valley*. Fannie Hardy Eckstorm, "The Indian Routes of Maine," unpublished manuscript in the University of Maine Library, Orono. Federal Writers, *Maine: A Guide "Down East"* (Boston, 1937), 384.

14. Hallett, 45. Deloraine P. Corey, *History of Malden, Massachusetts, 1633-1785* (Salem, 1899), 89. Henry M. Fenner, *History of Fall River* (New York, 1906), 8. Langdon B. Parsons, *History of Rye, New Hampshire* (Concord, 1905), and other local histories.

15. Williams, *Key*, 95. Quote by Hulbert, above.

16. Edward Winslow, in Nathaniel Morton, ed., *New England's Memorial*, 6th ed. (Boston, 1855), 492.

Bibliography

Agricultural and Botanical

Ames, Oakes. *Economic Annuals and Human Cultures*. Cambridge, Mass., Harvard University Botanical Museum, 1939.

Asch, John. *The Story of Plants*. New York, N.Y., Putnam's, 1948.

Bailey, Liberty H. *Manual of Cultivated Plants Most Commonly Grown in the United States and Canada*. Rev. ed. New York, N.Y., Macmillan, 1949.

Beadle, George W. "The Mystery of Maize." Field Museum of Natural History, *Bulletin*, 42 (1972), 1-11.

Biggar, J. Howard. "The Old and the New in Corn Culture." U.S. Department of Agriculture, *Report*, 1918.

Boswell, Victor R. "Fossils or Plants?" *American Vegetable Grower*, 12 (1965), 37.

Brand, Donald D. "The Origin and Early Distribution of New World Cultivated Plants." *Agricultural History*, 13 (April 1939), 109-117.

Britton, Nathaniel Lord, and Hon. Addison Brown. *An Illustrated Flora of the Northern United States and Canada*. 3 vols. 2nd rev. ed. New York, N.Y., Scribner's, 1913; reprint New York, N.Y., Dover, 1970.

Brown, William L., and Edgar Anderson. "The Northern Flint Corns." Missouri Botanical Garden, *Annals*, 34 (February 1947), 1-38.

Butler, Eva L. "Algonkian Culture and Use of Maize in Southern New England." Archeological Society of Connecticut, *Bulletin*, 22 (December 1948), 2-39.

———, and Wendell S. Hadlock. "Use of Birch-bark in the Northeast." Robert Abbe Museum, *Bulletin*, 7 (1957), Bar Harbor, Me.

Candolle, Alphonse de. *Origin of Cultivated Plants*. New York, N.Y., Appleton, 1887.

Carrier, Lyman. *The Beginnings of Agriculture in America*. New York, N.Y., McGraw-Hill, 1923.

Castetter, Edward F., and Willis H. Bell. *Pima and Papago Indian Agriculture*. Albuquerque, N.M., University of New Mexico Press, 1942.

———, and Willis H. Bell. *Yuman Indian Agriculture*. Albuquerque, N.M., University of New Mexico Press, 1951.

Ceci, Lynn. "Fish Fertilizer: A Native North American Practice?" *Science*, 188 (1975), 26-30.

Chamberlain, Lucia Sarah. "Plants Used by the Indians of Eastern North America." *American Naturalist*, 35. (1901), 1-10.

Corbett, L. C., et al. "Fruits and Vegetables." U.S. Department of Agriculture, *Agriculture Yearbook* (1925), 107-124.

Cutler, Manasseh. "An Account of Some of the Vegetable Productions Naturally Growing in This Part of America." American Academy of Arts and Sciences, *Memoirs*, 1 (1785), 396-493.

Delabarre, Edmund B., and Harris H. Wilder. "Indian Corn-hills in Massachusetts." *American Anthropologist*, 22 (1920), 203-225.

Dudley, Paul. "An Account of the Method of Making Sugar," quoted by A. E. Chamberlain in "Maple Sugar and the Indians." Ibid., 4 (1891), 382.

————. "Observations on Some of the Plants in New England." Massachusetts Historical Society, *Collections*, 1st series, 9 (1804), 193-200.

Edwards, Everett E. "The Agriculture of the American Indians Prior to the European Conquest." U.S. Department of Agriculture, *Bulletin*, 23 (2nd ed., 1934).

Emerson, George B. *A Report on the Trees and Shrubs Growing Naturally in the Forests of Massachusetts*. 2nd ed. 2 vols. Boston, Mass., Little, Brown, 1875.

Fernald, Merritt Lyndon, and Alfred Charles Kinsey. *Edible Wild Plants of Eastern North America*. Cornwall-on-Hudson, N.Y., Idlewild Press, 1943.

Fowler, William S. "Agricultural Tools and Techniques of the Northeast." Massachusetts Archaeological Society, *Bulletin*, 15, no. 3 (1954), 41-51.

————. "Comparative Study of Hoe and Spade Blades." Ibid., 35, nos. 1 and 2 (1973-74), 1-9.

————. "Did Lafitau Draw What He Saw?" Ibid., 21, nos. 3 and 4 (1960), 38-43.

————. "Triangular Hoes of the Northeast and Their Diffusion." Ibid., 9, no. 4 (1948), 83-88.

Galinat, Walton C. "Plant Habit and the Adaptation of Corn." University of Massachusetts Experiment Station, *Bulletin*, 565 (1967).

————. "The Origin of Sweet Corn." Ibid., 591 (1971).

————. "The Evolutionary Emergence of Maize." Torrey Botanical Club, *Bulletin*, 102, no. 6 (November-December 1975), 315-324.

————. "The Origin of Corn," in *Corn and Corn Improvement*, G. F. Sprague, ed. (Madison, Wisc., American Society of Agronomy, 1977), 1-47.

Garner, W. W., et al. "History and Status of Tobacco Culture." U.S. Department of Agriculture, *Agriculture Yearbook* (1922), 395-468.

Gentry, Howard Scott. "Origin of the Common Bean, *Phaseolus vulgaris*." *Economic Botany*, 23 (1969), 55-69.

Gilmore, Melvin R. "Indian Lore and Indian Gardens," in *Field and Camp Notebook*. Ithaca, N.Y., Slingerland-Comstock, 1930.

————. "Uses of Plants by the Indians of the Missouri River Region." U.S. Bureau of American Ethnology, *Annual Report*, 33 (1911-12), (Washington, D.C., 1919), 43-154.

Goode, G. Browne. "The Use of Agricultural Fertilizers by the American Indians and the Early English Colonists." *American Naturalist*, 14 (1880), 473-479.

Gray, Asa. *Manual of Botany*, Merritt Lyndon Fernald, ed. 8th ed. New York, N.Y., American Book Co., 1950.

————, and J. Hammond Trumbull. "Review of de Candolle's Origin of

Cultivated Plants." *American Journal of Science,* 3rd series, 25 (1883), 241-255, 370-379; 26 (1883), 128-138.

Gray, John C. "Remarks on New England Agriculture," in *Essays: Agricultural and Literary.* Boston, Mass., Little, Brown, 1856.

Gregory, James J. H. *Squashes: How to Grow Them.* New York, N. Y., Judd, 1867.

Grieve, Maud L. *A Modern Herbal.* New York, N.Y. Hafner Press, 1931, 1974.

Grobman, Alexander, et al. *Races of Maize in Peru.* National Academy of Sciences–National Research Council, *Publication,* 915, Washington, D.C., 1961.

Hausman, Ethel Hinckley. *The Illustrated Encyclopedia of American Wild Flowers.* Garden City, N.Y., Garden City Publishing Co., 1947.

Havard, Valery. "Drink Plants of the North American Indians." Torrey Botanical Club, *Bulletin,* 23 (1896), 33-46.

Haynes, Henry W. "Notes on Indian Hemp." Massachusetts Historical Society, *Proceedings,* 2nd series, 6 (1890), 34-36.

Heiser, Charles B., Jr. "The Sunflower among the North American Indians." American Philosophical Society, *Proceedings,* 95 (1951), 432-448.

Henshaw, H. W. "Indian Origin of Maple Sugar." *American Anthropologist,* 3 (1890), 341-351.

Holder, Charles F. "Indian Granaries." *Scientific American,* 89 (1903), 263.

Holmes, George K. "Aboriginal Agriculture—The American Indians," in *Cyclopedia of American Agriculture,* Liberty H. Bailey, ed. New York, N.Y., Macmillan, 1917, 4:24-39.

Hoskins, T. H., with Peol Susup. "An Indian on Indian Corn." *Garden and Forest,* 8 (1895), 23.

Hough, Walter. "The Development of Agriculture." *Scientific Monthly,* 29, no. 4 (1929), 304-316.

Jones, Henry Albert, and Joseph Tooker Rosa. *Truck Crop Plants.* New York, N.Y., McGraw-Hill, 1928.

Kalm, Peter. "Description of Sugar Making." *Agricultural History,* 13 (1939), 151-156.

Kaplan, Lawrence. "Archeology and Domestication in American Phaseolus (Beans)." *Economic Botany,* 19 (1965), 358-368.

Kempton, J. H. "Maize: Our Heritage from the Indian." Smithsonian Institution, *Annual Report,* 1937 (Washington, 1938), 385-408.

Laufer, Berthold. "The American Plant Migration." *Scientific Monthly,* 28 (1929), 239-251.

Lucas, Jannette May. *Indian Harvest: Wild Food Plants of America.* Philadelphia, Penn., Lippincott, 1945.

Mangelsdorf, Paul C. *Corn: Its Origin, Evolution, and Improvement.* Cambridge, Mass., Harvard University Press, 1974.

————, Richard E. MacNeish, and Walton C. Galinat. "Domestication of Corn." *Science*, 143 (1964), 538-545.

Martin, Richard. "The Origin and Evolution of the Cultivated Tobaccos." Unpublished manuscript, 1964.

Medsger, Oliver Perry. *Edible Wild Plants*. New York, N.Y., Macmillan, 1939.

Merriam, C. Hart. "The Acorn: A Possibly Neglected Source of Food." *National Geographic*, 34 (1918), 129-137.

Mood, Fulmer. "John Winthrop, Jr., on Indian Corn." *New England Quarterly*, 10 (1937), 121-133.

Murphey, Edith V. *Indian Uses of Native Plants*. Palm Desert, Cal., Desert Princes, 1959.

Nearing, Helen and Scott. *The Maple Sugar Book*. New York, N.Y., John Day, 1950.

Olday, Frederick C. "The Cultivated Cucurbits, Their Origin and Evolution." Unpublished Harvard University thesis, 1965.

Onion, Daniel K. "Corn in the Culture of the Mohawk Iroquois." *Economic Botany*, 18 (1964), 60-66.

Palmer, Edward. "Food Products of the North American Indians." U.S. Department of Agriculture, *Report*, 15 (1870), 404-428.

————. "Plants Used by Indians of the United States." *American Naturalist*, 12 (1878), 593-606, 646-655.

Phinney, S. B. "Cranberry Culture." U.S. Department of Agriculture, *Report* (1863), 131-139.

Ramsey, Elizabeth. *History of Tobacco Production in the Connecticut Valley*. Smith College Studies in History, 15. Northampton, Mass., Smith College Department of History, 1930.

Robert, Joseph C. *The Story of Tobacco in America*. New York, N.Y., Knopf, 1952.

Rostlund, Erhard. "The Evidence for the Use of Fish as Fertilizer in Aboriginal North America." *Journal of Geography*, 56 (1957), 222-228.

Russell, Howard S. "Indian Corn Cultivation" (letter). *Science,* 189, no. 4207 (Sept. 19, 1975), 944-946.

————. "New England Agriculture from Champlain and Others." Massachusetts Archaeological Society, *Bulletin*, 31, nos. 1 and 2 (1969-1970), 11-18.

Safford, William E. "Foods Discovered with America." *Scientific Monthly*, 21 (1925), 181-186.

Schuette, H. A. and Sybil C. "Maple Sugar: A Bibliography of Early Records [Part I]." Wisconsin Academy of Sciences, Arts, and Letters, *Transactions*, 29 (1935), 209-236.

————, and A. J. Ihde. "Maple Sugar: A Bibliography of Early Records, Part II." Ibid., 38 (1946), 89-184.

Schultes, Richard Evans. "The Widening Panorama in Medical Botany." *Rhodora*, 65 (1963), 97-120.

Scully, Virginia. *A Treasury of American Indian Herbs*. New York, N.Y., Crown, 1970.

Setchell, William Albert. "Aboriginal Tobaccos." *American Anthropologist*, new series, 23, no. 4 (1921), 397-414.

Smith, Huron H. "Ethnobotany of the Menomini Indians." Milwaukee Public Museum, *Bulletin*, 4, no. 1, 1923.

————. "Ethnobotany of the Meskwaki Indians." Ibid., no. 2, 1928.

————. "Ethnobotany of the Ojibwe." Ibid., no. 3, 1932.

Steeves, Taylor A. "Wild Rice—Indian Food and a Modern Delicacy." *Economic Botany*, 6 (1952), 107-142.

Sturtevant, E. Lewis. "Indian Corn and the Indian." *American Naturalist*, 19 (1885), 225-234.

————. "Kitchen Garden Esculents of American Origin." Ibid., 19 (1885), 444-457, 542-553, 658-669.

————. "Sturtevant's Notes on Edible Plants," Ulysses Prentiss Hedrick, ed. New York Agricultural Experiment Station, *Report*, 2, pt. 2, Albany, N.Y., Lyon, 1919.

Taylor, Lyda Averill. *Plants Used as Curatives by Certain Southeastern Tribes*. Cambridge, Mass., Harvard University Botanical Museum, 1940.

Walcott, Robert R. "Husbandry in Colonial New England." *New England Quarterly*, 9 (1936), 218-252.

Weatherwax, Paul. *Indian Corn in Old America*. New York, N.Y., Macmillan, 1954.

Weiner, Michael A. *Earth Medicine—Earth Foods: Plant Remedies, Drugs, and Natural Foods of the North American Indian*. New York, N.Y., Macmillan, 1972.

Wessell, Thomas R. "Agriculture and Iroquois Hegemony in New York, 1610-1779." *Maryland Historian*, 1, no. 2 (1970), 93-104.

Whitaker, Thomas W. "American Origin of Cultivated Cucurbits." Missouri Botanical Garden, *Annals*, 34 (1947), 101-107.

————. "Gourds and People." *American Horticultural Magazine*, 43 (October 1964), 207-213.

————, and Hugh C. Cutler. "Cucurbits and Cultures in the Americas." *Economic Botany*, 19 (1965), 344-349.

White, Mrs. Wilfrid O. "The Beach Plum." Garden Club of America, *Bulletin*, January 1940.

Winthrop, John. *Selections from an Ancient Catalogue of Objects of Natural History*. 1734; reprint New Haven, Conn., Hamlen, 1844.

Zevallos, Carlos M., et al. "The San Pablo Corn Kernel and Its Friends." *Science*, 196 (1977), 385-389.

Anthropological and Archaeological

Abbott, Charles C. *Primitive Industry: Or, Illustrations of the Handiwork in Stone, Bone and Clay of the Native Races of the Northern Atlantic Seaboard of America*. Salem, Mass., Bates, 1881.

Allen, Glover M. "Dogs of the American Aborigines, Living and Extinct." Museum of Comparative Zoology, Harvard University, *Bulletin*, 63, no. 9 (1920), 429-517.

Allen, Zachariah. *The Condition of Life, Habits, and Customs of the Native Indians of America and Their Treatment by the First Settlers*. Providence, R.I., Providence Press Co., 1880.

Allison, Roland. "Shell Heaps around Deer Island." Maine Archaeological Society, *Bulletin*, 2 (1964), 3-5; 12 (1975), 1-3.

Bailey, Alfred Goldsworthy. *The Conflict of European and Eastern Algonkian Cultures, 1504-1700*. New Brunswick Museum, Monograph Series, 2, Sackville, N.B., Tribune Press, 1937.

Ballard, Edward. "Character of the Penacooks." New Hampshire Historical Society, *Collections*, 8 (1866), 428-445.

Barratt, Joseph, ed. *The Indian of New-England and the North-eastern Provinces* . . . Middletown, Conn., Pelton, 1851.

Bennett, M. K. "The Food Economy of the New England Indians, 1605-75." *Journal of Political Economy*, 63 (1955), 369-397.

Borns, Harold W., Jr. "Possible Paleo-Indian Migration Routes in the Northeast: A Geological Approach." Massachusetts Archaeological Society, *Bulletin*, 34, nos. 1 and 2 (1972-73), 13-15.

Bourque, Bruce J. "Aboriginal Settlement and Subsistence on the Maine Coast." *Man in the Northeast*, 6 (1973), 3-20.

Brandon, William. *The Last Americans: The Indian in American Culture*. New York, N.Y., McGraw-Hill, 1973.

Brasser, Ted J. C. "The Coastal Algonkians" in *North American Indians in Historical Perspective*, Eleanore Burke Leacock and Nancy Oestreich Lurie, eds. New York, N.Y., Random House, 1971.

———. "Early Indian-European Contacts" in *Handbook of North American Indians: Volume 15, Northeast*, Bruce G. Trigger, ed. Washington, D.C., Smithsonian Institution (1978), 78-88.

———. "Mahican" in *Handbook of North American Indians*, 198-212.

Brooks, Jerome E. *The Mighty Leaf: Tobacco through the Centuries*. Boston, Mass., Little, Brown, 1952.

Brown, Percy S. "Indian Names in New Hampshire." *New Hampshire Archaeologist*, 7 (November 1953), 1-11.

Brown, Raymond H. "The Housatonic Indians." Massachusetts Archaeological Society, *Bulletin*, 19, no. 3 (1958), 44-50.

Browne, C. A. "The Chemical Industries of the American Aborigines." *Isis*, 23 (1935), 406-424.

Brownell, Charles De Wolf. *The Indian Races of North and South America* . . . Cincinnati, Ohio, Morse and Gordon, 1853.

Bullen, Ripley P. "Forts, Boundaries, or Ha-Has?" Massachusetts Archaeological Society, *Bulletin*, 4, no. 1 (1942), 1-12.

Burtt, J. Frederick. "Methods of Fishing Used by the Indians on the Merrimack River." *New Hampshire Archaeologist*, 2 (July 1951), 2-5.

———. "Religion of the North American Indians." Ibid., (December 1922), 15-21.

Bushnell, David I., Jr. *Native Villages and Village Sites East of the Mississippi*. Smithsonian Institution. Bureau of American Ethnology, *Bulletin*, 69, Washington, 1919.

———. "The Treatment of the Indians in Plymouth Colony." *New England Quarterly*, 26 (1953), 193-218.

Butler, Eva L. "Sweat-Houses in the Southern New England Area." Massachusetts Archaeological Society, *Bulletin*, 7, no. 1 (1945), 11-15.

———, and Wendell S. Hadlock. "Dogs of the Northeastern Woodland Indians." Ibid., 10, no. 2 (1949), 17-35.

———, and Wendell S. Hadlock. "Some Uses of Birch Bark in Northern New England." Ibid., 18, no. 4 (1957), 72-75.

Byers, Douglas S. "The Environment of the Northeast," in *Man in Northeastern North America*, Frederick Johnson, ed. Papers of the Robert S. Peabody Foundation for Archaeology, 3. (Andover, Mass., Phillips Academy, the Foundation, 1946).

———. "Ipswich B.C." Massachusetts Archaeological Society, *Bulletin*, 18, no. 3 (1957), 49-55.

———. "Notes on the Envronment of New England." Ibid., 8, no. 2 (1947), 29-31.

———. "Radiocarbon Dates from Bull Brook." Ibid., 20, no. 3 (1959), 33.

Carr, Lucien. "The Food of Certain American Indians and Their Methods of Preparing It." American Antiquarian Society, *Proceedings*, new series, 10 (1896), 155-190.

Carson, Jennie E. "Indians of New Hampshire." *New Hampshire Archaeologist*, 6 (1957), 10-16.

Cassedy, James H. *Demography in Early America: Beginnings of the Statistical Mind, 1600-1800*. Cambridge, Mass., Harvard University Press, 1969.

Castner, Harold W. *The Prehistoric Oyster Shell Heaps of the Damariscotta River*. Damariscotta, Me., 1948.

Catlin, George. *Letters and Notes on the Manners, Customs, and Condition of the North American Indians*. 2 vols. New York, N.Y., Wiley and Putnam, 3rd ed., 1844; reprinted Philadelphia, Penn. (under the title *North American Indians*), Leary, Stuart, 1913.

Chamberlain, Alexander F. "Algonkian Words in American English." *Journal of American Folklore*, 15 (1902), 240-267.

———. "The Contributions of the American Indian to Civilization." American Antiquarian Society, *Proceedings*, 16 (1905), 91-126.

———. "The Maple amongst the Algonkian Tribes." *American Anthropologist*, 4 (1891), 39-43.

———. "Maple Sugar and the Indians." Ibid., 4 (1891), 381-383.

————. "Wisdom of the North American Indian in Speech and Legend." American Antiquarian Society, *Proceedings*, new series, 23 (1913), 63-96.

Chase, Henry E. "Notes on the Wampanoag Indians." Smithsonian Institution, *Annual Report* (1883), (Washington, 1885), 878-907.

Chase, Levi Badger. *The Bay Path and Along the Way*. Norwood, Mass., author, 1919.

————. "Early Indian Trails." Worcester [Mass.] Society of Antiquity, *Collections*, 14 (1897), 105-126.

Clark, Grahame, and Stuart Piggott. *Prehistoric Societies*. History of Human Society Series. New York, N.Y., Knopf, 1965.

Coffin, Claude C. "Baldwin's Station—Indian Village Site." Archeological Society of Connecticut, *Bulletin*, 32 (1963), 27-57.

————. "Connecticut Indian Burials." Ibid., 32 (1963), 60-64.

————. "Early Man on the Housatonics." Ibid., *Newsletter*, 16 (1941), 6-7.

————. "Final Work at the Eagle Hill Site." Ibid., *Bulletin*, 19 (1946), 18-36.

————. "Rock Shelter Occupations by Connecticut Indians." Ibid., 32 (1963), 6-11.

————. "Seaside Indian Village Site: Fort Trumbull Beach." Ibid., 32 (1963), 12-25.

Cohen, Mark Nathan. *The Food Crisis in Prehistory: Overpopulation and the Origins of Agriculture*. New Haven., Conn., Yale University Press, 1977.

Collier, John. *The Indians of the Americas*. New York, N.Y., Norton, 1947.

Conkey, Laura E., Ethel Boissevain, and Ives Goddard. "Indians of Southern New England and Long Island: Late Period" in *Handbook of North American Indians: Volume 15, Northeast,* Bruce G. Trigger, ed. Washington, D.C., Smithsonian Institution (1978), 177-189.

Cook, Sherburne F. "Interracial Warfare and Population Decline among the New England Indians." *Ethnohistory*, 20, no. 1 (1973), 1-24.

Cooper, John M. "The Culture of the Northeastern Indian Hunters," in *Man in Northeastern North America*, Frederick Johnson, ed. Papers of the Robert S. Peabody Foundation for Archaeology, 3. (Andover, Mass., Phillips Academy, the Foundation, 1946), 272-305.

Cotton, Josiah. "Vocabulary of the Massachusetts (or Natick) Indian Language." Massachusetts Historical Society, *Collections*, 3rd series, 2 (1830), 147-257.

Cushing, Frank Hamilton. "Remarks on Shamanism." American Philosophical Society, *Proceedings*, 36 (1897), 183-192.

Daniels, Thomas E. *Vermont Indians*. Orwell, Vt., author, 1963.

Davis, Emily C. *Ancient Americans*. New York, N.Y., Holt, 1931.

Day, Gordon M. "The Eastern Boundary of Iroquoia-Abenaki Influence." *Man in the Northeast*, 1, no. 1 (March 1971), 7-13.

————. "The Indian as an Ecological Factor in the Northeastern Forest." *Ecology*, 34 (1953), 329-346.

————. "The Indian Occupation of Vermont." *Vermont History*, 33, no. 3 (1965), 365-374.

————. "Western Abenaki" in *Handbook of North American Indians: Volume 15,*

Northeast, Bruce G. Trigger, ed. Washington, D.C., Smithsonian Institution (1978), 148-159.

Dellenbaugh, Frederick S. *The North-Americans of Yesterday.* New York, N.Y., Putnam's, 1901.

Densmore, Frances. *Chippewa Customs.* Smithsonian Institution. Bureau of American Ethnology, *Bulletin,* 86, Washington, 1929.

Dincauze, Dena Ferran. *The Neville Site: 8000 Years at Amoskeag, Manchester, New Hampshire.* Peabody Museum, Harvard University, *Monographs,* 4, Cambridge, Mass., 1976.

Dodge, Ernest S. "Ethnology of Northern New England and the Maritime Provinces." Massachusetts Archaeological Society, *Bulletin,* 18, no. 4 (1957), 68-71.

Dorr, Henry C. "The Narragansetts." Rhode Island Historical Society, *Collections,* 7 (1885), 135-237.

Douglas, Frederic H. *American Indian Tobacco: Varieties, Cultivation, Methods of Use.* Denver Art Museum, *Indian Leaflet Series,* 22, April 1931.

―――. *Iroquoian and Algonkin Wampum: Manufacture and Uses.* Ibid., 31, September 1931.

―――. *Long Island Indian Culture.* Ibid., 50, June 1932.

―――. *New England Indian Houses, Forts, and Villages: Colonial Period.* Ibid., 39, January 1932.

―――. *The New England Tribes: Names and Locations.* Ibid., 27 and 28, July 1931.

Drake, Samuel G. *The Aboriginal Races of North America.* 15th ed. rev. New York, N.Y., Hurst, 1880.

Driver, Harold E. *Indians of North America.* Chicago, Ill., University of Chicago Press, 1961.

―――, ed. *The Americas on the Eve of Discovery.* Englewood Cliffs, N.J., Prentice-Hall, 1964.

Eckstorm, Fannie Hardy. "Review of Willoughby's 'Antiquities of the New England Indians'." *New England Quarterly,* 9 (1936), 346-348.

―――. "The Indians of Maine," in *Maine: A History,* Louis Clinton Hatch, ed. 5 vols. (New York, N.Y., American Historical Society, 1919), 1:43-64.

―――. "The Indian Routes of Maine." Unpublished Manuscript in the University of Maine Library, Orono.

―――. *Old John Neptune and Other Maine Indian Shamans.* Portland, Me., Southworth-Anthoensen Press, 1945.

Embree, Edwin R. *Indians of the Americas.* Boston, Mass., Houghton Mifflin, 1939.

Erickson, Vincent O. "Maliseet-Passamaquoddy" in *Handbook of North American Indians: Volume 15, Northeast,* Bruce G. Trigger, ed. Washington, D.C., Smithsonian Institution (1978), 123-136.

Fenton, William N. "Contacts Between Iroquois Herbalism and Colonial Medicine." Smithsonian Institution, *Annual Report* (1941), 503-526.

Ferguson, Chauncey C. "The Trail of the Indian." Massachusetts Archaeological Society, *Bulletin*, 13, no. 1 (1951), 11-13.

Fitting, James E. "Environmental Potential and the Postglacial Readaptation in Eastern North America." *American Antiquity*, 33 (1968), 441-445.

Flannery, Regina. *An Analysis of Coastal Algonquian Culture*. Anthropological Series, 7. Washington, D.C., Catholic University of America Press, 1939.

Fowler, William S. "Classification of Stone Implements of the Northeast." Massachusetts Archaeological Society, *Bulletin*, 25, no. 1 (1963), 1-29.

———. "The Diagnostic Stone Bowl Industry." Ibid., 36, nos. 3 and 4 (1975), 1-10.

———. "Eating Practices in Aboriginal New England." Ibid., 36, nos. 3 and 4 (1975), 21-27.

———. "Stone Bowl Making at the Westfield Quarry." Ibid., 30, no., (1968), 6-16.

———. "Stone Eating Utensils of Prehistoric New England." *American Antiquity*, 13 (1947-48), 146-163.

———. "Sweet-Meadow Brook: A Pottery Site in Rhode Island." Massachusetts Archaeological Society, *Bulletin*, 18, no. 1 (1956), 1-23.

———. *Ten Thousand Years in America*. New York, N.Y., Vantage Press, 1957.

———. "Two Indian Burials in North Middleboro." Massachusetts Archaeological Society, *Bulletin*, 35, nos. 3 and 4 (1974), 14-18.

———. "Woodworking: An Important Industry." Ibid., 23, nos. 3 and 4 (1962), 29-40.

Fulcher, L. Richard. "Stone Bowls on Cape Cod." Ibid., 36, nos. 1 and 2 (1974-75), 30-32.

Gahan, Laurence K. "The Nipmucks and Their Territory." Ibid., 2, no. 4 (1941), 2-6.

Goddard, Ives. "Eastern Algonquian Languages" in *Handbook of North American Indians: Volume 15, Northeast,* Bruce G. Trigger, ed. Washington, D.C., Smithsonian Institution (1978), 70-77.

Gookin, Warner F. "Metsoo'onk (Experience Mayhew's Word for Victuals)." Ibid., 12, no. 4 (1951), 58-60.

Griffin, James B. "The Northeast Woodlands Area," in *Prehistoric Man in the New World*, Jesse D. Jennings and Edward Norbeck, eds. Chicago, Ill., University of Chicago Press, 1964.

Haag, William G. "The Bering Strait Land Bridge." *Scientific American*, 206 (January 1962), 112-123.

Hadlock, Wendell, S. "War among the Northeastern Woodland Indians." *American Anthropologist*, 49, new series (1947), 204-221.

Hallett, Leaman F. "Cultural Traits of the Southern New England Indians." Massachusetts Archaeological Society, *Bulletin*, 15, no. 4 (1954), 59-64.

———. "Indian Games." Ibid., 16, no. 2 (1955), 25-28.

———. "Indian Trails and Their Importance to the Early Colonists." Ibid., 17, no. 3 (1956), 41-46.

————. "Medicine and Pharmacy of the New England Indians." Ibid., 17, no. 3 (1956), 46-49.

Hallock, William A. *The Venerable Mayhews and the Aboriginal Indians of Martha's Vineyard.* New York, N.Y., American Tract Society, 1874.

Hallowell, A. I. "Some Psychological Characteristics of the Northeastern Indians," in *Man in Northeastern North America*, Frederick Johnson, ed. Papers of the Robert S. Peabody Foundation for Archaeology, 3. (Andover, Mass., Phillips Academy, the Foundation, 1946), 195-225.

Harrington, M. R. *The Indians of New Jersey: Dickon among the Lenapes.* New Brunswick, N.J., Rutgers University Press, 1963.

————. "Some Seneca Corn-Foods and Their Preparation." *American Anthropologist*, new series, 10 (1908), 575-590.

Haviland, William A. "Men Hunted in Vermont in 4000 B.C." *Vermont Life,* 24 (Winter 1969), 53-55.

————. *The Original Vermonters.* In press.

Heiser, Charles B., Jr. "Cultivated Plants and Cultural Diffusion in Nuclear America." *American Anthropologist*, 67, no. 4 (1965), 930-949.

Hibben, Frank C. *Digging Up America.* New York, N.Y., Hill and Wang, 1960.

Hodge, Frederick Webb, ed. *Handbook of American Indians North of Mexico.* 2 vols. Smithsonian Institution. Bureau of American Ethnology, *Bulletin*, 30, Washington, 1907-10.

Holmes, Abiel. "A Memoir of the Moheagan Indians." Massachusetts Historical Society, *Collections*, 9 (1804), 75-99.

Howe, Henry F. "Archaeology of the Lower North River Valley." Massachusetts Archaeological Society, *Bulletin*, 10, no. 2 (1949), 39-43.

Howes, William J. "Aboriginal New England Pottery." Ibid., 5, no. 1 (1943), 1-5; 15, no. 2 (1954), 23-36, no. 4 (1954), 81-86; 16, no. 1 (1955), 9-19; 17, no. 3 (1956), 52-58.

————. "Guida Farm Pottery." Ibid., 21, no. 2 (1960), 27-31.

————. "The Importance of the Connecticut Valley . . . to the Indian." Ibid., 1, no. 4 (1940), 4-10.

————. "Iroquoian-Mohawk Pottery . . ." Ibid., 21, nos. 3 and 4 (1961), 56-61.

————. "Maine Coast Pottery." Ibid., 21, nos. 3 and 4 (1961), 54-56.

Huden, John C. "Indian Groups in Vermont." *New Hampshire Archaeologist*, 11 (October 1962), 8-11.

Hyde, George E. *Indians of the Woodlands: From Prehistoric Times to 1725.* Norman, Okla., University of Oklahoma Press, 1962.

James, George Wharton. *Indian Basketry.* 2nd ed. New York, N.Y., Henry Malkan, 1902.

Jenness, Diamond, *The Indians of Canada.* National Museum of Canada, *Bulletin*, 65, 3rd ed., 1953.

Jennings, Jesse D. *Prehistory of North America.* New York, N.Y., McGraw-Hill, 1968.

Johnson, F. Roy. *The Algonquians, Indians of That Part of the New World First Visited by the English.* Murphreesboro, N.C., Johnson Publishing Co., 1972.

Johnson, Frederick, ed. *Man in Northeastern North America.* Papers of the

Robert S. Peabody Foundation for Archaeology, 3. Andover, Mass., Phillips Academy, the Foundation, 1946.

Jones, Stuart E. "Indian Life before the Colonists Came." *National Geographic*, 92 (1947), 351-368.

Josephy, Alvin M., Jr. *The Indian Heritage of America*. New York, N.Y., Knopf, 1968.

Kellogg, Elijah. "Passamaquoddy Vocabulary." Massachusetts Historical Society, *Collections*, 3rd series, 3 (1833), 181-182.

Kennedy, Michael, ed. The Assiniboines. Norman, Okla., University of Oklahoma Press, 1961.

Kevitt, Chester B. "Aboriginal Dugout Discovered at Weymouth." Massachusetts Archaeological Society, *Bulletin*, 30, no. 1 (1968), 1-5.

Kihn, W. Langdon. "When Red Men Ruled Our Forests." *National Geographic*, 72 (1937), 551-590.

Kroeber, A. L. "Cultural and Natural Areas of Native North America," in *Ideas of Culture: Sources and Uses*, Frederick C. Gamst and Edward Norbeck, eds. New York, N.Y., Holt, Rinehart and Winston, 1976.

———. "Native American Population." *American Anthropologist*, new series, 36 (1934), 1-25.

Laurent, Stephen. "The Diet That Made the Red Man." *New Hampshire Archaeologist*, 9 (1959), 6-9.

Leland, Charles G. *The Algonquin Legends of New England*. Boston, Mass., Houghton, Mifflin, 1884.

MacGowan, Kenneth, and Joseph A. Hester, Jr. *Early Man in the New World*. Rev. ed. Garden City, N.Y., Doubleday, 1962.

MacNeish, Richard S. "Ancient Mesoamerican Civilization." *Science*, 143 (1964), 531-537.

———. "The Origins of New World Civilization." *Scientific American*, 211 (November 1964), 29-37.

McNickle, D'Arcy. "Americans Called Indians," in *North American Indians in Historical Perspective*, Eleanor Burke Leacock and Nancy Oestreich Lurie, eds. New York, N.Y., Random House, 1971.

———. *They Came Here First: The Epic of the American Indian*. Philadelphia, Penn., Lippincott, 1949.

Maddox, John Lee. *The Medicine Man*. New York, N.Y., Macmillan, 1923.

Martin, Calvin S. "The European Impact on the Culture of a Northeastern Algonquian Tribe: An Ecological Interpretation." *William and Mary Quarterly*, 3rd series, 31 (1974), 3-26.

Martin, Paul S., George I. Quimby, and Donald Collier. *Indians before Columbus: Twenty Thousand Years of North American History Revealed by Archeology*. Chicago, Ill., University of Chicago Press, 1947.

Mason, Otis Tufton. "Aboriginal American Basketry: Studies in a Textile Art without Machinery." U.S. National Museum. *Annual Report* (1902), (Washington, 1904), 171-548.

————. Aboriginal Skin-dressing." Ibid., (1889), (Washington, 1891), 553-589.

————. *Woman's Share in Primitive Culture.* New York, N.Y., 1894.

Miller, William J. *Notes Concerning the Wampanoag Tribe of Indians.* Providence, R.I., 1880.

Moorehead, Warren K. *A Report on the Archaeology of Maine.* Andover, Mass., Andover Press, 1922.

Morgan, Lewis H. *Houses and House-Life of the American Aborigines.* Contributions to North American Ethnology, 4. Washington, D.C., 1881.

Needham, Walter, and Barrows Mussey. *A Book of Country Things.* Brattleboro, Vt., Stephen Greene Press, 1965.

Nicolar, Joseph. *The Life and Traditions of the Red Man.* Old Town, Me., 1893.

Palmer, Rose A. *The North American Indians.* Smithsonian Scientific Series, 4. Washington, D.C., Smithsonian Institution, 1929.

Parker, Arthur C. *Iroquois Uses of Maize and Other Food Plants.* New York State Museum, *Bulletin*, 144, Albany, 1910.

Payne, Edward Waldron. *The Immortal Stone Age.* Chicago, Ill., Lightner, 1938.

Potter, C. E. "Appendix to 'Language of the Abnaquies'." Maine Historical Society, *Collections*, 4 (1850), 189-193.

Powell, J. W. U.S. Bureau of American Ethnology, *Annual Report*, 14 (1892), 288-290.

Price, Chester B. "Historic Indian Trails of New Hampshire." *New Hampshire Archaeologist*, 8 (1956), 2-13.

Prince, J. Dyneley. "The Passamaquoddy Wampum Records." American Philosophical Society, *Proceedings*, 36 (1897), 479-495.

Pulling, H. E. "Farmers before Columbus." Unpublished lecture before the New England Section, American Chemical Society, September 18, 1936.

Pumphrey, Stanley. *Indian Civilization.* Philadelphia, Penn., 1877.

Rainey, Froelich G. "A Compilation of Historical Data Contributing to the Ethnography of Connecticut and Southern New England Indians." Archeological Society of Connecticut, *Bulletin*, 3 (1936), 1-49.

Rau, Charles. "Ancient Aboriginal Trade in North America." Smithsonian Institution, *Annual Report* (1872), 348-394.

Ritchie, William A. *The Archaeology of Martha's Vineyard.* American Museum of Natural History. Garden City, N.Y., Natural History Press, 1969.

————. *The Archaeology of New York State.* American Museum of Natural History. Garden City, N.Y., Natural History Press, 1965.

Robbins, Maurice. "Some Indian Burials from Southeastern Massachusetts." Massachusetts Archaeological Society, *Bulletin*, 20, no. 2 (1959), 17-32.

————. "Some Indian Burials . . .: Part 2, The Wapanucket Burials." Ibid., 20, no. 4 (1959), 61-67.

Russell, Howard S. "How Aboriginal Planters Stored Food." Ibid., 23, nos. 3 and 4 (1962), 47-49.

Salwen, Bert. "Indians of Southern New England and Long Island: Early Period" in *Handbook of North American Indians: Volume 15, Northeast,* Bruce G. Trigger, ed. Washington, D.C., Smithsonian Institution (1978), 160-176.

————. "A Tentative 'in situ' Solution to the Mohegan-Pequot Problem" in *Connecticut Valley Indians,* William R. Young, ed. Springfield, Mass., Science Museum Publications, new series, 1, no. 1, 1969.

Sherman, Charles F. "Habitations, Summer and Winter Sites." Massachusetts Archaeological Society, *Bulletin,* 6, no. 1 (1944), 10-14.

————. "Pottery Traits of the Plymouth District." Ibid., 8, no. 2 (1947), 27-29.

Simmons, William S. *Cautantowwit's House.* Providence, R.I., Brown University Press, 1970.

————. "Narragansett" in *Handbook of North American Indians: Volume 15, Northeast,* Bruce G. Trigger, ed. Washington, D.C., Smithsonian Institution (1978), 190-197.

Skinner, Alanson. "Some Wyandot Corn Foods." Milwaukee Public Museum, *Yearbook,* 3 (n.d.), 109-112.

Sleeper, Myron O. "Indian Place Names in New England." Massachusetts Archaeological Society, *Bulletin,* 10, no. 4 (1949), 89-93.

Smith, C. Earle, Jr. "The Archeological Record of Cultivated Crops of New World Origins." *Economic Botany,* 19 (1965), 323-334.

Smith, Nicholas N. "Indian Medicine: Fact or Fiction?" Massachusetts Archaeological Society, *Bulletin,* 26, no. 1 (1964), 13-17.

————. "Smoking Habits of the Wabanaki." Ibid., 18, no. 4 (1957), 76-77.

Snow, Dean R. "Eastern Abenaki" in *Handbook of North American Indians: Volume 15, Northeast,* Bruce G. Trigger, ed. Washington, D.C., Smithsonian Institution (1978), 137-147.

————. "Late Prehistory of the East Coast" in *Handbook of North American Indians,* 58-69.

————. "A Middle Woodland Site on the Coast of Maine." Maine Archaeological Society, *Bulletin,* 10, nos. 1 and 2 (1970), 1-10.

————. *A Summary of Excavations at the Hathaway Site in Passadumkeag, Maine, 1902, 1947, and 1968.* Orono, Me., University of Maine Department of Anthropology, 1969.

————. "Wabanaki 'Family Hunting Territories'." *American Anthropologist,* new series, 70 (1968), 1143-1151.

Speck, Frank G. "The Family Hunting Band as the Basis of Algonkian Social Organization." *American Anthropologist,* new series, 17 (1915), 289-305.

————. *Gourds of the Southeastern Indians.* Boston, Mass., New England Gourd Society, 1941.

————. "Native Tribes and Dialects of Connecticut." U.S. Bureau of American Ethnology, *Annual Reports,* 43 (1925-26), 199-287.

————. "A Note on the Hassanamisco Band of Nipmuc." Massachusetts Archaeological Society, *Bulletin,* 4, no. 4 (1943), 49-56.

————. *Penobscot Man: The Life History of a Forest Tribe in Maine.* Philadelphia, Penn., University of Pennsylvania Press, 1940.

————. "Reflections upon the Past and Present of the Massachusetts Indians." Massachusetts Archaeological Society, *Bulletin*, 4, no. 3 (1943), 33-38.

————. "Territorial Subdivisions and Boundaries of the Wampanoag, Massachusett, and Nauset Indians," in *Indian Notes and Monographs*, 44. (New York, N.Y., Heye Foundation, 1928), 7-152.

————, and Loren C. Eiseley. "The Significance of Hunting Territory Systems of the Algonkian in Social Theory." *American Anthropologist,* 41, new series (1939), 269-280.

Starbird, Charles M. *The Indians of the Androscoggin Valley*. Lewiston, Me., Lewiston Journal Printshop, 1928.

Stirling, M. W., W. Langdon Kuhn, et al. *Indians of the Americas*. Washington, D.C., National Geographic Society, 1955.

Stone, Eric. *Medicine among the American Indians*. New York, N.Y., Hoeber, 1932.

Stout, A. B. "Vegetable Foods of the American Indians." New York Botanical Garden, *Bulletin*, 15 (1914), 50-60.

Sturtevant, William C. "Lafitau's Hoes." *American Antiquity*, 33 (1968), 93-95.

Swanton, John R. *The Indians of the Southeastern United States*. U.S. Bureau of American Ethnology, *Bulletin*, 137, Washington, 1946.

————. *The Indian Tribes of North America*. Ibid., 145, Washington, 1953, reprinted 1968.

Tantaquidgeon, Gladys. *Folk Medicine of the Delaware and Related Algonkian Indians*. Harrisburg, Penn., Pennsylvania Historical and Museum Commission, 1972.

————. "Mohegan Medicinal Practices, Weather-lore, and Superstitions." U.S. Bureau of American Ethnology, *Annual Report*, 43 (1928), 264-279.

Thomas, Peter A. "Contrastive Subsistence Strategies and Land Use as Factors for Understanding Indian-White Relations in New England." *Ethnohistory*, 23 (1976), 1-18.

————. "Squakheag Ethnohistory: A Preliminary Study of Culture Conflict on the Seventeenth Century Frontier." *Man in the Northeast*, 5 (1973), 27-36.

Tolman, Adams. *Indian Relics in Concord*. Concord, Mass., Concord Antiquarian Society, 1901-1902.

Torrey, Howard. "Indian Rocks of Cape Cod." Massachusetts Archaeological Society, *Bulletin*, 14, special no. (1953), 19-67.

Towle, Margaret A. *The Ethnobotany of Pre-Columbian Peru*. Viking Fund Publications in Anthropology, 30. New York, N.Y., Wenner-Gren Foundation for Anthropological Research, 1961.

Travers, Milton A. *The Wampanoag Indian Federation of the Algonquin Nation*. New Bedford, Mass., Reynolds-DeWalt, 1957.

Trumbull, James Hammond. "The Indian Tongue and Its Literature," in *The Memorial History of Boston*, Justin Winsor, ed. (Boston, Mass., 1880), 1:465-480.

————. *Natick Dictionary*. Smithsonian Institution. Bureau of American Ethnology, *Bulletin*, 25, Washington, 1903.

———. "On the Composition of Indian Geographical Names." Connecticut Historical Society, *Collections*, 2 (1870), 1-50.

———. "On Words Derived from Indian Languages of North America." American Philological Association, *Transactions*, 3 (1872), 19-32.

———, ed. *Williams' Key into the Language of America.* (Providence, R.I., Narragansett Club, 1864), 1:1-29.

Tylor, Edward B. "Primitive Society Part II." *Contemporary Review*, 22 (1873), 53-72.

Underhill, Ruth M. *Red Man's America.* Chicago, Ill., University of Chicago Press, 1953, 1971.

Vogel, Virgil J. *American Indian Medicine.* Norman, Okla., University of Oklahoma Press, 1970.

Washburn, Wilcomb E. *The Indian in America.* New York, N.Y., Harper and Row, 1975.

———. "Seventeenth-Century Indian Wars" in *Handbook of North American Indians: Volume 15, Northeast,* Bruce G. Trigger, ed. Washington, D.C., Smithsonian Institution (1978), 89-100.

Waugh, F. W. *Iroquois Foods and Food Preparation.* Geological Survey of Canada, Anthropological Series, 12, *Memoir*, 86, Ottawa, 1916.

Wentworth, Edward N. "Dried Meat—Early Man's Travel Ration." *Agricultural History*, 30 (1956), 2-10.

Wertenbacker, Thomas Jefferson. *The First Americans, 1607-1690.* New York, N.Y., Macmillan, 1929.

Weslager, C. A. *Magic Medicines of the Indians.* Somerset, N.J., Middle Atlantic Press, 1973.

West, George A. *Tobacco, Pipes and Smoking Customs of the American Indians,* 2 vols. Milwaukee Public Museum, *Bulletin*, 17 (1934).

White, Owen T. "Some Aspects of Indian Culture in New England." Archeological Society of Connecticut, *Newsletter*, 16 (1941), 3-5.

Wilbur, C. Keith. *The New England Indians.* Chester, Conn., Globe Pequot Press, 1978.

Wilder, Harris Hawthorne. "Notes on the Indians of Southern Massachusetts." *American Anthropologist*, new series, 25 (1923), 197-218.

Will, George F., and George E. Hyde. *Corn among the Indians of the Upper Missouri.* St. Louis, Mo., 1917; reprint Lincoln, Neb., University of Nebraska Press, 1964.

Willey, Gordon R. *An Introduction to American Archaeology, I: North and Middle America.* Englewood Cliffs, N.J., Prentice-Hall, 1966.

Willis, Wm. "The Language of the Abnaquies or Eastern Indians." Maine Historical Society, *Collections*, 4 (1856), 93-117.

Willoughby, Charles C. *Antiquities of the New England Indians.* Cambridge, Mass., Peabody Museum of American Archaeology and Ethnology, Harvard University, 1935.

————. "Houses and Gardens of the New England Indians." *American Anthropologist*, 8, new series (1906), 115-132.

————. "Prehistoric Workshops at Mt. Kineo, Maine." *American Naturalist*, 35 (1901), 213-219.

————. "The Wilderness and the Indian," in *Commonwealth History of Massachusetts*. Albert Bushnell Hart, ed. 5 vols. (New York, N.Y., States History Co., 1927-30), 1:127-158.

Wissler, Clark. *The American Indian*. New York, N.Y., Oxford University Press, 3rd ed., 1938; reprint Gloucester, Mass., Peter Smith, 1957.

————. *Indians of the United States*. Garden City, N.Y., Doubleday, 1940, rev. ed., 1966.

Wojta, J. F. "A Visit to the Indian Sugar Bush Ceremonials." *Wisconsin Archaeologist*, 11, no. 4 (1932), 172-175.

Young, William R., ed. *The Connecticut Valley Indian: An Introduction to Their Archaeology and History*. Science Museum Bulletin, *Publications*, new series, 1, no. 1. Springfield, Mass., 1969.

Youngken, Heber W. "The Drugs of the American Indian." *American Journal of Pharmacy*, 96 (1924), 485-502; 97, no. 3 (1925), 158-185, 257-271.

Historical and Geographical

Abbott, Jacob. *American History*. 8 vols. New York, N.Y., Sheldon, 1860-65.

Adair, James. *History of the American Indians*, Samuel C. Williams, ed. Johnson City, Tenn., Watauga, 1930.

Adams, Sherman W., and H. R. Stiles. *The History of Ancient Wethersfield, Connecticut*. New York, N.Y., Grafton, 1904.

Alden, Timothy. "Memorabilia of Yarmouth." Massachusetts Historical Society, *Collections*, 1st series, 5 (1798), 54-60.

Allen, Wilkes. "A Memoir of the Pawtuckett Indians," in *The History of Chelmsford . . ., 1653-1820*. (Haverhill, Mass., Green, 1820), 140-161.

American Heritage. *Book of Indians*, Alvin M. Josephy, ed. New York, N.Y., American Heritage Publishing Co., 1961.

Anderson, Edgar, and William L. Brown. "The History of the Common Maize Varieties of the United States Corn Belt." *Agricultural History*, 26 (1952), 2-8.

Andrews, Charles M. *Colonial Folkways*. New Haven, Conn., 1920.

Arber, Edward, ed. *The Story of the Pilgrim Fathers, 1606-1623 A.D.: As Told by Themselves, Their Friends, and Their Enemies*. Boston, Mass., Houghton, Mifflin, 1897.

Arnold, Samuel Greene. *History of the State of Rhode Island and Providence Plantations*. 2 vols. New York, N.Y., Appleton, 1859-60.

Arnow, Harriette S. *Seedtime on the Cumberland*. New York, N.Y., Macmillan, 1960.

Atwater, Edward E. *History of the Colony of New Haven to Its Absorption into Connecticut*. New Haven, Conn., author, 1881.

Ayres, Harral. *The Great Trail of New England*. Boston, Mass., Meador, 1940.

Bacon, Edwin M. *The Connecticut River and the Valley of the Connecticut*. New York, N.Y., Putnam's, 1906.

Baker, Virginia. *Massasoit's Town, Sowams in Pokonoket*. Warren, R.I., author, 1904.

Banks, Charles Edward. *The History of Martha's Vineyard*. 3 vols. Boston, Mass., Dean, 1911-25.

Barber, John W. *Historical Collections of Connecticut*. 2nd ed. New Haven, Conn., n.p., 1836, 1856.

———. *Historical Collections . . .[of] Massachusetts*. Worcester, Mass., Lazell, 1844.

———, ed. *The History and Antiquities of New England, New York, and New Jersey*. Worcester, Mass., Dorr, Howland, 1841.

Barry, John Stetson. *The History of Massachusetts*. 3 vols. (Boston, Mass., Phillips, Sampson, 1855), Vol. 1.

Bicknell, Thomas Williams. *The History of the State of Rhode Island and Providence Plantations*. 5 vols. (New York, N.Y., American Historical Society, 1920), Vol. 1.

Blair, Peter H. *Roman Britain and Early England, 55 B.C.-A.D. 871*. New York, N.Y., Norton, 1966.

Bolton, Charles Knowles. *The Real Founders of New England*. Boston, Mass., Faxon, 1929.

Boorstin, Daniel J. *The Americans: The Colonial Experience*. New York, N.Y., Random House, 1958.

[Bourne, Benjamin]. *An Account of the Settlement of the Town of Bristol in the State of Rhode-Island*. Providence, R.I., Bennett Wheeler, 1785.

Bouton, Nathaniel. *History of Concord . . . 1725-1853, with a "History of the Ancient Penacooks."* Concord, N.H., Sanborn, 1856.

Bowen, Clarence Winthrop. *Woodstock: An Historical Sketch*. New York, N.Y., Putnam's, 1886.

Bowler, William H. "The History of Indian Corn." Tenth U.S. Census, *Miscellaneous Documents*, 13, pt. 3 (1880).

Bradford, William. "A Descriptive and Historical Account of New England in Verse." Massachusetts Historical Society, *Collections*, 3 (1794), 77-84.

———. *"Of Plimouth Plantation," from the Original Manuscript*. Boston, Mass., Wright and Potter, 1898.

"A Brief Narrative of . . . Nanhiganset [Narragansett] Country." Massachusetts Historical Society, *Collections*, 3rd series, 1 (1825), 209-228.

Browne, William B. *The Mohawk Trail*. Pittsfield, Mass., Sun, 1920.

Bynner, Edward L. "Topography and Landmarks of the Colonial Period," in *The Memorial History of Boston . . . , 1630-1880*, Justin Winsor, ed. (Boston, Mass., Osgood, 1880), 521-556.

Cabot, Mary R., comp. and ed. *Annals of Brattleboro, 1681-1895*. 2 vols. Brattleboro, Vt., Hildreth, 1921-22.

Cambridge, Mass. *The Records of the Town of Cambridge (formerly Newtowne),*

Massachusetts, 1630-1703: Records of the Town Meetings, and of the Selectmen . . . Cambridge, Mass., 1901.

Campbell, Mildred. *The English Yeoman under Elizabeth and the Early Stuarts.* New Haven, Conn., Yale University Press, 1942.

Carroll, Charles F. *The Timber Economy of Puritan New England.* Providence, R.I., Brown University Press, 1973.

Caulkins, Frances M. *History of New London, Conn. . . . , 1612-1860.* New London, Conn., Utley, 1895.

Church, Benjamin. *The History of King Philip's War*, Henry M. Dexter, ed. 2 vols. (Boston, Mass., Wiggin, 1865), Vol. 1.

Clap, Roger. *Memoirs, 1630.* Boston, Mass., 1731; reprinted in Dorchester Antiquarian and Historical Society, *Collections*, 1 (1844).

Clark, George Faber. *A History of. . . Norton, . . . Massachusetts.* Boston, Mass., Crosby, Nichols, 1859.

Clark, William Horace. *The History of Winthrop, Massachusetts, 1630-1952.* Winthrop, Mass., Winthrop Centennial Committee, 1952.

Comer, William R. *Landmarks "in the Old Bay State."* Wellesley, Mass., author, 1911.

Connole, Dennis A. "Land Occupied by the Nipmuck Indians of Central New England 1600-1700." Massachusetts Archaeological Society, *Bulletin*, 38, nos. 1 and 2 (1976), 14-20.

Corey, Deloraine Pendre. *The History of Malden, Massachusetts, 1633-1785.* Malden, Mass., author, 1899.

Crockett, Walter Hill. *Vermont, the Green Mountain State.* 5 vols. New York, N.Y., Century History Co., 1921.

Currier, John J. *History of Newbury, Mass., 1635-1902.* Boston, Mass., Damrell and Upham, 1902.

Day, Clarence A. *A History of Maine Agriculture, 1604-1860.* Orono, Me., University Press, 1954.

DeCosta, B. F. "The Sagadahoc Colony." Massachusetts Historical Society, *Proceedings*, 18 (1880), 82-117.

DeForest, John W. *History of the Indians of Connecticut . . . to 1850.* Hartford, Conn., Hamersley, 1851.

Dixon, Roland Burrage. "The Early Migrations of the Indians of New England and the Maritime Provinces." American Antiquarian Society, *Proceedings*, new series, 24 (1914), 65-76.

Drake, Samuel G. *Indian Captivities, or, Life in the Wigwam.* New York, N.Y., Miller, Orton, and Mulligan, 1855.

Duffy, John. *The Healers: The Rise of the Medical Establishment.* New York, N.Y., McGraw-Hill, 1976.

Dunbar, Seymour. *A History of Travel in America.* Indianapolis, Ind., Bobbs-Merrill, 4 vols., 1915; reprint in 1 vol. New York, N.Y., Tudor, 1937.

Edwards, Everett E. *American Indian Contributions to Civilization.* U.S. Department of Agriculture, Bureau of Agricultural Economics, pamphlet, 1934.

Ellis, George H. "The Indians of Eastern Massachusetts," in *The Memorial History of Boston . . . ,1630-1880*, Justin Winsor, ed. 4 vols. (Boston, Mass., Osgood, 1880-81), 1:240-294.

Fairbridge, Rhodes W. "Recent World-Wide Sea-Level Changes and Their Possible Significance to New England Archaeology." Massachusetts Archaeological Society, *Bulletin*, 21, nos. 3 and 4 (1960), 49-51.

Felt, Joseph B. *Annals of Salem*. 2nd ed. 2 vols. Salem, Mass., Ives, 1845.

Fenner, Henry M. *History of Fall River*. New York, N.Y., Smiley, 1906.

Ferguson, C. C. "Some Observations in Regard to Our Earliest Indian Inhabitants." Worcester Historical Society, *Publications*, new series, 2, no. 4 (1939), 193-204.

Fessenden, G. M. *The History of Warren, R. I. . . .* Providence, R.I., Brown, 1845, supplement.

Forbes, Allan, comp. *Other Indian Events of New England*. Boston, Mass., State Street Trust Co., 1941.

———, comp. *Some Indian Events of New England*. Boston, Mass., State Street Trust Company, 1934.

Ford, George H., comp. *Historical Sketches of the Town of Milford*. New Haven, Conn., Tuttle, Morehouse and Taylor, 1914.

Foster, William E., ed. "Early Attempts at Rhode Island History." Rhode Island Historical Society, *Collections*, 7 (1885), 5-109.

Freeland, Mary DeW. *The Records of Oxford, Mass., Including Chapters of Nipmuck . . . History . . .* Albany, N.Y., Munsell's, 1894.

Freeman, Frederick. *The History of Cape Cod*. 2 vols. Boston, Mass., Rand and Avery, 1858-62.

Garcilasco de la Vega. *The Royal Commentaries of Peru*, Sir Paul Rycaut, tr. London, 1688.

Gomme, George Laurence. *The Village Community*. New York, N.Y., Scribner and Welford, 1890.

Gookin, Daniel. "An Historical Account of . . . the Christian Indians in New England, in . . . 1675, 1676, 1677." American Antiquarian Society, *Transactions and Collections*, 2 (1836), 423-534.

———. *Historical Collections of the Indians in New England*, Jeffrey H. Fiske, ed. 1792; reprint n.p., Towtaid, 1970.

Gookin, Warner F., and Philip L. Barbour. *Bartholomew Gosnold, Discoverer and Planter*. Hamden, Conn., Archon, 1963.

Green, Mason A. *Springfield, 1634-1886: History of Town and City*. Springfield, Mass., Nicholas, 1888.

[Gregory, J. H.] "Some Essex County Indians." *Essex Antiquarian*, 5 (1901), 39-40.

Griffin, Simon G. *A History of . . . Keene from 1732 . . . to 1874*. Keene, N.H., Sentinel, 1904.

Hallett, Leaman F. "The Colonial Invasion of Hereditary Lands." Massachusetts Archaeological Society, *Bulletin*, 20, no. 3 (1959), 34-37.

Hamilton, Edward Pierce. *A History of Milton*. Milton, Mass., Milton Historical Society, 1957.

Hanson, Elizabeth. *An Account of the Captivity of Elizabeth Hanson*. London, Clark, 1760.

Hanson, John W. *History of . . . Norridgewock and Canaan*. Boston, Mass., author, 1849.

Hart, Albert Bushnell, ed. *Commonwealth History of Massachusetts*. 5 vols. New York, N.Y., States History Co., 1927-30.

Hatch, Louis C., ed. *Maine: A History*. 5 vols. New York, N.Y., American Historical Society, 1919.

Hedrick, Ulysses Prentiss. *A History of Agriculture in the State of New York*. Albany, N.Y., New York State Agricultural Society, 1933.

———. *A History of Horticulture in America to 1860*. New York, Oxford University Press, 1950.

Holland, Josiah Gilbert. *History of Western Massachusetts*. 2 vols. Springfield, Mass., Bowles, 1855.

Holmes, George K. "Some Features of Tobacco History." American Historical Association, *Annual Report*, 1 (1919), 385-407.

———. "Three Centuries of Tobacco." U.S. Department of Agriculture, *Yearbook*, (1919), 151-175.

Hoornbeck, Billee. "An Investigation into the Cause or Causes of the Epidemic Which Decimated the Indian Population of New England, 1616-1619." *New Hampshire Archaeologist*, 19 (1976-77), 35-46.

Hopkins, Samuel. *Historical Memoirs, Relating to the Housatunnuk Indians*. Boston, Mass., Kneeland, 1753.

Hopkins, Stephen. "An Historical Account of the Planting and Growth of Providence," in *Early Attempts at Rhode Island History*, William E. Foster, ed. Rhode Island Historical Society, *Collections*, 7 (1885), 15-107.

Howe, George. *Mount Hope: A New England Chronicle*. New York, N.Y., Viking, 1959.

Howe, Henry F. *Prologue to New England*. New York, N.Y., Farrar and Rinehart, 1943.

———. *Salt Rivers of the Massachusetts Shore*. New York, N.Y., Rinehart, 1951.

Hoyt, Epaphras. *Antiquarian Researches: Comprising a History of the Indian Wars in the Country Bordering Connecticut River . . .* Greenfield, Mass., Phelps, 1824.

Hubbard, William. "A General History of New England . . . " 2nd ed. Massachusetts Historical Society, *Collections*, 2nd series, 5 (1848), 7-304; 6 (1848), 305-676.

———. *A Narrative of the Indian Wars in New England, . . . 1607-1677*. Worcester, Mass., Greenleaf, 1801.

Huden, John C. *Indian Place Names of New England*. New York, N.Y., Heye Foundation, 1962.

Hudson, Alfred Sereno. *The History of Concord, Massachusetts*. Concord, Mass., Erudite Press, 1904.

———. *The History of Sudbury, Massachusetts*. Boston, Mass., Blodgett, 1889.

Hulbert, Archer Butler. *Historic Highways of America*. Vols. 1 and 2 (of 16 vols.) Cleveland, Ohio, Clark, 1902-05.

———. *Soil: Its Influence on the History of the United States*. New Haven, Conn., Yale University Press, 1930.

Hutchinson, Thomas. *The History of the Colony and Province of Massachusetts Bay*, Lawrence S. Mayo, ed. 3 vols. Cambridge, Mass., Harvard University Press, 1936.

———. "Hutchinson Papers." Massachusetts Historical Society, *Collections*, 3rd series, 1 (1825), 1-152.

James, Sydney V. *Colonial Rhode Island: A History*. New York, N.Y., Scribner's, 1975.

Jameson, J. Franklin, ed., *Narratives of New Netherland, 1609-1664*. New York, N.Y., Scribner's, 1909.

Jenkins, Edward H. *A History of Connecticut Agriculture*. New Haven, Conn., Connecticut Agricultural Experiment Station, 1925?.

Jennings, Francis. *The Invasion of America: Indians, Colonialism, and the Cant of Conquest*. Chapel Hill, N.C., University of North Carolina Press, 1975.

Johnson, Edward, *Wonder-Working Providence of Sions Saviour in New England*. London, 1654; reprint Andover, Mass., 1867.

Jones, Electa F. *Stockbridge, Past and Present: or, Records of an Old Mission Station*. Springfield, Mass., 1854.

Judd, Sylvester. *History of Hadley*. New ed. Springfield, Mass., 1905.

Kittredge, Henry C. *Cape Cod: Its People and Their History*. Boston, Mass., Houghton Mifflin, 1930.

Knowles, James D. *Memoir of Roger Williams*. Boston, Mass., 1834.

Knowles, Nathaniel. "The Torture of Captives by the Indians of Eastern North America." American Philosophical Society, *Proceedings*, 82 (1940), 151-225.

La Farge, Oliver. *A Pictorial History of the American Indian*. New York, N.Y., Crown, 1956.

Larned, Ellen D. *History of Windham County, Connecticut*. 2 vols. Worcester, Mass., 1874-80.

Leach, Douglas E. *Flintlock and Tomahawk: New England in King Philip's War*. New York, N.Y., Macmillan, 1958.

Lechford, Thomas. *Plain Dealing: or, News from New England*, J. Hammond Trumbull, ed. 1642; reprinted Boston, Mass., 1867.

Lee, W. Storrs. *The Yankees of Connecticut*. New York, N.Y., Holt, 1957.

Lincoln, Charles H., ed. *Narratives of the Indian Wars*. New York, N.Y., Scribner's, 1913.

Livermore, S. T. *A History of Block Island . . .* Hartford, Conn., 1877.

Lurie, Nancy O. "Indian Cultural Adjustment to European Civilization," in *Seventeenth-Century America*, James M. Smith, ed. Chapel Hill, N.C., University of North Carolina Press, 1959.

McDonald, Adrian Francis. *The History of Tobacco Production in Connecticut.* New Haven, Conn., Yale University Press, 1936.

McKeen, John. "Remarks on the Voyage of George Waymouth to the Coast of Maine, 1605." Maine Historical Society, *Collections*, 5 (1857), 309-338.

Marlowe, George Francis. *The Old Bay Paths.* New York, N.Y., Hastings House, 1942.

Mason, Gregory. "Native American Food." *Natural History*, 37 (1936), 309-318.

Mather, Cotton. *Magnalia Christi Americana.* 7 books in 1 vol. (London, 1702), 7:41.

May, Ralph. *Early Portsmouth History.* Boston, Mass., Goodspeed, 1926.

Mead, Spencer P. *Historie of . . . Greenwich . . . Connecticut.* New York, N.Y., 1911.

Miller, William Davis. *Ancient Paths to Pequot.* Society of Colonial Wars, Pamphlet, June 15, 1936.

———. *The Narragansett Planters.* American Antiquarian Society, *Proceedings*, new series, 43 (1934), 48-115.

Mirick, Benjamin L. *The History of Haverhill, Massachusetts.* Haverhill, Mass., 1832.

Morison, Samuel Eliot. *The European Discovery of America: The Northern Voyages, A.D. 500-1600.* New York, N.Y., Oxford University Press, 1971.

———. *The Story of the "Old Colony" of New Plymouth, 1620-1692.* New York, N.Y., Knopf, 1956.

Morton, Nathaniel, ed. *New England's Memorial.* 6th ed. Boston, Mass., 1855.

Mourt's Relation, or Journal of the Plantation at Plymouth (probably written by William Bradford and Edward Winslow), Henry Martyn Dexter, ed. Boston, Mass., 1865.

Munro, Wilfred H. *The History of Bristol, R.I.: The Story of the Mount Hope Lands.* Providence, R.I., 1880.

Neal, Daniel. *The History of New-England . . . to 1700.* 2 vols. London, 1720.

New England's First Fruits. London, 1643; reprinted New York, N.Y., 1865.

[Newhall, James R. (Obadiah Oldpath)]. *Lin̄: or Jewels of the Third Plantation.* Lynn, Mass., 1862.

Niles, Grace Greylock. *The Hoosac Valley: Its Legends and Its History.* New York, N.Y., Putnam's, 1912.

North American Indians in Historical Perspective. Eleanore Burke Leacock and Nancy Oestreich Lurie, eds. New York, N.Y., Random House, 1971.

Nourse, Henry S. *History of the Town of Harvard, Massachusetts, 1732-1893.* Harvard, Mass., 1894.

Orcutt, Samuel. *The History of the Old Town of Derby, Connecticut, 1642-1880.* Springfield, Mass., 1880.

———. *The Indians of the Housatonic and Naugatuck Valleys.* Hartford, Conn., 1882.

Paine, Josiah. *A History of Harwich, Barnstable County, Massachusetts, 1620-1800*. Rutland, Vt., Tuttle, 1937.

Parsons, Herbert Collins. *A Puritan Outpost: A History of . . . Northfield, Massachusetts*. New York, N.Y., Macmillan, 1937.

Parsons, Langdon B. *History of . . . Rye, New Hampshire*. Concord, N.H., 1905.

Payne, Edward John. *History of the New World Called America*. 2 vols. New York, N.Y., 1892-99.

Peale, Arthur L. *Uncas and the Mohegan-Pequot*. Boston, Mass., Meador, 1939.

Pearce, Roy H. *The Savages of America*. Rev. ed. Baltimore, Md., Johns Hopkins Press, 1965.

Peirce, Ebenezer W. *Indian History, Biography and Genealogy* . . . North Abington, Mass., Z. G. Mitchell, 1878.

Penhallow, Samuel. *The History of the Wars of New-England with the Eastern Indians*. Boston, Mass., 1726; reprinted in New Hampshire Historical Society, *Collections*, 1 (1824), 14-132.

Phelps, Noah A. *History of Simsbury, Granby, and Canton*. Hartford, Conn., 1845.

Phillips, James Duncan. *Salem in the Seventeenth Century*. Boston, Mass., Houghton Mifflin, 1933.

Pierce, George W. "History of Winchester," in *History of Cheshire and Sullivan Counties, New Hampshire*, D. Hamilton Hurd, ed. (Philadelphia, Penn., Lewis, 1886), 541-585.

Potter, Chandler E. *The History of Manchester, . . . N.H.* Manchester, N.H., 1856.

Potter, Elisha R., Jr. "The Early History of Narragansett," Rhode Island Historical Society, *Collections*, 3 (1835), 1-315.

Powers, Grant. *Historical Sketches of . . . Coos Country*. Haverhill, N.H., 1841; reprint 1880.

Pratt, Enoch. *A Comprehensive History of . . . Eastham, Wellfleet, and Orleans*. Yarmouth, Mass., 1844.

Prince, Thomas. "Annals of New-England," Boston, Mass., 1736; reprinted in Massachusetts Historical Society, *Collections*, 2nd series, 7 (1826), 189-295.

Proctor, Mary A. *The Indians of the Winnipesaukee and Pemigewasset Valleys*. Franklin, N.H., Towne and Robie, 1931.

Prowse, D. W. *A History of Newfoundland . . .* New York, N.Y., Macmillan, 1895.

Quinebaug Historical Society, Leaflets, Sturbridge, Mass.

Rantoul, Robert, Sr. "Essex County and the Indians." Essex Institute, *Historical Collections*, 19 (1882), 126-142.

Ray, Roger B. "Maine Indians' Concept of Land Tenure." Maine Historical Society, *Quarterly*, 13, no. 1 (1973), 28-51.

Ricketson, Daniel. *The History of New Bedford, . . . Massachusetts*. New Bedford, Mass., 1858.

Rider, Sidney S. *The Lands of Rhode Island . . .* Providence, R.I., 1904.

Robbins, Maurice. "Historical Approach to Titicut." Massachusetts Archaeological Society, *Bulletin*, 11, no. 3 (1950), 48-73.
———. "Indians of the Old Colony." Ibid., 17, no. 4 (1956), 59-74.
Ruttenber, Edward M. *History of the Indian Tribes of Hudson's River*. Albany, N.Y., 1872.

Saltonstall, Nathaniel. "The Present State of New England . . .," in *Narratives of the Indian Wars, 1675-1699*, Charles H. Lincoln, ed. (New York, N.Y., Scribner's, 1913), 21-74.
Sanborn, Edwin D. *History of New Hampshire*. Manchester, N.H., 1875.
Sauer, Carl O. "A Geographic Sketch of Early Man in America." *Geographic Review*, 34 (1944), 529-573.
Schorger, A. W. *The Wild Turkey: Its History and Domestication*. Norman, Okla., University of Oklahoma Press, 1966.
Sedgwick, Charles F. *General History . . . of Sharon . . . Conn*. 3rd ed. Amenia, N.Y., 1898.
Seebohm, Mabel E. *The Evolution of the English Farm*. London, 1927.
Sewall, Rufus King. *Ancient Dominions of Maine*. Bath, Me., 1859.
Shattuck, Lemuel. *A History of the Town of Concord, . . . Massachusetts*. Boston, Mass., 1835.
Sheldon, George. *A History of Deerfield, Massachusetts*. 2 vols. Deerfield, Mass., 1895-96.
Shipton, Clifford K. "The New England Frontier." *New England Quarterly*, 10 (1937), 25-36
———. *Roger Conant, A Founder of Massachusetts*. Cambridge, Mass., Harvard University Press, 1944.
Smith, Bradford. *Captain John Smith: His Life and Legend*. Philadelphia, Penn., Lippincott, 1953.
Smith, Chard Powers. *The Housatonic, Puritan River*. New York, N.Y., Rinehart, 1946.
Smith, Colonel James. "An Account of the . . . Life and Travels . . . During his Captivity with the Indians . . . 1755-59," in *Indian Captivities*, Samuel G. Drake, ed. New York, N.Y., Miler, Orton, and Mulligan, 1851.
Smith, Ralph D. *The History of Guilford, Connecticut*. Albany, N.Y., 1877.
Smith, Robinson V. "New Hampshire Remembers the Indians." *Historical New Hampshire*, 7 (October 1952), 1-31.
Smith, William C. *A History of Chatham, Massachusetts*. Hyannis, Mass., 1909.
Spiess, Mathias. *The Indians of Connecticut*. New Haven, Conn., Yale University Press, 1933.
Spinden, Herbert J. "Thank the American Indian." *Scientific American*, 138 (1928), 330-332.
Sprague, John Francis. *Sebastian Ralé: A Maine Tragedy of the Eighteenth Century*. Boston, Mass., 1906.
Squires, James Duane. *The Granite State of the United States*. New York, N.Y., American Historical Co., 1956.
Stackpole, Everett S. *History of New Hampshire*. 4 vols. New York, N.Y., American Historical Society, 1916.

Stiles, Henry R. *The History of Ancient Windsor, Connecticut.* 2 vols. Albany, N.Y., 1863.

Stoehr, Ruth M. "Favorite American Foods and the Role They Have Played in History." *Western Pennsylvania Historical Magazine,* 40, no. 2 (1957), 89-100.

Stone, William L. *The Life and Times of Sir William Johnson, Bart.* 2 vols. Albany, N.Y., 1865.

Strachey, William. *The Historie of Travaile into Virginia Britannia,* R. H. Major, ed. London, 1849.

Strock, Daniel, Jr. *Pictorial History of King Philip's War.* Hartford, Conn., 1851.

Sullivan, James, "The History of the Penobscot Indians." Massachusetts Historical Society, *Collections,* 9 (1804), 207-232.

Swift, Charles F. *History of Old Yarmouth.* Yarmouth Port, Mass., 1884.

Swift, Samuel. *History of the Town of Middlebury, . . . Vermont.* Middlebury, Vt., 1859.

Teele, A. K. *Noted Men and Historical Narrations of Ancient Milton.* Boston, Mass., 1900.

Temple, J. H. *History of Framingham, Massachusetts.* Framingham, Mass., 1887.

————. *History of North Brookfield, Massachusetts.* North Brookfield, Mass., 1887.

Thatcher, Benjamin B. *Indian Biography.* 2 vols. New York, N.Y., 1832.

Thomson, Betty F. *The Changing Face of New England.* New York, N.Y., Macmillan, 1958.

Thompson, Francis McGee. *History of Greenfield, . . . Massachusetts.* 3 vols. Greenfield, Mass., Morey, 1904.

Thornton, J. Wingate. "Ancient Pemaquid." Maine Historical Society, *Collections,* 5 (1857), 139-305.

Tilton, George H. *A History of Rehoboth, Massachusetts . . . 1643-1918.* Boston, Mass., 1918.

Tompson, Benjamin, *New-England's Crisis.* Boston, Mass., 1894.

Tooker, W. W. "Roger Williams Vindicated." Rhode Island Historical Society, *Publications,* new series, 2 (1894), 61-67.

Trumbull, Benjamin. *A Complete History of Connecticut.* New Haven, Conn., 1797, 1818.

Tustin, Josiah P. *A Discourse Delivered . . . in Warren, R.I.* Providence, R.I., Brown, 1845.

Underhill, John. "History of the Pequot War," in *Nevves from America,* London, 1638; reprinted in Massachusetts Historical Society, *Collections,* 3rd series, 6 (1837), 1-28.

Usher, Roland G. *The Pilgrims and Their History.* New York, N.Y., Macmillan, 1918.

Vaughan, Alden T. *New England Frontier: Puritans and Indians, 1620-1675.* Boston, Mass., Little, Brown, 1965.

Verrill, A. Hyatt. *Foods America Gave the World.* Boston, Mass., Page, 1937.

———. *The Heart of Old New England*. New York, Dodd, Mead, 1936.

———, and Ruth Verrill. *America's Ancient Civilizations*. New York, N.Y., Putnam's, 1953.

Vincent, Philip. "A True Relation of the Late Battell . . . (Pequot War)." Massachusetts Historical Society, *Collections*, 3rd series, 6 (1837), 29-43.

Vuilleumier, Marion. *Indians on Olde Cape Cod*. Taunton, Mass., Sullwold, 1970.

Washburn, Wilcomb E. "The Moral and Legal Justifications for Dispossessing the Indians," in *Seventeenth-Century America*, James M. Smith, ed. Chapel Hill, N.C., University of North Carolina Press, 1959.

Watson, W. L. "A Short History of Jamestown . . ." Rhode Island Historical Society, *Collections, 26 (1933)*, 40-59.

Weeks, Alvin G. *Massasoit of the Wampanoags*. Fall River, Mass., author, 1919.

Wells, Daniel White, and Reuben Field Wells. *A History of Hatfield, Massachusetts*. Springfield, Mass., 1910.

Wells, Frederic P. *History of Newbury, Vermont*. St. Johnsbury, Vt., 1902.

Weston, Thomas. *History of the Town of Middleboro, Massachusetts*. Boston, Mass., 1906.

Wheeler, Richard A. *The Pequot Indians: An Historical Sketch*. Westerly, R.I., Utter, [187-?].

White, John. *The Planters Plea, 1630*. Rockport, Mass., Sandy Bay Historical Society and Museum, 1930.

Williamson, William D. *The History of the State of Maine*. 2 vols. (Hallowell, Me., 1832), Vol. 2.

Winsor, Justin, ed. *The Memorial History of Boston . . . 1630-1880*. 4 vols. Boston, Mass., Osgood, 1880-81.

———, ed. *Narrative and Critical History of America*. 8 vols. Boston, Mass., Osgood, 1885, Vols. 3 and 4.

———. "The New England Indians—Bibliography." Massachusetts Historical Society, *Proceedings*, 2nd series, 10 (1895), 327-359.

Winthrop, John. *The History of New England from 1630 to 1649*, James Savage, ed. 2 vols. Boston, Mass., Phelps and Farnham, 1825.

Wright, Albert H. "Early Records of the Wild Turkey." *The Auk*, 21, no. 3 (1914), 334-362.

Wroth, Lawrence C. *The Voyages of Giovanni da Verrazzano, 1542-1528*. New Haven, Conn., Yale University Press, 1970.

Young, Alexander, ed. *Chronicles of the First Planters of the Colony of Massachusetts Bay from 1623 to 1636*. Boston, Mass., Little and Brown, 1846.

———. *Chronicles of the Pilgrim Fathers of the Colony of Plymouth from 1602 to 1625*. 2d ed. Boston, Mass., Little and Brown, 1844.

Reference

The Animal Kingdom. Frederick Drimmer, ed. 3 vols. Garden City, N.Y., Doubleday, 1954.

Bailey, Liberty H., ed. *Cyclopedia of American Agriculture.* 4 vols., 5th ed. New York, N.Y., Macmillan, 1917.

Compton's Pictured Encyclopedia . . . Guy S. Ford, ed. Chicago, Ill., Compton, 1933.
Connecticut Register and Manual Memorial. Hartford, Conn., 1842.
Corswant, Willy. *A Dictionary of Life in Bible Times.* New York, N.Y., Oxford, 1960.

Eastern States Archeological Federation. *An Anthropological Bibliography of the Eastern Seaboard.* Irving Rouse and John M. Goggin, eds. New Haven, Conn., Eastern States Archeological Federation, 1947.
————. *Archaeological Bibliography for Eastern North America.* Roger W. Moeller and John Reid, comps.; Roger W. Moeller, ed. Attleboro, Mass. and Washington, Conn., Eastern States Archeological Federation and American Archaeological Institute, 1977.
Edwards, Everett E., and Wayne D. Rasmussen, comps. *A Bibliography on the Agriculture of the American Indians.* U.S. Department of Agriculture, *Miscellaneous Publication*, 447, Washington, 1942.

Federal Writers' Project, American Guide Series. Boston, Mass., Houghton Mifflin.
   Connecticut: A Guide to Its Roads, Lore, and People. 1938.
   Maine: A Guide "Down East." 1937.
   Massachusetts: A Guide to Its Places and People. 1937.
   New Hampshire: A Guide to the Granite State. 1938.
   Rhode Island: A Guide to the Smallest State. 1937.
   Vermont: A Guide to the Green Mountain State. 1937.

Handbook of North American Indians: Volume 15, Northeast. Bruce G. Trigger, ed. Washington, D.C., Smithsonian Institution, 1978.

Lane, Evelyn M. "Indians of Early New England: Their Character and Customs, with Bibliography of Items in Springfield and Holyoke Libraries," manuscript. Springfield, Mass., 1943.

Maine Historical Society. Library. *The Indians of Maine, Preliminary Inventory of Material.* Portland, Me., Maine Historical Society, 1969.
Massachusetts (Colony). *Records of the Governor and Company of the Massachusetts Bay in New England.* Nathaniel B. Shurtleff, ed. 2 vols. Boston, Mass., White, 1853.
Miller, Madeleine S., and J. Lane Miller. *Harper's Bible Dictionary.* 3rd ed. New York, N.Y., Harper, 1955.
Moeller, Roger W., and John Reid, comps. *Archaeological Bibiography for Eastern North America. See under* Eastern States Archeological Federation.

The Pageant of America. Ralph Henry Gabriel, ed. 15 vols. New Haven, Conn., Yale University Press, 1925-29.

Pilling, James Constantine. *Bibliography of the Algonquian Languages*. Smithsonian Institution, Bureau of American Ethnology, *Bulletin*, 13, Washington, 1891.

Sargent, Porter E. *A Handbook of New England*. Boston, Mass., Sargent, 1916.

Stoutenburgh, John L. *Dictionary of the American Indian*. New York, N.Y., Philosophical Library, 1960.

Sturtevant, William C. *Preliminary Bibliography on North American Indian Agriculture*. Southeastern Archaeological Conference, *Bulletin*, 3, Cambridge, 1965.

Travel and Observation

Alsberg, Henry G., ed. *The American Guide: A Source Book and Complete Travel Guide for the United States*. New York, N.Y., Hastings House, 1949.

Apes, William (of the Pequod Tribe). *A Son of the Forest—The Experience of William Apes, A Native of the Forest*. New York, N.Y., author, 1829.

Ayres, Harral. "Historic Journeys of Pioneer Years: Southern New England Trails and Activities." Massachusetts Archaeological Society, *Bulletin*, 6, no. 1 (1944), 1-10.

Bakeless, John. *The Eyes of Discovery*. Philadelphia, Penn., Lippincott, 1950.

Bartram, John. *Observations on the Inhabitants, Climate, Soil, Rivers, Productions, Animals, and Other Matters* . . . London, 1751; reprinted, Geneva, N.Y., Humphrey, 1895.

Biard, Pierre. Writings in *Jesuit Relations*, ed. Reuben Gold Thwaites. 73 vols. (Cleveland, Ohio, Burrows, 1896-1901), 3:101.

Bowles, Ella Shannon. *Let Me Show You New Hampshire*. New York, N.Y., Knopf, 1938.

Brereton, M. John. "A Brief and True Relation of the Discovery of the North Part of Virginia . . . London, 1602." Massachusetts Historical Society, *Collections*, 3rd series, 8 (1843), 83-123.

Browne, Edmund. "Report on Massachusetts." Colonial Society of Massachusetts, *Transactions*, 7 (1900), 76-80.

Burrage, Henry S., ed. *Early English and French Voyages Chiefly from Hakluyt, 1534-1608*. New York, N.Y., Scribner's, 1906.

Cartier, Jacques. "Discovery of the St. Lawrence (1534-1535)," in *American History Told by Contemporaries*, Albert Bushnell Hart, ed. 5 vols. (New York, N.Y., Macmillan, 1897-1929), 1:107-112.

———. "Second Voyage," in *Trois Voyages au Canada*, Bertrand Guégan, ed. Paris, Éditions du Carrefour, 1929.

Carver, Jonathan. *Travels through the Interior Parts of North America* . . . *1766-1768*. London, author, 1778.

Caswell, Harriet S. *Our Life among the Iroquois Indians*. Boston, Mass., Congregational Sunday School and Publishing Society, 1892.

Champlain, [Sieur] Samuel de. *Les Voyages de la Novvelle France Occidentale, dicte Canada*. Paris, 1632.

———. *Voyages*, tr. Charles Pomeroy Otis. 3 vols. Boston, Mass., Prince Society, 1878-82.

———. *Voyages*, ed. W. L. Grant. New York, New York, Scribner's, 1907.

Coleman, Emma L. *New England Captives Carried to Canada Between 1677 and 1760* . . . 2 vols. Portland, Me., Southworth Press, 1925.

Curtis, Natalie. *The Indian's Book*. New York, N.Y., Harper, 1907.

Danckaerts, Jasper, and Peter Sluyter. "Journal of a Voyage to New York . . . in 1679-80." Long Island Historical Society, *Memoirs* 1, Brooklyn, N.Y., 1867.

Davies, J. "A Relation of a Voyage to Sagadahoc 1607-1608," in *Early English and French Voyages, Chiefly from Hakluyt, 1534-1608*, Henry S. Burrage, ed. New York, N.Y., Scribner's, 1906.

Denys, Nicolas. *The Description and Natural History of the Coasts of North America (Acadia)*. Toronto, Champlain Society, 1908.

Dermer, Thomas. "Letter Describing His Passage from Maine to Virginia, A.D. 1619." New York Historical Society, *Collections*, 2nd series, 1 (1841), 343-354.

Diéreville, Sieur de. *Relation of the Voyage to Port Royal in Acadia or New France*. Toronto, Champlain Society, 1933.

Donck, Adriaen van der. "Description of the New Netherlands." New-York Historical Society, *Collections,* 2nd series, 1 (1841), 125-242.

Dunton, John. "Journal in Massachusetts, 1686." Massachusetts Historical Society, *Collections*, 2nd series, 2 (1814), 97-124.

Dwight, Timothy. *Travels in New-England and New-York*. 4 vols. London, Baynes, 1823.

Eastman, Charles A. *Indian Boyhood*. Boston, Mass., Little, Brown, 1924.

Gorges, Ferdinando (the Younger). "A Description of New-England" in his *America Painted to the Life*. London, T.J. for Nath. Brook, 1659.

Gosnold, Master Bartholomew. "Letter to His Father. Touching His First Voyage to Virginia, 1602." Massachusetts Historical Society, *Collections*, 3rd series, 8 (1843), 69-72.

Grant, Mrs. Anne. *Memoirs of an American Lady*. 2 vols. New York, N.Y., Dodd, Mead, 1901.

Graves, Thomas. "Letter from New England," in *Chronicles of the First Planters of the Colony of Massachusetts Bay,* Alexander Young, ed. (Boston, Mass., Little and Brown, 1846), 152-153.

Hard, Walter. *The Connecticut*. Rivers of America Series. New York, N.Y., Rinehart, 1947.

Hariot, Thomas. *A Briefe and True Report of the New Found Land of Virginia*. Facsimile of first edition of 1588. New York, N.Y., Dodd, Mead, 1903.

Harmon, Daniel Williams. *A Journal of Voyages and Travels in the Interior of North America*. New York, N.Y., Barnes, 1903.

Harris, John. *Navigantium atque Itinerantum Bibliotheca*, 2, *Lahontan's Voyage*. London, Bennet, 1705.

Haugen, Einar. *Voyages to Vinland*. New York, N.Y., Knopf, 1942.

Heckewelder, John. "History, Manners and Customs of the Indian Nations . . . [of] Pennsylvania . . ." American Philosophical Society, History and Literary Committee, *Transactions*, 1 (1819), 24-347.

Hennepin, Louis. *A New Discovery of a Vast Country in America*, Reuben Gold Thwaites, ed. 2 vols. Chicago, Ill., McClurg, 1903.

Henry, Alexander. *(Fur Trader of the Northwest), Manuscript Journals, . . . 1789-1814*, Elliott Coues, ed. 3 vols. New York, N.Y., Harper, 1897.

Higginson, Francis. "New-England's Plantation," in *Chronicles of the First Planters of the Colony of Massachusetts Bay*, Alexander Young, ed., (Boston, Little and Brown, 1846), 238-268.

How, Nehemiah. "A Narrative of the Captivity of . . ., 1745-1748," in *Tragedies of the Wilderness*, Samuel G. Drake, ed. Boston, Mass., 1878, 127-138.

Hunter, John D. *Memoirs of a Captivity among the Indians of North America*. London, Longman et al., 1823.

The Jesuit Relations and Allied Documents, Travels and Explorations of the Jesuit Missionaries in New France, 1610-1791, Reuben Gold Thwaites, ed. 73 vols. Cleveland, Ohio, 1896-1901.

Josselyn, John. *An Account of Two Voyages to New-England* . . . London, 1674; reprint Boston, Mass., Veazie, 1865.

————. *New-England's Rarities Discovered* . . . Edward Tuckerman, ed., Boston, Mass., Veazie, 1865.

Jouvency, Joseph. Writings in *Jesuit Relations*, Reuben Gold Thwaites, ed. 73 vols. (Cleveland, Ohio, 1896-1901), 1:257.

Kalm, Peter. *A Journey into North America*. New York, N.Y., 1837.

————. "Travels into North America," in *Pinkerton's Travels*, John R. Forster, tr. (London, 1812), 374-700.

Laet, John de. "Extracts from 'The New World,' 1625, 1630, 1634, 1640." New-York Historical Society, *Collections*, 2nd series, 1 (1841), 281-316.

Lafitau, Joseph. *Moeurs des Sauvages Ameriquains*. Books I and II. Paris, 1724.

Lahontan, [Louis Armand] Baron de. *New Voyages to North-America*, Reuben Gold Thwaites, ed. 2 vols. 1703; reprint Chicago, Ill., McClurg, 1905.

Lee, Samuel, *Letters of Samuel Lee and Samuel Sewall Relating to New England and the Indians*, George Lyman Kittredge, ed. Colonial Society of Massachusetts, *Publications*, 14 (1912), 142-186.

Le Jeune, Paul. Writings in *Jesuit Relations*, Reuben Gold Thwaites, ed. 73 vols. (Cleveland, Ohio, 1896-1901), Vols. 5-8, 10, 12, 16, and 17.

Lescarbot, Marc. *Nova Francia: A Description of Acadia, 1606*, P. Erondelle, tr. London, 1609; reprint London, Routledge, 1928.

Levett, Christopher. "A Voyage into New England." Massachusetts Historical Society, *Collections*, 3rd series, 8 (1843), 159-190.

Lincoln. Benjamin. "Journal of a Treaty Held in 1793, with the Indian Tribes North-west of the Ohio . . ." Ibid., 3rd series, 5 (1836), 109-176.

Long, John. *Voyages and Travels . . . 1768-1788,* Milo Milton Quaife, ed. Chicago, Ill., 1922.

Lorant, Stefan, ed. *The New World: The First Pictures of America*. New York, N.Y., Duell, Sloan, and Pearce, 1946.

McKenney, Thomas L. *History of the Indian Tribes of North America*. 3 vols. Philadelphia, Penn., 1836-44.

———. *Memoirs . . ., with Sketches of Travels among the Northern and Southern Indians*. New York, N.Y., 1846.

———. *Sketches of a Tour to the Lakes, of the Character and Customs of the Chippeway Indians* . . . Baltimore, Md., 1827.

Mereness, Newton D. *Travels in the American Colonies, 1690-1783*. New York, N.Y., 1916.

Morrell, William. "Poem on New England." Massachusetts Historical Society, *Collections*, 1 (1792), 125-139.

Morton, Thomas. *Manners and Customs of the Indians*. Old South Leaflet, 4, no. 87, Boston, Mass., 1897.

———. *The New English Canaan*, Charles Francis Adams, Jr., introd. Boston, Mass., Prince Society, 1883.

Pastorius, Francis Daniel. *Description of Pennsylvania (1700)*. Old South Leaflet, 4, no. 95, Boston, Mass., 1898.

Pory, John. *Lost Description of Plymouth Colony*, Champlin Burrage, ed. Boston, Mass., Houghton Mifflin, 1918.

Pratt, Phinehas. "A Declaration of the Affairs of the English People That First Inhabited New England." Massachusetts Historical Society, *Collections,* 4th series, 4 (1858), 474-487.

Quanapaug, James. "James Quanapaug's Information." Ibid., 1st series, 6 (1799), 205-208.

Ralé, Sebastian. "Letter to His Brother," in *Sebastian Ralé: A Maine Tragedy of the Eighteenth Century*, John F. Sprague, ed. Boston, Mass., 1906.

Rasieres, Isaack de. "Letter to Samuel Blommaert," in *Narratives of New Netherland, 1609-1664*, J. Franklin Jameson, ed. New York, N.Y., Scribner's, 1909.

Rosier, James. "A True Relation of the Most Prosperous Voyage . . . 1605 by Captain George Waymouth." Massachusetts Historical Society, *Collections*, 3rd series, 8 (1843), 125-157.

Rowlandson, Mary. *The Narrative of the Captivity and Restoration of Mrs. Mary Rowlandson*. Lancaster, Mass., [Cambridge, J. Wilson and Son], 1903.

Sagard, F. Gabriel. "Le Grand Voyage Fait au Pays des Hurons," in *Trois Voyages au Canada*, Bertrand Guégan, ed. Paris, Editions du Carrefour, 1929.

Schemel, Emma, tr. and ed. "A Swiss Surgeon Visits Rhode Island, 1661-1662." *New England Quarterly*, 10 (1937), 536-548.

Schoolcraft, Henry R. *The American Indians: Their History, Condition and Prospects*. Rev. ed. Rochester, N.Y., 1851.

Smith, James, *An Account of the Remarkable Occurrences . . . during His Captivity with the Indians in the Years 1755-59*. Lexington, Kty., 1799; reprint Cincinnati, Ohio, Robert Clarke, 1870.

Smith, John. "A Description of New-England." Massachusetts Historical Society, *Collections*, 3rd series, 6 (1837), 103-140.

Stiles, Ezra. *Extracts from the Itineraries . . . 1755-1794*, Franklin Bowditch Dexter, ed. New Haven, Conn., Yale University Press, 1916.

Tanner, John. *A Narrative of the Captivity and Adventures of . . .*, Edwin James, ed. New York, N.Y., 1830.

Tenesles, Nicola, *The Indian of New-England and the North-eastern Provinces . . .*, Joseph Barratt, ed., Middletown, Conn., Pelton, 1851.

Thoreau, Henry David. *Writings*, Bradford Torrey and Franklin B. Sanborn, eds. 20 vols. Boston, Mass., Houghton Mifflin, 1906.

Verazzano [Verrazano], John de. "The Voyage of . . . along the Coast of North America," Joseph G. Cogswell, tr. New-York Historical Society, *Collections*, 2nd series, 1 (1841), 37-67.

Vries, David Pieterszen de. "Extracts from the Second Voyage to the Coast of America." New-York Historical Society, *Collections*, 2nd series (1841), 258-260.

———. "Extracts from the Voyages of . . ." Ibid., 2nd series, 1 (1841), 243-280.

Ward, Edward. "A Trip to New-England," in *Boston in 1682 and 1699*, George P. Winship, ed. (Providence, R.I., 1905), 29-70.

Wassenaer, Nicolaes Van. "Historisch Verhael," in *Narratives of New Netherland*, J. Franklin Jameson, ed., New York, N.Y., Scribner's, 1909.

Waymouth, George. "Voyage." Massachusetts Historical Society, *Collections*, 3rd series, 8 (1843), 125-157.

Wheeler, Thomas. ". . . Narrative of an Expedition . . . into the Nipmuck Country . . . 1675." New Hampshire Historical Society, *Collections*, 2 (1827), 2-23.

Williams, Roger. "A Key into the . . . Language of the Natives in That Part of America Called New England . . ." Massachusetts Historical Society, *Collections*, 3 (1794), reprinted 1810, 203-238.

———. "An Helpe to the Native Language . . . , (Commonly Called Williams' *Key*)," in *Writings*, J. Hammond Trumbull, ed. 6 vols. (Providence, R.I., Narragansett Club, 1864), 1:1-219.

———. *Complete Writings*. 7 vols. New York, N.Y., Russell and Russell, 1963.

———. *Letters*, John Russell Bartlett, ed., Providence, R.I., Narragansett Club, 1874.

Wilson, James Grant. "Arent Van Curler and His Journal." American Historical Association, *Annual Report* (1895), 79-101.

Winship, George Parker, ed. *Sailors Narratives of Voyages along the New England Coast, 1524-1624*. Boston, Mass., Houghton Mifflin, 1905.

Winslow, Edward. "Account of the Natives of New England," in *New England's Memorial*, Nathaniel Morton, ed. 6th ed. (Boston, Mass., Congregational Board of Publication, 1855), 486-494.

———. "Good News from New England." Massachusetts Historical Society, *Collections*, 8 (1802), 239-276; *Collections*, 2nd series, 9 (1832), 74-104.

Wood, William. "Description of Massachusetts," in *Chronicles of the First Planters of the Colony of Massachusetts Bay*, Alexander Young, ed. (Boston, Little and Brown, 1846), 389-415.

———. *New England's Prospect*. London, 1635; reprint Boston, Mass., Prince Society, 1865.

Index

Library of Congress Cataloging in Publication Data

Russell, Howard S
    Indian New England before the Mayflower.

    Bibliography: p.237
    Includes index.
    1. Indians of North America—New England—History. I. Title.
E78.N5R87   974'.00497   79-63082
ISBN 0-87451-162-3

DATE DUE			
DEC 2 1981			
OC 31 '83			
NO 12 '84			
AP 29 '85			
EE 3 '86			
MR 17 '86			
DEC 1 9 1988			